高级商务英语系列教材

总主编：叶兴国　王光林

第二版

高级商务笔译
Business English Translation

主　编：温建平　吴　朋
编　者：叶　泉　胡筱颖　郭　义
　　　　吴　朋　温建平

外语教学与研究出版社
FOREIGN LANGUAGE TEACHING AND RESEARCH PRESS
北京 BEIJING

图书在版编目(CIP)数据

高级商务笔译 / 温建平，吴朋主编；叶泉等编 . -- 2 版 . -- 北京：外语教学与研究出版社，2024.9（2025.2重印）. --（高级商务英语系列教材 / 叶兴国，王光林总主编）. -- ISBN 978-7-5213-5432-4

I. F7

中国国家版本馆 CIP 数据核字第 20246Z9W52 号

出 版 人	王　芳
项目策划	万健玲
责任编辑	刘小萌
责任校对	危阿莹
封面设计	高黛琳
版式设计	付玉梅
出版发行	外语教学与研究出版社
社　　址	北京市西三环北路 19 号（100089）
网　　址	https://www.fltrp.com
印　　刷	河北虎彩印刷有限公司
开　　本	787×1092　1/16
印　　张	12.5
字　　数	312 千字
版　　次	2024 年 9 月第 2 版
印　　次	2025 年 2 月第 3 次印刷
书　　号	ISBN 978-7-5213-5432-4
定　　价	45.90 元

如有图书采购需求，图书内容或印刷装订等问题，侵权、盗版书籍等线索，请拨打以下电话或关注官方服务号：
客服电话：400 898 7008
官方服务号：微信搜索并关注公众号"外研社官方服务号"
外研社购书网址：https://fltrp.tmall.com

物料号：354320001

序　言

　　我国的外语教育为国家的经济社会发展作出了重要贡献。新中国成立以来，特别是改革开放以来，各项事业迅速发展。以便于量化的出口贸易为例，我国出口贸易占全球出口贸易的份额已从1949年的不到1%增至2023年的约14%；同期，美德日三国的出口贸易份额分别从各自的最高水平降至2023年的约9%、7%和3%。在这个过程中，我国的外语专业人才发挥了不可替代的重要作用。然而，我们应该认识到，相较于人口分别约占全球总人口4.2%、1%和1.5%的美德日三国，我国人口占全球总人口的17%以上，而出口贸易额仅占全球出口贸易总额的约14%。我们应识破所谓的"产能过剩"话语陷阱，深切认识到在贸易大国向贸易强国的发展进程中，商务英语专业教育任重道远。

　　当前，世界之变、时代之变、历史之变正在以前所未有的方式展开。经济全球化意味着生产全球化、贸易全球化、资本全球化和科技全球化；全球治理意味着共商共建共享、国际关系民主化以及权利和义务相平衡；人类命运共同体理念的核心在于建设一个持久和平、普遍安全、共同繁荣、开放包容、清洁美丽的世界；实现"一带一路"倡议的路径是"五通"，即政策沟通、设施联通、贸易畅通、资金融通、民心相通。要实现上述目标，包括商务英语专业人才在内的高水平外语专业人才比以往任何时候都更加不可或缺。习近平总书记2021年9月25日在给北京外国语大学老教授的回信中指出，"深化中外交流，增进各国人民友谊，推动构建人类命运共同体，讲好中国故事，需要大批外语人才，外语院校大有可为"，同时提出"提高育人水平，努力培养更多有家国情怀、有全球视野、有专业本领的复合型人才，在推动中国更好走向世界、世界更好了解中国上作出新的贡献"的新要求，为我们搞好外语教育提供重要指示和根本遵循。

　　截至2023年，我国已连续七年保持全球货物贸易第一大国地位，但人均进出口额依然很低。新科技革命和产业变革正在改变和颠覆、重构和重塑人类的生产模式、生活方式、教学方式和价值观，新技术对大学的教育功能、师生关系、课程体系和教育体制带来了深刻的影响和挑战，但很多外语院系的教育教学形态远未达到教育部提出的网络化、数字化、智能化和个性化的要求。全国设立商务英语专业的院校数量已从2012年的几十所增至2024年的400多所，但规模扩张与质量提升之间的矛盾依然存在。

　　当今时代是一个高等教育质量保障运动方兴未艾的时代。联合国教科文组织举办的首届世界高等教育大会明确提出："提高质量是21世纪的时代命题，由数量向质量的转移，标志着一个时代的结束和另一个时代的开始。谁轻视质量，谁将被淘汰出局。"自

2017年9月中共中央、国务院颁布《关于开展质量提升行动的指导意见》以来，教育部打出了一套质量提升的"组合拳"，深入贯彻落实该文件精神。2018年，教育部颁布《普通高等学校本科专业类教学质量国家标准》；推出高等教育人才培养的中国方案，即"新时代高教40条"。2019年，教育部等13个部门联合启动"六卓越一拔尖"计划2.0，全面推进新工科、新医科、新农科、新文科建设，掀起"质量革命"；启动一流本科专业和一流本科课程"双万计划"；制定并印发《普通高等学校教材管理办法》。2020年，教育部高等学校外国语言文学类专业教学指导委员会正式颁布《普通高等学校本科外国语言文学类专业教学指南》。

为贯彻落实教育部文件的相关要求，我们对"高级商务英语系列教材"进行了修订，更新部分内容。在本系列教材的编写和修订过程中，我们坚持遵循以下原则：

1. 商务英语专业教育应该全面贯彻党的教育方针，落实立德树人根本任务，培养学生成为担当中华民族复兴大任的时代新人。

2. 商务英语专业教育应该服务国家需求，与国家的战略意图相吻合，聚焦"适应国家经济社会对外开放的要求，培养大批具有国际视野、通晓国际规则、能够参与国际事务和国际竞争的国际化人才"的要求。

3. 商务英语教材应该主动适应国际商务领域正在发生的深刻变化，努力克服教材内容滞后于国际商务实际的通病。

4. 商务英语教材应该涵盖国际商务的主要方面。

5. 商务英语教学应该坚持以"学生中心、产出导向、持续改进"为核心内容的OBE（outcome-based education）理念。

本系列教材涵盖国际商务的方方面面。我们把国际商务定义为任何为了满足个人和机构需要而进行的跨境商业交易。具体地说，国际商务包括商品、资本、服务、人员和技术的国际流通，知识产权（包括专利、商标、技术、版权等）的跨境交易，实物资产和金融资产投资，用于当地销售或出口的来料加工或组装，跨国采购和零售，在国外设立的仓储和分销系统等。商务包括贸易和投资，以及与贸易和投资有关的方方面面。就所涉及的领域而言，商务涉及营销、金融、税收、结算、跨国公司管理、对外直接投资、知识产权、电子商务、贸易法律和跨文化交际等领域。就所涉及的行业而言，商务不仅涉及贸易和投资，还涉及运输、旅游、银行、广告、零售、批发、保险、电信、航空、海运、咨询、会计等行业。上述领域和行业都是商务的组成部分，上述环境中使用的英语就是商务英语。基于以上考虑，本系列教材包括《高级综合商务英语（1—2）》《高级商务英语阅读（1—2）》《高级商务英语听说（1—2）》《高级商务英语写作》《新编进出口英语函电》《高级商务笔译》《高级商务口译》《管理学导论》《国际商法教程》《国际商务导论》《国际商务管理》《国际会计教程》等。

在商务英语教学过程中，教师应落实以"学生中心、产出导向、持续改进"为核心内容的 OBE 理念。具体地讲，教师应该聚焦四个问题：我们想让学生取得的学习成果是什么？为什么要让学生取得这样的学习成果？如何有效地帮助学生取得这些学习成果？如何知道学生已经取得了这些学习成果？在教学设计时应该重点确定四个对应关系：内外需求与培养目标的对应关系，培养目标与毕业要求的对应关系，毕业要求与课程体系的对应关系，毕业要求与教学内容的对应关系。在教学中应该努力实现五个转变：从灌输课堂向对话课堂转变，从封闭课堂向开放课堂转变，从知识课堂向能力课堂转变，从重学轻思向学思结合转变，从重教轻学向以学为主转变。

  本系列教材主要供高等院校英语专业、商务英语专业和财经类专业学生使用，也可供具有相当英文水平的商界从业人员使用。

  本系列教材的编写人员都具有长期教授商务英语的经验，主要来自上海对外经贸大学、上海交通大学、西安交通大学、上海外国语大学、广东外语外贸大学、上海电力大学、香港中文大学、悉尼大学、昆士兰大学等院校。在教材编写和修订过程中，我们得到了许多专家学者的关心、指导和帮助。在此，谨向他们表示衷心的感谢。

  由于编者水平有限，书中难免有不妥甚至错误之处。我们恳切地希望大家提出宝贵意见。

叶兴国

上海对外经贸大学教授

原中国国际贸易学会商务英语研究会理事长

编写说明

党的二十大报告指出，要"加强国际传播能力建设，全面提升国际传播效能，形成同我国综合国力和国际地位相匹配的国际话语权。"为了推进国家翻译能力建设，提高学生讲好中国故事、传播中国文化的能力已经成为外语学科人才培养的重要指标之一。随着我国对外交往的不断扩大和全球贸易地位的不断提高，商务文本的翻译实践大量增加，商务翻译的人才需求不断增长。为满足服务国家经济战略和国际传播能力建设对人才的需求，本教材专注于商务翻译，通过选择经典商务语篇，讲解其中涉及的翻译技巧，增强翻译与商务的紧密结合，提升兼具商务知识和翻译能力的人才培养的效果。

对商务英语翻译而言，英语是基础，翻译是落脚点，商务知识是内容拓展。知识是可以通过学习者的学习过程获取的，而能力是需要培养的。掌握知识的目的在于提高能力，提高能力可以更好地运用知识，二者是并行不悖的关系，即：商务英语翻译＝商务（知识）＋英语（基本功／技能）＋翻译（技能／能力）。这些认识决定了商务英语翻译教学的内容体系和功能，也决定了编写翻译教材的理念应该是：把知识传授、思维训练和能力培养有机结合起来，帮助学生在实践中运用学到的语言知识，使知识最终转化成语言运用能力。

基于此，本教材以翻译活动的各个层面为脉络，以商务英语文本为主要翻译对象，让学生在学习翻译的过程中，了解并熟悉商务英语文本的特点，并掌握商务知识；在了解商务英语特征的同时，了解翻译的基本技能和方法，了解商务文本翻译与文化背景的关系，了解翻译的难点和关键所在，并通过商务文本的翻译训练，提高学生对翻译的感悟能力，打好翻译基础。本教材不是就商务谈商务，也不是就翻译论翻译，而是以商务英语为媒介来阐释翻译技巧和方法。在内容方面突出商务特色，强调商务英语专业基础知识的重要性，注重选材的实用性、时代性、灵活性和规范性。在技巧上注重学习方法的习得和思维方式的转换，以实现提高学生翻译能力和商务英语知识水平的双重目的。

本教材共有 12 章，在内容安排上遵循以下逻辑：
- 从翻译中易出现的问题出发，指出提升翻译能力的对策；
- 从英汉语言对比角度讨论英汉语言在诸多方面的异同，让学生了解翻译技巧的理据，也为后面的学习安排作好铺垫；

- 从翻译中的转换、衔接与连贯、信息的拆分与融合等技能层面为学生提供指导和帮助；
- 从意义、语境、文化三个相对宏观的层面阐述翻译与三者之间的关系，帮助学生从更宽广的视角来理解翻译的实质，了解影响翻译的诸多因素，以达到提高翻译水平和翻译能力的最终目标；
- 根据教学经验归纳总结学生翻译作业中出现的典型问题，分析出现这些问题的根源并指出避免这些问题的方法。

本教材的特点体现在以下方面：

1. 采用翻译和商务主题双主线进行编排。商务英语翻译涉及翻译本身的特点，也涉及广泛的商务主题。因此，每一章中既有翻译知识讲座——让学生了解翻译的过程、翻译中遇到的问题、应该注意的事项以及翻译的对策，同时也有商务知识讲座和商务语篇翻译与解析——通过介绍商务主题知识、词汇特点等内容，让学生在翻译学习中了解商务内容，掌握翻译技能。

2. 以问题为切入点展开翻译知识讲解。编者根据多年的翻译教学经验，选择最能体现各章翻译技能要求与特点且有一定难度的句子翻译作为开篇，以引起学生对该章翻译问题的关注。

3. 选材注重实用性、时代性、灵活性、规范性。本教材从国外纸媒或网媒上选择较新的资料作为译例或练习题，力求体现现代社会商务英语的发展状况。另外，为了体现举例的典型性，编者采用了少量的其他语篇（如散文），以便让读者能从这些实例中更深刻地理解翻译的特色。

4. 翻译练习类型多样。每章配有与本章翻译知识讲座和商务语篇翻译相关的各类练习，便于从多个方面检验学生的学习效果。通过问题导入、思考题和摘录商务语篇中的句子或词组等练习，提倡反思式学习，加深学生对翻译过程的理解，帮助其提高对翻译及语言材料的敏感性；商务术语翻译旨在帮助学生拓展并积累相关商务主题的常用术语；句子和篇章翻译要求学生在具体语境中翻译词汇和句子，以此提高学生对翻译连贯性、逻辑性、词义的灵活性和语境因素的认识与把握，同时提升其翻译技能。

5. 翻译名家介绍增强了翻译课程的育人效果。根据课程思政的要求，每章增加了对我国著名翻译家的介绍，通过介绍他们的学术观点和翻译实例，帮助学生了解翻译的职业道德、翻译家的情怀、翻译在"四史"中的作用等，培养学生立足中国大地、服务国家战略的政治意识和文化自觉，更好地树立文化自信和专业自信，成为讲好中国故事、传播好中国声音的使者。

基于本教材的特点，编者对使用者提出以下建议：

1. 多动手实践。翻译是一项实践性很强的技能，熟能生巧。希望学生能认真对待教材中的多种练习形式，根据要求进行翻译、比较和思考。这对认识翻译中的问题和翻译实质、提升翻译能力都很有益处。

2. 认真阅读教材内容，积极拓展课外知识，注意打好英汉双语语言基本功。

3. 对参考译文不能盲信盲从。在原文理解层面不可避免地存在"一千个读者就有一千个哈姆雷特"的现象，译者解读的不同必然会带来译文的不同。在语言表达层面，也存在译者的先在知识对翻译选择的影响和译者的审美水平对译文措辞的影响等诸多因素。因此并不存在所谓唯一的标准译文。本教材中提供的"参考译文"仅供参照比较。翻译应强调"同归"而"殊途"，"一致"而"百虑"，学习者要学会在比较中鉴别，在比较中选择，在比较中提高。

上海对外经贸大学的多位教师参与了本教材的编写，温建平编写了第1、9、12章，胡筱颖编写了第2、3章，叶泉编写了第4、5、8章，郭义编写了第6、7章，吴朋编写了第10、11章。

在本教材编写过程中，编者采用了一些在翻译教学过程中收集到的学生翻译实例，这些实例虽然有些问题或者错误，但是却给了编者很多思考和灵感，也使编者尽可能做到有的放矢，提高本教材的针对性和实用性。责任编辑在审稿过程中曾先后提出多条意见和建议供编者思考。谨此一并致谢。

由于编者水平有限，加之时间仓促，难免会有疏漏之处，恳请各位专家、学者和读者不吝赐教。

温建平　吴　朋

2024年3月

目 录

第 1 章　提升商务翻译能力的路径　　1

第 2 章　英汉语言特点对比　　17

第 3 章　商务词汇的翻译　　33

第 4 章　句子的翻译　　46

第 5 章　主语和谓语的翻译　　62

第 6 章　翻译中的转换　　74

第 7 章　信息的拆分与融合　　88

第 8 章　翻译中的衔接与连贯　　102

第 9 章　翻译中的意义再现　　115

第10章　翻译与语境　　127

第11章　翻译中的文化因素　　138

第12章　翻译症与对策　　150

附录 1　商务语篇翻译参考译文　　164

附录 2　参考文献　　184

第 1 章　提升商务翻译能力的路径

> Some people imagine that the greatest problem in translating is to find the right words and constructions in the receptor or target language. On the contrary, the most difficult task for the translator is to understand thoroughly the designative and associative meanings of the text to be translated.
>
> —Eugene A. Nida

问题导入

1. 阅读下面这段文字，并将其译成汉语。

   Even the best corporate names are under attack these days. Still, those companies are reaping the benefits of the years they spent building customer trust and honing images of quality and dependability. To weather an extended bout of distrust and instability, strong brands are crucial. Companies will also have to work doubly hard to keep them intact.

   译文 _____
   _____
   _____

2. 从翻译的角度说明有哪些需要注意的单词和短语。至少列出五个。
   _____
   _____

翻译知识讲座

提升商务翻译能力的路径

"懂外语就能翻译"的无师自通论一直是语言学习中的一大误区。有人认为，翻译既然是两种语言之间的转换，因此只要掌握了母语和一门外语，就可以从事翻译工作。似乎只要学过外语，便可借助词典进行母语和外语之间的翻译，与翻译相关的问题也能够迎刃而解。这些认识上的误区直接导致了翻译教学与学习中的诸多问题。

翻译初学者在实际翻译过程中容易出现眼高手低的情况，认为只要看得懂就能翻得出。在具体操作中，他们往往对原文亦步亦趋，不敢越雷池一步，做不到灵活变通。其翻译常常直接照搬词典释义，脱离原文语境，或者拘泥于原文语法结构，逐字逐句进行对应。这仅是普遍存在的一般性问题。具体到商务翻译，由于涉及商务文本的特殊性质，学习者又对英汉语言差异和相关商务知识掌握不足，因此翻译中还容易忽视英汉文本单复数差异问题、数字和日期的包含或排除问题以及否定的范围问题等，从而落入翻译陷阱，导致沟通失误。

本章主要就翻译初学者存在的问题针对性地提出以下几条提升商务翻译能力的路径。

1. 多动手，提升语言意识

语言基本功是做好翻译的前提和基础，如果不能透彻理解语言，或缺乏扎实的语言基本功，就很难做好翻译。理解和翻译不仅需要译者的源语基本功，也需要译者对译入语具有很好的驾驭能力，否则翻译时会感到力不从心。

翻译过程中，译者常会发现自己对语言的掌握不够到位或不够准确。翻译是一种语言输出技能，没有丰富有效的语言输入，就不可能产生有效的语言输出。第二语言习得理论认为，输入是输出的基石，而只有输入被内化为纳入（intake），才能转化成输出。从语言学习规律来看，语言知识的记忆是非常必要的，但记忆中的词汇和语言结构往往都是消极知识，而且具有一定的模糊性，并不能保证正确地使用语言。只有通过语言使用，这种记忆才能得到检验和强化，消极词汇和语言结构才能转化成学习者可以自由支配的积极知识。同理，只有通过大量的翻译实践，才能提高学习者对翻译的感性认识和对翻译理论与技巧的领悟能力。

在翻译实践中，学习者会接触到丰富的语言材料，遇到各种各样的问题，并对无意中发现的诸多问题形成朦胧的认识和看法。翻译过程可以唤起学习者对两种语言的注意，关注那些一般语言学习中容易被忽视的语言现象，将隐性知识转化为语言中的显性知识，并通过语言的实际运用最终将其内化，从而提升语言意识，强化对语言功能和形式的认识与敏感性，最终达到提升翻译能力的目的。

例 1 A good book is often the best urn of a life enshrining the best that life could think out; for the world of a man's life is, for the most part, but the world of his thoughts. Thus the best books are treasuries of good words, the golden thoughts, which, remembered and cherished, become our constant companions and comforters. "They are never alone," said Sir Philip Sidney, "that are accompanied by noble thoughts."

参考译文： 好书常如最精美的宝器，珍藏着人的一生思想的精华。人生的境界，主要就在于他思想的境界。所以，最好的书是金玉良言的宝库，若将其中的崇高思想铭记于心，就成为我们忠实的伴侣和永恒的慰藉。菲利普·锡德尼爵士说得好："有高尚思想作伴的人永不孤独。"（王克礼译）

上述译例选自散文名篇，从中我们可以领略到贴切的用词、得体的结构、美妙的语音和灵动的思想，更令人惊叹的是译文语言形式与思想内容的绝妙结合，真可谓悦耳动心，美不胜收。翻译学习者若能在加强实践的同时，多观摩诵读名家译文，一定能够终身受益。

下面一例选自商务文本，但其精准恰当的用词同样令人耳目一新，也值得我们观摩学习。

例 2 Even the best corporate names are under attack these days. Still, those companies are reaping the benefits of the years they spent building customer trust and honing images of quality and dependability. To weather an extended bout of distrust and instability, strong brands are crucial. Companies will also have to work doubly hard to keep them intact.

参考译文： 现在即使是最著名的公司品牌也饱受非难。然而，这些公司已经开始收获多年来苦心经营建立起来的客户信任以及所营造的优质可靠的企业形象给他们带来的益处。要经受住不断的信任危机和动荡不安，就必须有强大的品牌形象。这些公司还需要付出双倍的努力方可维护其品牌形象。

在《英译中国现代散文选》序言中，翻译家张培基将自己娴熟高超的英语水平归功于自幼开始的散文背诵。他这样写道："当时我们都觉得压力很大，但苦尽甘来，事后莫不感到受用不尽。这九十六篇短文装在头脑里，使我增加了对英语和散文的兴趣，增加了语感，慢慢悟出了写文章的路子。从那以后，在我从事翻译或写作时，过去熟读的点点滴滴会不知不觉地出现在脑子里面。"因此，不论是商务翻译还是一般翻译，都需要大量阅读，要学会从语言材料中汲取营养。

2. 勤思考，培养语言认知方式

要学好翻译，除具备扎实的源语和译语基本功，还必须能够在双语之间进行转换，这两种能力体现在理解原文信息，并按照译入语思维方式及语言特点再现原文信息这两个环节。翻译离不开意义，而意义的载体是具体的词汇和句法结构。由于语言是以认知为基础的，不同的语言使用者具有不同的认知方式，因此使用中的语言往往具有动态性，不同的概念可以用同一个词汇来表达，同一概念也可以用不同的词汇来表示，这些都蕴含着不同的认知方式。因此，在翻译过程中，需要转换的不仅是语言事实及词汇和结构本身所表达的意义，而且还包括这些词汇和结构的安排方式以及其中隐含的意义。换言之，翻译不仅要再现语言形式的字面意义，而且要传递其中所蕴含的言外之意和隐含信息。

我们曾对学习者处理翻译作业中某些词语的方式进行过观察，结果表明，多数学习者都倾向于直接套用词典释义，尤其是词典所列举的前几条释义，而做不到根据上下文引申出词语的动态意义。初学者容易把翻译完全视为单纯的语言形式转换，而很少去思考语言形式背后所隐含的丰富信息及其与所在语言环境的关系。因此，认知方式的培养是提升翻译能力不可或缺的方面。

例3 If a communication, because of an ambiguity, seems inconsistent with prior communications, the receiving party may question the sincerity of the other party. When such inconsistencies accumulate, trust between the parties may *erode*, and the relationship may *wither*.

参考译文： 如果语义模糊造成后面的交流与之前的交流有出入，接受方就可能会质疑另一方的诚意。如果连续出现这种情况，彼此间的信任就会减弱，彼此间的关系就可能疏远。

在本例中，以斜体标注的词汇 erode 和 wither 对学习者而言并不属于生僻词汇，甚至可以说比较熟悉。但如果将它们删除，并要求学习者根据上下文填写合适的词汇，可能很少有人会想到它们。这表明，对多数学习者而言，这两个词都属于消极词汇，尚不能灵活运用其引申后的词义。这两个词的基本意义虽然都可以在词典中查找出来，但词典释义无法直接搬进译文。如果能从认知的角度来理解词典中各种释义之间的关联，并结合具体上下文将词义进行动态引申，我们就能正确理解原文意义，并给出符合译入语习惯的译文。

认知学习方式是一种通过理解和应用已有知识来促进学习的方法，它可以教会学习者根据已有知识激活相应的思维技巧和推理规则，从而有意识地利用构词、语义变化和文化背景等相关知识对未知信息进行思考和推理，有利于学习者感知和内化认知规律，主动使用语言学习策略。因此，学习者的进步不是 1+1 = 2 的累加，而是体现为 1+1 > 2 的增效效应。

在翻译实践中，译者面对的是作者对语言的创造性使用。在不同作者的笔下，同一个词汇或结构被置于不同的语言环境，也往往被赋予不同的含义并具有作者的个性特征。就翻译而言，如不能准确把握作者赋予词汇的特殊含义，就无法准确再现原文的真正意义和作者的真正意图，就会丧失翻译过程中的创造性，这样译出来的东西就像是"鸟的标本"，一根羽毛不少，但不能飞翔，没有灵魂和灵性。

由此可见，认知是语言学习的钥匙，学习者在翻译学习中应该着力培养自己的认知方式和对词汇意义的感悟能力。只有这样，才能根据不同的语境或上下文准确理解词汇和语言结构，从而提升翻译能力。

3. 常比较，提升思维转换能力

从语言和思维的关系来看，语言离不开思维，任何语言都是由词汇和语法规则构成的符号系统，而词汇和语法规则是思维的结果，词汇的意义正是概括了的思维和概念，语法结构则是思维逻辑的表现。同时，思维活动总是借助语言来实现，语言是思维的"物质外壳"，是思维的现实化。英汉两种语言之间的差异实质上是两种语言所蕴含的思维差异，因此，英汉两种语言之间的翻译必然会涉及不同思维方式的转换。

一位苏联语言学家曾经指出："最适合的外语学习方法是可以使学生悟到母语的语法结构，使其自动转移到外语上的方法。""本族语对外语学习的影响有两个方面：有利的一面——正迁移；无利的一面——负迁移，或叫干扰。恰到好处的对比教学利于充分发挥正迁移和克服负迁移。"（范维杰，1994）只有这样，才能"在目的语学习的过程中，目的语与母语水平的提高相得益彰；目的语文化与母语文化的鉴赏力相互促进；学习者自身的潜能得以充分发挥。"（高一虹，1994）可以这样说，认识两种语言的差异无疑是从根本上提升翻译能力的必由之路。

例 4 Any business is only as good as the people who comprise the organization. Therefore, an excellent employee is a pearl of great price.

原译1 做生意就如同与组成这个团体中的人打交道。因而，一名优秀的员工就如同一颗价值不菲的珍珠。

原译2 实际上，任何企业都是由工作人员所组成的。因此，卓尔不群的员工对公司而言是无价之宝。

原译3 任何公司的好坏取决于其人员构成。因此，一名优秀的员工对于公司来说相当于无价之宝。

原译4 优秀的企业需要优秀的人才来运营和管理，因此，一个出色的雇员就是公司的无价之宝。

原译5 任何一家企业都仅是和构成这个组织的成员那样优秀。因此，一名出色的雇员就如无价之宝。

原译6 一些企业的好坏取决于其员工素质的高低。因此，一个优秀的员工犹如一颗无价珍珠。

在上述六个译文中，前半句翻译都有问题，原译 1 和原译 2 没有正确理解原文结构，忽视了 as good as 这个词组；原译 3 和原译 4 虽然注意到了这个词组，但是仅仅从 good 一词的本义来推演该词组的意义，理解上出现偏差；原译 5 和原译 6 虽然理解正确，但译文仍没能摆脱原文思维方式和语言结构的束缚。

参考译文： 员工的素质决定企业的品质。因此，优秀员工是企业的无价之宝。

不同语言的特点或独特之处是翻译技巧得以产生的理论依据。语言的独特性使得我们无法在英汉两种语言之间寻求语言结构的绝对对等，而必须深刻领会英语原文的言内、言外意义，然后再从汉语中寻求功能相当的表达形式来再现原文的意义。因此可以说，英汉翻译是对英语原文信息内容高度融合，并根据汉语特点寻找适当表达形式的复杂过程。

4. 广阅读，拓展商务知识和相关文化知识

除了上述三个方面，翻译学习者还应该具备宽广的知识面，即所谓"通百艺而专一长"（knowing something of everything and everything of something）。在商务翻译中，不仅涉及英汉两种语言本身的知识，还涉及商务知识和文化背景知识。我们知道，缺乏语言知识，会造成理解不到位，吃不透原文，译文会出现"词懂句不通，文懂意不明"、译文受原文思维束缚等情况。假如不了解所译内容涉及的商务知识和文化背景知识，翻译时就无法做到灵活变通，更无法做到游刃有余，译文就会出现不准确、不符合商务文本特点等问题。

例 5 This procedure can result in high costs for bridging maturity gaps in situations where sudden and unexpected changes in interest rates occur that can momentarily influence the market quotations for swap transactions.

参考译文： 如果利率突然发生意想不到的变化，可能会暂时影响掉期交易的市场报价，这种程序可能会拉高弥补到期日缺口的成本。

阅读这个句子，会发现没有什么生词，但是试着去翻译时，会发现这些词汇的词义累加起来并不能形成有意义的句子，那是因为句子中包含商务术语，需要运用相应的商务知识才能正确理解。maturity 不是我们所熟悉的"成熟""长成"之意，而是指"保险单等的到期（应付款）"，maturity gap 的意思是"到期日缺口"，是指金融机构以市场价值计价的资产与负债加权平均到期日之间的差额。quotation 也不是我们所熟悉的"引语"之意，而是指"报价"。swap transaction 合起来的意思是"掉期交易"，是指交易双方约定在未来某一时期相互交换某种资产的交易形式。

翻译作为跨文化交流的手段，与文化有着密不可分的联系。王佐良先生曾经说过，翻译者"处理的是个别的词，他面对的则是两大片文化"。商务翻译还同时关涉商务活动，更需要双方在相互理解的基础上产生共情共鸣，避免文化误读和文化冲突，跨越文化障碍，实现跨文化商务沟通的顺畅进行。

例 6 Most companies realize that the only way to do business effectively in other cultures is to adapt to those cultures. The phrase "think globally, act locally" is often used to describe this approach. The first step that a web business usually takes to reach potential customers in other countries, and thus in other cultures, is to provide local language versions of its website.

参考译文： 很多公司都认识到，在异国文化背景中有效从事商务活动的唯一途径便是适应该文化。"国际化思考，本地化行动"这一说法经常用于描述这种文化适应。要想赢得其他国家（因而也是其他文化）的潜在客户，网络营销的第一步就是要用当地语言创建网站。

在国际商务活动中，一个企业的成功，不仅取决于它的生产能力，还取决于它的国际视野和跨文化沟通能力。一个企业要想拓展业务，扩大经济收益，不仅要具备强大的经济实力、高端的技术和出色的管理水平，而且必须具有全球视野，对目标市场的文化有深入的理解。跨国文化差异研究专家曾经说过，跨国公司的失败几乎都是忽略文化差异所致。因此，作为跨国商务活动桥梁的译者，要扩展文化知识，对文化差异了然于胸。

5. 严要求，培养高度的责任心

翻译是一项要求很高的工作，其中甘苦只有译者自知。在翻译过程中，一个句子，甚至一个词汇都可能成为棘手的问题，稍有不慎，便有可能会出错。因此，翻译大家无不具有严谨的作风。严复在《天演论·译例言》中曾经感慨"一名之立，旬月踟蹰"，鲁迅也曾经感叹"词典不离手，冷汗不离身"，而在他们笔下都产生了不朽的译著。为了减少翻译中的失误，译者应该做到以下三点：

（1）养成自上而下理解、自下而上转换的习惯。在理解原文时，译者要从整体的角度去把握局部的意义，包括用词、搭配关系和句式安排，同时还要悉心体会作者在语言选择时所参照的聚合关系，实现自上而下的理解。假如仅仅孤立地看待词句，而不能把这些因素置于原作的整体语境中，或不参照聚合关系这一坐标，就很难体会作者在语言链中的良苦用心与真实意图。而在翻译转换过程中，译者则必须将自己对原作信息的全方位把握重新整合，选择恰当的、能够体现原作者思想精髓的词汇、搭配和句式等来实现语言形式的转换，自下而上进行译文的重构。

（2）将译文审校作为翻译的重要步骤。不少初学者总是对自己充满信心，对自己的译文非常满意，一旦翻译完成，就觉得万事大吉。然而，这种做法可能会导致一些错漏被忽视。译文审校不仅包括对语法、拼写和标点等的检查，更要对译文质量进行评估，包括其准确性、合理性以及是否符合目标语文化等。译者需要把译文审校视为翻译流程中必不可少的一环。

（3）用逻辑来检验译文的准确性。匈牙利翻译家拉多·久吉尔说过："翻译是逻辑活动，翻译作品是逻辑活动的产物。"语言表达清晰，推理合情合理，文通字顺、文气贯通，语言就合乎逻辑性。因此，逻辑是检验译文准确性的重要标准。

例7 Given risk conditions, capital flows to where it can earn the highest rate of return.

原译1 鉴于存在风险因素，资本总会流向回报率最高的地方。
原译2 鉴于风险的因素，资金通常都流向它能够获得最高的回报率的地方。
原译3 将风险因素考虑在内，资金流入了能产生最高回报的地方。
原译4 考虑到风险因素，资本主要流向获利多、风险小的地区。

从微观层面上讲，原译1"鉴于存在风险因素"和原译2"鉴于风险的因素"两个表述语义非常模糊，指向性不明，"虽译犹不译也"。原译2和原译3都将capital译为"资金"，不符合原文的意义。原译4中"获利多、风险小"有过译之嫌，也与风险投资的特点相悖。从宏观层面上讲，四个译文逗号前后的内容不连贯，都存在逻辑关系上不协调的问题，读起来让人难以理解。其实这句话揭示了资本的本质，风险投资之所以被称为风险投资，是因为这种投资行为有很多不确定性，给投资及其回报带来很大的风险，或者说逐利性是资本的本质特征。翻译本句话时，需要从逻辑上进行梳理，而运用恰当的连接词，可以帮助我们将其关系理顺。

参考译文： 即使存在风险因素，资本依然会流向回报率最高的领域。

综上所述，翻译是对译者综合能力要求很高的一项工作。译者的功力绝非一朝一夕可以练就，而是需要通过译者在长期的翻译实践中不断提升对语言的认知和感悟能力，增强对源语和目的语之间差异的认识，有意识地培养两种语言之间的转换能力以及实现上述转换所需的思维能力和文化能力。

The Psychological Contract

(1) <u>One concept that has been useful in discussing employees' relationships with organizations is that of a psychological contract, which refers to the unwritten expectations employees and employers have about the nature of their work relationships</u>. Because the psychological contract is individual and subjective in nature, it focuses on expectations about "fairness" that may not be defined clearly by employees.

Both tangible items (such as wages, benefits, employee productivity, and attendance) and intangible items (such as loyalty, fair treatment, and job security) are encompassed by unwritten psychological contracts between employers and employees. Many employers may attempt to (2) <u>detail</u> their expectations through employee handbooks and policy manuals, but those materials are (2) <u>only</u> part of the total "contractual" relationship.

(3) <u>At one time, employees exchanged their efforts and capabilities for a secure job that offered rising pay, good benefits, and career progression within the organization</u>. But as organizations have downsized and cut workers who have given long and loyal service, a growing number of employees question whether they should be loyal to their employers. Closely related to the psychological contract is psychological ownership. When individuals feel that they have some control and perceived rights in the organization, they are more likely to be committed to the organization. How employee expectations have changed in psychological contracts is a question in discussion.

Employers provide	Employees contribute
Competitive compensation and benefits	Continuous skill improvement and increased productivity
Career development opportunities	Reasonable time with organization
Flexibility to balance work and family life	Extra effort when needed

Two factors affecting the relationship between individuals and organizations are economic changes and the expectations of different generations of individuals. These factors affect the psychological contract in a number of ways.

The ebb and flow of the economy is a major factor affecting employee expectations. Just consider the "employment world" when the dot-com and technology boom was underway. Many individuals, especially younger ones with technology backgrounds, expected and demanded high starting salaries, (4) <u>hiring bonuses, stock options</u>, relaxed and casual workplaces, and frequent career promotions or changes. However, when the dot-com bubble burst, these same individuals had to face a different job market and employers offering different rewards and job environments.

Much has been written about the differing expectations of individuals in different generations. Many of these observations give only generalizations about individuals in the various age groups. Some of the common generational labels are:

- Matures (born 1909–1945)
- Baby boomers (born 1946–1964)
- Generation X (born 1965–1980)
- Generation Y (born 1981–1996)

Rather than identifying the characteristics cited for each of these groups, it is most important here to emphasize that people's expectations differ between generations, (5) as well as within these generational labels. For employers, the differing expectations present challenges. For instance, many of the baby boomers and matures are concerned about security and experience, whereas the younger generation Ys expect to be rewarded quickly, and tend to be more questioning about why managers and organizations make the decisions they do. Also, consider the dynamics of a mature manager directing Generation X and Y individuals, or Generation X managers supervising older, more experienced baby boomers. These generational differences are likely to continue to create challenges and conflicts in organizations because of the differing expectations that various individuals have. One of the most noticeable differences is in loyalty to organizations.

Employees do believe in psychological contracts and hope their employers will (6) honor that side of the "agreement." Many employees still want security and stability, interesting work, a supervisor they respect, and competitive pay and benefits. If these elements are not provided, employees may feel a diminished need to contribute to organizational performance. (7) When organizations merge, lay off large numbers of employees, outsource work, and use large numbers of temporary and part-time workers, employees see fewer reasons to give their loyalty to employers in return for this loss of job security. (8) This decline is evident in some American firms, where significant staff cutbacks and declines in stock prices have demoralized many of the remaining staff members. More employers are finding that in tight labor markets, turnover of key people occurs more frequently when employee loyalty is low, which in turn emphasizes the importance of a loyal and committed workforce.

A study on psychological contracts has identified what employees value most and how they respond when their expectations are and are not met. The study found that discrepancies between what the individuals valued and the employers provided were related to lower job satisfaction and higher intention to leave. Thus, the research has confirmed what many would logically think, that is, individuals whose psychological contract "obligations" are not being fulfilled by their employers are more dissatisfied with their jobs and are more likely to leave. Finally, employees expect their employers to provide feedback on individual performance through performance appraisal systems and provide career development opportunities. Employers who understand the "new" psychological contracts expected by employees are more likely to have satisfied employees who stay longer.

难点解析

（1）本句是一个较长的复合句，结构复杂严谨，环环相扣，充分体现了英语句式的形合（hypotaxis）特点。该句实现形合的手段是三个从句引导词（同位语引导词 that、表语引导词 that 和定语从句引导词 which），翻译时要充分考虑汉语和英语句式结构上的不同，把英语通过引导词连接起来的形合结构转换为汉语的意合结构（parataxis），化长为短，化繁为简，运用"拆译法"将原文分译为两句。

（2）detail 在这里用作动词，意为"详述、详细说明"。另外应注意将 only 一词所蕴含的语气翻译出来。

（3）词组 at one time 意为"在过去某个时间"，可以引申为"过去"。exchange...for 本义为"用……换取/交换"，此处不应受字面意义束缚，可适当变换措辞。career progression within the organization 指在某人供职的组织内部得到提拔。

（4）hiring bonus 译为"入职安置费"，指员工入职上岗后的经费补贴，是吸引人才的有效手段。stock option 指股票期权，又称经理股票期权（executive stock option），是指公司授予高级管理人员、技术骨干等雇员在未来一定时间内以某一特定价格购买一定数量公司股票的权利。股票期权制度在激励企业经营者、减少治理成本、改善治理结构、促进稳健经营等方面具有优越性。该制度在欧美企业界获得极大发展，被认为是一项创造财富、提升生产力的高效率制度。

（5）翻译时 as well as 结构较难安排。译者应摆脱原文结构的束缚，透彻理解原文意义，然后根据汉语行文特点进行转换。

（6）honor 为动词，意思是"执行、承认……的有效性"。

（7）这句话较长，涉及组织的一些行为，需要根据语篇内容所涉及的领域进行翻译，merge 指企业合并，outsource 指业务外包。see fewer reasons to 可以译成"就更没有理由……"。

（8）significant staff cutbacks 意为"大量裁员"。demoralize 意为"使士气低迷"，翻译时需要进行调整，否则就会造成译文的翻译腔。

商务知识讲座

人力资源管理

美国知名管理学者托马斯·彼得斯说过："企业或事业唯一真正的资源是人，管理就是充分开发人力资源以做好工作。"在知识经济时代，人力资源越来越成为组织发展和提高绩效最重要的资源。

广义的人力资源是指能够推动整个经济和社会发展，具有劳动能力（体力、智力）的人口总和。从社会的角度来看，人力资源是指在一定的实践和一定的经济范围内，整个社会所能够利用来提供产品或服务的所有体力和脑力的总和；从企业的角度来看，人力资源是指一家企业所能够获得、开发、保持和利用的所有体力和脑力的总和。人力资源作为社会经济资源中的一个特殊部分，具有以下特点：

1. 能动性：人不同于自然界的其他生物，因为人具有思想、感情，具有主观能动性，能够有目的地进行活动，能动地改造客观世界，可以通过各种学习和培训实现自我强化，可以选择适合自己的职业并从事创造性的劳动。

2. 动态性：人的劳动能力会随着时间而变化。

3. 再生性和增值性：虽然人力资源在使用中会出现损耗，但是人可以通过不断学习更新知识、提高技能、积累经验，实现自我更新、自我提高。人力资源的这种再生不同于一般生物资源的再生，它会受到人类意识的支配和人类活动的影响。

4. 社会性：每个人的价值观和行为方式都会受到其民族文化和社会环境的影响，从而具有不同特征。

人力资源管理（Human Resources Management，HRM）是为实现组织的战略目标，采用现代管理方法，对人力资源的获取、开发、保持和利用等方面进行的计划、组织、指挥、控制和协调等一系列活动。它以组织中人与人的关系的调整、人与事的配合为研究对象，以实现充分开发人力资源、挖掘人的潜能、调动人的主观能动性和工作积极性、提高工作效率的目标。人力资源管理的核心是人职匹配，使人与岗位互相满足对方的要求。

人力资源管理的发展经历了从经验管理到科学管理到文化管理三个阶段。弗雷德里克·W. 泰勒曾致力于解决美国工厂在生产过程中遇到的实际问题，逐渐形成了广为人知的四项"科学管理原则"，实现了企业管理从经验到科学的转变，极大地提高了工作效率。科学管理依靠金字塔式等级森严的组织和行政命令的方式，实行集中和统一的指挥和控制，权力和责任大都集中在上层，在提升效率的同时，其弊端也逐步显露。20世纪80年代兴起的企业文化理论注重满足员工的社交、自尊、自我价值实现等高层次的精神需求，成为激励员工绩效、赢得组织发展优势的关键手段。而大量跨国公司建立之后实行的分权管理为不同民族、不同语言和不同文化背景的跨国公司员工认同企业文化提供了土壤，成为凝聚人心的重要力量。

人力资源管理有三个目标：

1. 取得人力资源最大的使用价值：人力资源管理的首要目标就是把人与事适当地配合起来，使事得其人，人尽其才，人事相宜，共同发展，充分体现组织管理的"大高低"原则，即大价值、高效能、低成本。具体可以用以下两个公式表示：

人的使用价值最大化 = 人的有效技能的最大发挥

人的有效技能 = 人的劳动技能 × 适用率 × 发挥率 × 有效率

2. 最大程度发挥人的主观能动性：工作表现是能力和激励的乘积，因此，人力资源管理就是要通过促进人与人之间关系的和谐，增进合作，发挥员工的主观能动性，提高工作效率。

3. 培养全面发展的人：员工的素质和能力的高低极大地影响着组织的绩效，因此，培养高素质、全面发展的人应该成为组织的出发点和重要目标。

知识化、全球化和信息化的环境促使人力资源管理逐渐成为企业战略管理的组成部分，凸显了人力资源管理在企业价值链中的重要作用。充分信任员工，实行员工自我管理，体现人本管理思想，创建学习型组织，重视员工的终身学习，使员工实现自我价值，逐渐成为人力资源管理的发展趋势，也成为培养组织持续的创造力、凝聚力和竞争力的重要保证。

翻译练习

I. 思考题

1. 结合翻译实践谈谈翻译对语言学习的促进作用。
2. 举例说明你是如何利用认知学习方式推断词汇在上下文中的具体含义的。

II. 从"The Psychological Contract"中摘录给你深刻印象的句子或词组。

1. _____
2. _____
3. _____
4. _____
5. _____

III. 商务术语翻译

360-degree performance appraisal	
balanced scorecard	
bona fide occupational qualification (BFOQ)	
career planning	
content validity	
corporate culture	
cost-benefit analysis	
critical incident method	
direct financial compensation	
employee empowerment	

employee stock ownership plan (ESOP)	
ergonomics	
external equity	
externship	
glass ceiling	
grievance procedure	
human capital	
incentive compensation	
internal equity	
job description	
job enlargement	
job enrichment	
learning organization	
management by objective (MBO)	
merit pay	
nepotism	
organization development (OD)	
pay equity	
performance appraisal (PA)	
phased retirement	
profit sharing	
psychological contract	
quality circle	
rating scale method	
recruitment	
role conflict	
self-assessment	

strategic human resource management	
stress management program	
succession planning	
survey feedback	
wellness program	
workflow analysis	

IV. 句子翻译

1. In the 21st century the business environment has become extremely competitive and continuous improvement is no longer an option; it has become a necessity. One area where organizations of any size can create changes is in their utilization of human resources. People are a company's greatest asset.

2. Changing outdated structures and even more archaic attitudes can help attract, motivate, and retain the employees who have the vision, skills, and determination to adapt to a constantly changing world.

3. The use of external motivation, such as large bonuses, can be counterproductive because such bonuses foster personal greed rather than corporate conscience and promote competition rather than collaborative working practices. Intrinsic rewards, on the other hand, are more sustainable and help employees focus on the job rather than on the reward.

4. Leadership is all about getting people consistently to give their best, helping them grow to their fullest potential, and motivating them to work toward a common good.

5. A leader who has respect for other people at all levels of an organization, for the work they do, and for their abilities, aspirations, and needs, will find that respect is returned.

6. Helping people learn new skills and try out different jobs within an organization can be a form of intrinsic motivation and may aid in retention of staff who might otherwise leave to seek new challenges elsewhere.

7. One theory of human motivation developed by Abraham Maslow has received a great deal of exposure. In this theory, Maslow classified human needs into five categories that ascend in a definite order. Until more basic needs are adequately fulfilled, a person will not strive to meet higher needs. Maslow's well-known hierarchy is composed of: (1) physiological needs, (2) safety and security needs, (3) belonging and love needs, (4) esteem needs, and (5) self-actualization needs.

8. The pressure of modern life, coupled with the demands of a job, can lead to emotional imbalances that are collectively labeled stress. Not all stress is unpleasant. To be alive

means to respond to the stress of achievement and the excitement of a challenge. In fact, evidence indicates that people need a certain amount of stimulation, and that monotony can bring on some of the same problems as overwork. The term "stress" usually refers to excessive stress.
9. Excellent management involves maximizing performance to achieve specific organizational goals. While many managers know the goals they want to reach and how their employees fall short, they struggle when it comes to changing employee behavior to get the results they want.
10. In its most basic sense, job satisfaction is a positive emotional state resulting from evaluating one's job experiences. Job dissatisfaction occurs when one's expectations are not met. For example, if an employee expects clean and safe working conditions of the job, then the employee is likely to be dissatisfied if the workplace is dirty and dangerous.

V. 篇章翻译

There are various points in a career trajectory where problems can occur, from recruitment, training, and mentorship to promotion and retention. Recruitment can be particularly difficult because a new employee is an unknown factor. The evidence that many companies are failing to recruit the right people is the number of people who are patently in the wrong job! One reason for this is that organizations make job offers based on past performance rather than on realistic assessment of future potential.

The mismatch between an individual and their position within a company may, however, be due to factors other than poor recruitment practices. Employees can be promoted into positions that no longer match their skills; rigidity in organizational structures may inhibit opportunities for employees, particularly women, who need to balance work and family responsibilities; and organizational reward structures can encourage people to take jobs for the wrong reasons.

Failing to promote employees with the aptitude and skills to be effective managers can be just as big a mistake as promoting the wrong people. Recent evidence indicates that organizations with women in top management positions outperform those with more traditional, male-dominated leadership structures.

However, many women who begin their careers on an equal footing with their male colleagues fail to reach the highest level of management because of rigid organizational structures that inhibit an achievable work-life balance. Although many companies are beginning to recognize the value of a more flexible approach to working, employees who take advantage of this are often seen as less committed or ambitious.

翻译名家

王佐良（1916—1995），著名教育家、翻译家、诗人和英国文学研究专家。1939年毕业于西南联合大学外语系（原清华大学外语系），1947年赴英国牛津大学攻读英国文学研究生。1949年9月他怀着一颗赤子之心，毅然决然放弃了留法读博的机会，选择回国，把余生都献给了我国的外语教育事业。

王佐良率先倡导英语专业学生要了解欧洲文化及其与中国文化的差异，强调中国文化对中文译者素养的重要性。他认为"通过文化来学习语言，语言也会学得更好"，"文化知识和文化修养有助于人的性情、趣味、道德、价值标准等的提高，也就是人的素养的提高"。他很早就提出了译者的跨文化素养对翻译的重要作用，译者不仅需要了解外国文化，还必须了解自己民族的文化，因为翻译不仅仅是双语交流，更是一种跨文化交流，翻译的目的是突破语言障碍，实现并促进文化交流。"翻译者必须是一个真正意义的文化人"，因为"他处理的是个别的词，他面对的则是两大片文化"。

王佐良还在文学、哲学、语言学以及西方文化领域造诣极深，译作甚丰，且篇篇是精品。他翻译的《一朵红红的玫瑰》（"A Red, Red Rose"）和培根的《谈读书》（"Of Studies"）因其译文精美而广为传颂，值得研读。

第 2 章　英汉语言特点对比

> 每个字在一国语言中都有很长久的历史，在历史过程中，它和许多事物情境发生联想，和那一国的人民生活状态打成一片，它有一种特殊的情感氛围。
>
> ——朱光潜

问题导入

1. 翻译下面的句子。

   Probably through oversight, the check was not signed, and we are returning it to you for your kind signature.

   译文　_____

   _____

   _____

2. 思考译文和原文在词汇、主客体、句子结构等方面的异同，并说明你在翻译时就选词和句子结构方面所作的调整。

   相同点：_____

   不同点：_____

   调整：_____

翻译知识讲座

英汉语言特点对比

翻译从表面上看是不同语言之间的转换过程，但究其内涵我们会发现，语言超越了简单的符号系统，它体现了使用该语言的民族所特有的世界观、哲学观、道德观、宗教信仰、思维方式等深层文化内涵。因此，翻译不只是语言之间的转化，更是通过这种转换实现不同语言和文化之间的对话与沟通。

在翻译过程中，首先需要关注意义的理解与传达。语言并非孤立存在，它产生并深植于特定的文化之中，需要将其与文化背景相结合才能表达意义，确定对语言文字的正确理解与表达。其次，译者需要掌握对比方法，熟练进行源语与译语之间的对比分析。具体而言，译者在翻译的过程中，需要深入理解两种语言之间的共性和特性，通过对比分析找出翻译中存在的客观规律，确立翻译的科学依据。同时根据源语和译语之间的深层次文化异同，考虑目标读者和翻译目的，选择适当的翻译策略（如归化与异化）、翻译方法（如直译与意译）和翻译技巧（如省译、增译或改译），确保信息准确传递，并达到最佳的可读性。本章将从词汇、句法和语篇三个层面来简要概述英汉两种语言的差异。

1. 英汉词汇对比

词汇是语言中最小的完整语义单位，是构成句子最基本的单位，反映文化特质最为直接。词汇概念意义的产生，词义的发展、演进、延伸和消失，都是文化发展演进的直接体现。根据利奇（Leech, 1974）对词汇意义的七种类型划分，词汇的概念意义、内涵意义、风格意义、情感意义、联想意义、搭配意义和主题意义都与词汇所在的文化有直接的关系。奈达（Nida, 1993）认为，语言在文化中的作用以及文化对词汇意义、习语含义的影响非常普遍，因此，要正确理解文本，译者必须理解其中涉及的文化背景。在翻译过程中，英汉两种语言在词汇层面的对应关系大致分为以下三种情况：完全对应、不完全对应、完全不对应。

（1）完全对应

人类在漫长的进化、发展过程中，不同民族、不同文化之间有许多相似甚至相同的生活体验，反映在语言上，便是不同的语言系统中有部分词汇的意义基本相同，这也是不同民族、不同文化之间可以交流的基础。在英汉两种语言系统中，词义完全对应关系一般存在于部分常用词汇，如 apple—苹果，banana—香蕉，peach—桃子，river—河，bird—鸟，fish—鱼，jump—跳，run—跑，walk—走，write—写，peace—和平，war—战争；部分专业技术术语，如 economy—经济，market—市场，science—科学，technology—技术，cost—成本，fund—基金，consultation—协商，patent—专利，industrialization—工业化；还有部分专有名词，如 World Health Organization (WHO)—世界卫生组织，Sea Waybill (SWB)—海运单，Ex Works (EXW)—工厂交货，consumer surplus—消费者剩余，exclusive right—独家经营/专营权，invitation of tender—招标，等等。但是即使是这类常用词汇、专业技术术语和专有名词，在具体使用过程中也时常存在意义范围拓宽的情况，比如英语词汇 stop 与汉语的"停"是完全对应关系，但是不能把"停车"简单地译为 stop the car。完全对应是英汉两种语言中极为少见的现象，绝大部分情况下，英汉两种语言都没有严格的一一对应关系，这一点需要引起我们的高度重视。

（2）不完全对应

所谓不完全对应，是指一种语言的词汇在另一种语言中有多个同义词，或者一种语言的词汇同时与另一种语言中的多个词汇的某个或某几个意义有对应关系。一般而言，词义不完全对应主要表现在概念意义的不完全对应以及附加意义（包括内涵意义、风格意义、情感意义、联想意义、搭配意义和主题意义）的不完全对应。

概念意义是语言交际的核心因素，是语言不可或缺的基本组成部分，也是最基础、最根本的意义。概念意义是抽象的，与客观事物并不发生直接的联系。概念意义表达或理解有误，往往会引起交际冲突。英汉两种语言中，概念意义不完全对应的情况极为常见，以亲属称谓语为例，英语中的 aunt 在汉语中就有"阿姨""姨妈""舅妈""姑妈""伯母""婶娘"等称谓与之对应；英语中的 cousin 在汉语中有"堂兄""堂弟""表哥""表弟""堂姐""堂妹""表姐""表妹"等对应称谓；英语中的 brother-in-law 在汉语中则有"内兄""内弟""襟兄""襟弟""姐夫""妹夫"等称谓与之对应。而汉语中的"说"，在英语中也有很多词汇与之对应，如 speak、say、talk、murmur、mumble、exclaim、announce、shout、retort 等。

附加意义是由概念意义衍生出的意义，往往与客观事物的本质特性或特点相关。在英汉两种语言中，尽管有许多词汇的概念意义相同或相似，但内涵意义、风格意义、情感意义、联想意义、搭配意义和主题意义等附加意义却因文化差异而不同。英汉双语中，有些词汇有着相同或者相似的概念意义，但它们在英语中有附加意义，而在汉语中则没有，反之亦然。比如英语中的 white elephant 与汉语中"白象"的概念意义基本无差，但是 white elephant 在英语中的联想意义是"昂贵而无用的东西"，在汉语中则没有这样的附加意义；英语中的 pine 与汉语的"松"，英语中的 crane 与汉语的"鹤"，都属于有相同的概念意义，而汉语中的"松""鹤"都有"长寿"的附加意义，但在英语中则没有。

有些词汇有着相同或者相似的概念意义，然而在英汉双语中的联想意义不同。如英语中用 as wise as an owl 来表扬人聪明，而汉语中会说"机灵得像个猴"；英语中用 as stupid as a goose 来形容人蠢笨，而汉语中会说"笨得像头猪"；英语中用 cry up wine and sell vinegar 来表示里外不一、名不副实，对应的汉语则是"挂羊头卖狗肉"；英语用 as strong as a horse 来形容人健壮，而汉语则说"健壮如牛"。还有些词汇的附加意义不同，比如英语中的 peasant 与汉语中的"农民"所体现的附加意义并不完全相同，peasant 常为贬义，有乡巴佬、缺乏教养之意，而"农民"通常包含勤劳、朴实等寓意，并无贬义；英语中的 propaganda 一词通常含有贬义，而汉语中的"宣传"则往往是中性词；英语中的 individualism 更倾向于褒义，而汉语中的"个人主义"则常被视为贬义。简而言之，英汉两种语言的词汇普遍存在词汇意义不完全对应的情况，这主要源于中西方在生活环境、神话传说、历史事件、文学经典、宗教信仰、文化心理以及政治、经济与社会制度等各方面的显著差异。

在商务英语中，不完全对应关系往往是由一词多义现象引起的，具体表现为某些词汇在普通英语和商务英语中的词义不同，如 negotiation 在一般情境下与汉语词汇"谈判""协商"对应，而在国际贸易情境下，商务术语 negotiation 为"议付"之意。

例1 By irrevocable sight letter of credit payable against presentation of the shipping documents as stipulated under Clause (3)(A) of the Terms of Delivery of this Contract to be opened with Citibank, San Francisco by the Buyers in favor of the Sellers to reach the Sellers 30 days before the date of shipment and to remain valid for negotiation in China till the 15th day after shipment.

参考译文： 用由买方通过花旗银行旧金山分行开立的以卖方为抬头（或受益人）的、凭本合同交货条款第（3）(A)条所列装运单据（提示）付款的不可撤销即期信用证支付，该信用证应在装运期前30天开到卖方，其有效期应到装运后第15天止，在中国议付。

又如，surplus一词在普通英语中为"剩余、剩余额"之意，但是在商务术语中，有"顺差"之意。

例2 The RMB has been under a lot of pressure to appreciate in recent years. Part of the reason is that China's international balance of payments maintains a large number of surpluses.

参考译文： 近年来人民币升值压力加大，其中一个原因是中国的国际收支出现了高额顺差。

英语中business一词的释义较为丰富，各释义间存在着某种意义关联，可以根据语境翻译成不同的汉语词汇，这和汉语词汇之间就形成了一对多的不完全对应关系，而这些汉语词汇又可以与英语中的其他词汇或表达形成对应关系。

举例	汉语释义	本例中英语同义表达
It's been a pleasure to do business with you. She works in the computer business.	商业、买卖、生意	commerce, trade
Is the trip to Rome business or pleasure?	商务、公事	work
Her task was to drum up (increase) business.	营业额、贸易额	turnover
She works in a family business.	商业机构、企业、公司、商店、工厂	company, enterprise
It's the business of the police to protect the community.	职责	responsibility
He has some unfinished business to deal with.	要事	important matters
The plane crash was a terrible business.	事情	event
We're grateful for your business.	惠顾、光顾	being a customer

（3）完全不对应

完全不对应，又称词汇空缺现象，是指源语中的指称对象在目标语文化中不存在或者与目标语文化中的可比对象有明显不同，由此导致一种语言的某一词汇在另一种语言中无法找到对应形式。词汇空缺本质上是不同民族文化的空缺，英语中有的词汇有某种文化意义，但汉语的对应词无特定的文化意义，如Halloween、Achilles' Heel、Easter、Valentine's Day等。同样，在汉语中，有些词汇有某种文化意义，但英语无对应的文化意义，如"粽子""饺子""火锅""京剧""相声""太极拳""拜年""压岁钱""石库门""四合院"等，均无法在英语中找到对应词语。除了这些反映中国传统文化的词汇之外，在中国近年来的社会、文化、经济的发展历程中，也出现了许多反映中国特色现象的词汇，例如"美丽中国""绿色发展""新发展理念""一带一路""人类命运共同体""大湾区"等，在英语中也都无法找到契合的对应词汇，只能根据汉语意思，用恰当的英语进行解释、翻译。

除了上述英汉词汇对应的三种情况外，英汉词汇的对应关系还会基于语境的不同而变化。英语词汇 play 可以搭配乐器、球类和游戏，但在汉语中则需要视不同的语境对应不同的汉语词汇，如 play the piano 对应"弹钢琴"，play the violin 对应"拉小提琴"，play the flute 则变成了"吹笛子"；play volleyball 对应"打排球"，play football 对应"踢足球"；play chess 对应"下棋"，play cards 对应"打牌"，而 play a game 则对应"玩游戏"。汉语中的"送"可以搭配人、物，但需要视不同的语境对应不同的英语词汇，如"开车送你上学"对应 drive you to school，"送你一张生日贺卡"对应 give you a birthday card，"送货上门"对应 deliver the goods to the door，"送客人到门口"则对应 accompany the guest to the door。除此以外，词汇含义的广狭、感情色彩的褒贬、文体意义的差别都会受到语境的制约，因此，译者在翻译过程中不能脱离词汇的语境来选择和明确具体的词义。

2. 英汉句法对比

词汇是能独立运用的最小语言单位，但句子才是语言表达的基本单位，对于初学翻译者而言，句子是较为理想的翻译单位。因此，翻译过程中，对英汉两种语言的句法结构进行对比分析是十分必要的。

从句法角度来看，语言可分为综合型语言和分析型语言两大类。英语是一种由综合型向分析型过渡的语言，仍然保存着丰富的形态变化手段，而汉语则是典型的分析型语言，主要借助分析性语法手段（如词序、辅助词等）来表示词与词之间的语法关系。英汉语句法的根本差异体现为语言形态丰富与否。从基本句式来看，英语基本句式是主谓结构，并在此结构上扩展，而汉语不仅有主谓结构，还有话题—评述句和非主谓句；英语长句的结构多为多枝共干结构，而汉语长句则多为竹节型结构，包含多个短小流水句。从语态来看，英语被动态使用普遍，而汉语被动态使用较为受限。从句子的扩展方向来看，英语句子具有向右扩展的特征，多为右分支结构，左短右长、头轻脚重，定语和中心语形态变化机制丰富，定语在中心语之后；而汉语句子则具有向左扩展的特征，多为左分支结构，句首开放态势、头大尾小，定语和中心语的位置相对固定，定语在中心语之前。鉴于本书第四章中会有更详尽的句子翻译相关内容，本节只简要介绍英汉语句法的差异。

（1）形合与意合：逻辑思维与形象思维

英语文化倾向于逻辑思维，中国传统文化更侧重形象思维，这种思维模式的差异在英汉句子结构中体现尤为突出。英语以句子的结构形式为中心，重心焦点明显，句子内部或句子之间的关系为显性 (overtness)，依靠句法手段 (syntactic devices) 或词汇手段 (lexical devices) 予以表现，以形制意，句法有形合 (hypotaxis) 特征。汉语以话题为中心，没有明显的重心焦点，句子内部或句子之间的关系呈隐性（covertness），依靠语义手段（semantic devices）进行连接，以意驭形，句法属意合（parataxis）。

从语法理解的实际步骤来看，英语行文是一种"结构—语义"过程：先根据形态（首先是动词、名词及主谓一致关系）找出主语和谓语动词，在此基础上建立起句子的基本框架并借助形合手段进行扩展。汉语行文则是"语义—结构"过程：句子大致呈现为线性结构，句子的成分之间缺乏显性的形态标志，要厘清句子成分之间的结构关系必须先从语义入手，了解字词的意义。

例 3 We are proud of the progress we've made and are 100% committed to raising the bar on ourselves in the important quest of building and maintaining a healthy and balanced world that meets society's evolving needs.

例 3 句子结构清晰，基本框架为主谓宾结构，后置定语从句对宾语 progress 进行修饰和限定，状语成分 in the important quest of 中，介词 of 的宾语结构中也带有 that 引导的定语从句对 world 进行修饰和限定。译成汉语时，应根据形合与意合方面的差异性进行转换。

参考译文： 我们为取得的成绩感到自豪。今后，我们将不断提升自己，致力于建立和维护世界的健康平衡发展，以满足人们不断提高的需求。

在翻译实践中，处理英语形合和汉语意合的差别时，不应局限于句内，而应根据前后句的语法关系、整个段落的主题等来综合考量。

例 4 We define sustainability as meeting today's needs without compromising the future's. This applies to all facets of our business—from engineering environmentally responsible products to creating equal opportunities for our employees and for those in our communities.

参考译文： 我们认为，可持续发展应该是在不牺牲未来利益的前提下满足当下需求，这一理念应该适用于方方面面，包括研发环保产品、为员工和全社会提供均等机会等。

上例中有两处易出现对原文理解的偏差，从而导致译文的不准确。一处是第一句中 the future's 后面省略掉的名词指的是什么；另一处是第二句中的代词 this 和 those 指代的分别是什么。通过对英语原文的语法分析，第一句中省略的名词是 needs，而第二句中的代词 this 指代的是 sustainability，those 则指代的是 people。

（2）物称与人称：客体意识与主体意识

西方传统思维以自然为认知对象，因此英语注重客体意识，主张保持主体和客体二者之间的距离，以实现人对客体对象的冷静剖析。英语句子结构重物称，倾向于从客观视角表达事物如何作用于人的感知。而汉语则注重主体思维，句子结构重人称，倾向于从主观视角出发来叙述客观事物。另外，儒家文化崇尚"天人合一"，把自然与人看成是一个整体，因此汉语一般对思维的主体和客体不加区分，在语言上则表现为汉语句子常以有生命的名词作主语。请见下例：

例 5 To overcome some of these challenges, Scope 3 emissions are calculated according to the Greenhouse Gas Protocol Corporate Value Chain (Scope 3) Accounting and Reporting Standard.

参考译文： 为了克服上述困难，我们根据《温室气体核算体系：企业价值链（范围三）核算和报告标准》计算了范围三的排放量。

此例句中，源语文本的主语是 Scope 3 emissions，属于物称主语，体现了文本的客观视角，译文在处理的时候使用了人称主语"我们"，从人的角度来审视、处理问题。再如：

例 6 A subset of these volatile organic compound emissions is defined by the local environmental protection department as hazardous air pollutants.

参考译文： 当地环保部门称，这些挥发性有机化合物排放到大气中的气体为有害空气污染物。

此例中，源语文本的主语是 a subset of these volatile organic compound emissions，属物称主语，配合被动语态的使用，凸显出文本的正式性。译文将源语文本中的 the local environmental protection department 用作主语，配合谓语动词"称"的使用。另外，需要提醒的是，翻译中遇到专有名词，需查证权威工具书或者网站，使用规范译名。

（3）句首重心与句尾重心：直线思维与环形思维

如前所述，英语句子通常为右分支结构，其语义重心一般置于句首，即先阐述观点或结论，再列举原因、条件、事实等。具体表现为先陈述要点，再展开细节内容，体现的是一种直线思维。然而汉语句子的左分支结构和话题—评述结构则常常将语义重心置于句末，即先讲事实、原因，再给出态度或结果。具体表现为先关注事物的环境和外围因素，再深入到具体事物和中心事件，体现的是一种环形思维。句首语义重心与句尾语义重心是英汉句子结构另一个明显区别，在进行英汉双语转换时，译者必须按照目标语的思维方式和表达习惯相应调整句子重心的位置。

例 7 Rather than limiting financial institutions to mere transactional agents in climate finance, Socially Responsible Investment envisions a much more active and enlightened role for them.

参考译文： 社会责任投资这一概念把金融机构塑造为一个更为主动、更富创意的参与者，而非将其局限于充当气候金融业务代理人这一简单角色。

本例英语文本中的 rather than 引导的是分词结构，按照英语的语言习惯，这个分词结构既可放主句前也可放主句后，但作者选择将 rather than 引导的分词结构放在句首，说明这是本句的语义重心所在。相反，汉语的语义重心通常在句尾，讲述者倾向于娓娓道来，逐渐引出重心。因此，本例中 rather than 之后的分词结构在翻译成汉语时，我们需要对语序作相应调整。

例 8 Notice is hereby given that regular meetings of the Board of Trustees of Sublette County School District #1, State of Wyoming, are scheduled to be held each month in the Boardroom of the Administration Building in Pinedale, Wyoming, and such meetings are open to the public.

参考译文： 怀俄明州萨布莱特县第一学区董事会的定期会议定于每月在怀俄明州派恩代尔行政大楼的会议室举行，这些会议向公众开放。特此通告。

本例中，英语的句首语义重心 notice is hereby given 在翻译成中文时遵循英汉句法的规则，在译文中被转移至句尾，实现了汉语的句尾重心。

3. 英汉语篇对比

语篇是按照一定的思维模式组织起来的，中西方思维结构的差异导致了汉英语篇结构的差异。总的来说，英汉语篇对比主要体现在以下两个方面：

（1）衔接手段：理性思维与悟性思维

韩礼德和哈桑（Halliday & Hasan, 1976）将英语语篇的衔接手段分为五种，即照应（reference）、替代（substitution）、省略（ellipsis）、连接（conjunction）、词汇衔接（lexical cohesion），其中词汇衔接又分为复现（reiteration）和同现（collocation）。与英语不同，汉语主要使用重复作为语篇的衔接手段（潘文国，1997）。虽然英语和汉语中都存在照应关系，但是英语语篇的照应关系为显性，而汉语语篇的照应关系为隐性。除此之外，英语语篇中照应手段的使用频率大大高于汉语语篇的使用频率。

例9 Since the 1990s, our company has been focused on "Design for Sustainability" because we recognize that our products have environmental, social, and economic effects throughout their life cycle. Design for Sustainability consists of criteria for each phase of the corporation's product design and delivery process. Design teams are required to respond to each criterion before being permitted to pass to the next phase of the process. We developed the criteria based on global standards, market trends, and quantitative analysis.

参考译文：公司认识到产品在整个生命周期中会给环境、社会和经济带来负面影响，所以自20世纪90年代以来，我们一直专注于"可持续设计"。可持续设计包括产品设计和交付过程中每个阶段的可持续性标准。设计团队在进入下一个阶段前，需要对本阶段的标准进行考量，考量通过后方可进入下一阶段。这些标准是我们参考了全球标准、市场趋势以及量化分析制定出来的。

在上例英语文本中，Design for Sustainability 在第一句首次出现，紧接着第二句的开头处进行了重复，以实现原文的照应关系。中文译文使用了重复关键词的衔接手段，即重复"可持续设计"，强调了本语段的中心词；英语语篇文本中分别使用了代词 our、we、their 等显性照应手段，而中文则省译，使用了隐性照应。

（2）语篇推进方式：直线思维和环形思维

英语的段落是一个完整的统一体，强调段落一致性，大部分段落都有一个非常明显的主题句，段与段之间连接清晰。这是英语直线思维模式在语篇结构上的体现。而汉语的曲线思维模式反映在语篇结构中，则讲究"起、承、转、合"，汉语篇章结构在形式上不像英语那样有严密的逻辑性，段落里不一定有主题句，段落之间主要依赖于意义的关联，形散神不散，只要话题相关、语义相关，就可以构成一个段落。基于对英汉两种语言使用者思维模式差异的认识，译者在翻译过程中应留心调整语篇结构，提高译文的可读性。

翻译的实质就是通过原文的形式（表层结构）来理解原文的内容（深层意义），最终以译文形式把原文内容再现出来，就此而言，翻译离不开比较与对比。事实上，翻译理论、方法和技巧的形成即是建立在语言对比基础上的，因此学习英汉翻译，深入分析并对比语言差异性具有重要意义。

International Trade

International trade is the process of exchanging goods or services between two or more countries, involving the use of two or more currencies. (1) <u>International trade produces a more efficient employment of the productive forces of the world</u>.

Why does international trade occur? The answer (2) <u>follows directly from</u> our definition of international trade—both parties to the transaction, who happen to reside in two different countries, believe they benefit from a voluntary exchange. Behind this simple truth lies much economic theory, business practice, government policy, and international conflict.

The benefits derived from the development of international trade are numerous. International trade permits a wider consumer choice and higher levels of consumer satisfaction. (3) <u>Lower production costs</u>, through economies of scale, result in (3) <u>lower prices</u> to the consumers. International trade increases competition and prevents the monopolistic control of the home market by local exporters. (4) <u>It also provides a stimulus to economic growth, developing technology, and raising living standards</u>.

Overall, it provides wealth to the economy and extends opportunities to exchange ideas and develop the infrastructure of a country or region and its resource. Trade develops beneficial links between countries and (5) <u>encourages tourism and education</u>. (5) <u>This brings both political and economic stability to a country or region</u>. International trade plays an important role in the fight against poverty by helping drive economic growth and provide jobs. Countries that have entered export markets, increased their reliance on imports, and strengthened their investment climate so as to become more internationally competitive have tended to grow faster than those that have not.

International trade has important direct and indirect effects on national economies. On the one hand, exports spark additional economic activity in the domestic economy. On the other hand, so do imports. To illustrate, (6) <u>Southcorp's wine exports generated orders for its Australian suppliers—as well as its international suppliers, such as cork suppliers and grape harvester manufacturers—along with wages for its Australian workers and dividend payments for its shareholders, all of which in turn created income for local car dealers, supermarkets, and others</u>. Imports can also put pressure on domestic suppliers to cut their prices and improve their competitiveness.

(7) <u>Failure</u> to respond to foreign competition may lead to factories shutting down and workers becoming unemployed. Imports also generate jobs and stimulate competition. While exports feature prominently in discussions on world trade, it must never be forgotten that every export is also an import. Probably because of the (7) <u>emphasis</u> that

nations place on their balance of payments, where exports are regarded more positively than imports, imports have developed something of a "bad reputation." Of course, to view imports as "bad" is a foolish notion. As consumers, few of us would like to be without Japanese and German technology, American entertainment, French wines, and the occasional trip to a Pacific atoll or an exotic Asian holiday spot. Without importing these goods or services, our lives as consumers would be miserable and our factories out of date. This point should be remembered when we discuss the theories put forward for international trade and investment. And always remember, every export is also an import!

(8) <u>The rapid growth in international trade and specialization raises the question of the economic reasons for trade</u>. Why does Japan export mainly manufactured goods and import principally raw materials? Why is agriculture of the US so different from that of the Netherlands? But most important of all, do countries gain or lose from opening up their boundaries to international trade? The key to such questions lies in the theory of comparative advantage. (9) <u>This principle holds that a nation can raise its standard and real income by specializing in the production of those commodities or services in which it has the highest productivity or comparative advantage</u>. The benefits of specialization may also be affected by transport costs. Goods and raw materials have to be transported around the world and the cost of the transport narrows the limits between which it will prove profitable to trade.

Extending the principle of comparative advantages a little further, where a country has absolute advantage in the production of two or more products, it is still beneficial to trade. For example, the US may have a higher output per worker (or per unit output) than the rest of the world both in steel and computers. However, it might still benefit the US to engage in trade—exporting computers (in which it is relatively more productive) and importing steel (in which it is relatively less productive). Similarly, a country will gain by trading with the US, even if it is absolutely less efficient in the production of a range of goods.

难点解析

（1）produce 的本义为"生产；引起；提出"等，此处与 a more efficient employment of the productive forces 搭配，转换时应依据上下文确定词义范围，并根据汉语表达习惯和搭配要求进行翻译，可译为"使生产力得到更加有效的利用"等。

（2）follow directly from 本义为"从……直接得出……"，为紧凑起见，翻译时不必拘泥于原文结构，可根据汉语习惯进行调整。当然，保留原文结构，将其译为"答案可从我们为国际贸易所下的定义中直接得出"亦无大碍。

（3）汉语更倾向于动态表达，两个比较级 lower 都可译为动词。

（4）本句中的 provides a stimulus 也可以合并译为汉语中的动词"刺激、激励"，同时 stimulus to 后面有多个宾语，但是在汉语中由于不同名词要求搭配的动词不同，所以此处需要根据汉语搭配习惯将其译为不同的动词。

（5）由于英语和汉语在表达习惯上的差异，增词和减词都是常见的翻译变通手段，比如 encourages tourism and education，可根据汉语表达习惯译为"促进旅游业和教育事业的发展"。此外，合句法也是常见的处理手段，此处指示代词 this 指代上句内容，翻译时不必拘泥于这两个句子中间的句号，可以考虑合而为一。

（6）本句较长，运用了丰富的衔接手段，如 as well as、such as、along with、its、all of which 等，还使用了插入语，因此结构较为复杂，给翻译带来不小的困难。翻译时要先对句子的结构进行划分调整，然后根据汉语习惯重新组织，此外还应注意 generated 一词的理解与表达。

（7）英语为名词优势语言，汉语为动词优势语言，鉴于此，英汉翻译过程中，不少英语名词（尤其是抽象名词）往往可以或需要译为汉语动词。failure 和 emphasis 均为抽象名词，实际上相当于动词的功能，翻译时注意转换为动词。

（8）下文中的三个问句均是对本句中 question of the economic reasons for trade 的补充说明，因此翻译时可以将四个句子合并起来，用冒号引出具体问题（即三个问句）。

（9）本句是英语中典型的树状结构，呈三角形，主句（this principle holds）很短，是三角形的顶部，也是树的主干部分，宾语从句很长，而且其中还镶嵌着 by 介词短语和 which 引导的从句，构成了三角形的底部，也是树的枝叶部分。翻译时首先要考虑句子结构上的调整，将原句中 by 所引导的动名词短语提前，体现汉语"因为怎样，所以结果怎样"的惯用逻辑。

商务知识讲座

国际贸易

国际贸易是指世界各国或地区之间货物、知识和服务的交换，是国家或地区之间劳动分工的表现，反映了世界各国或地区在经济上的相互依赖。

贸易是在一定历史条件下产生和发展起来的，其产生与人类历史上的三次社会大分工密切相关。第一次社会大分工是畜牧部落从其他部落中分离出来，牲畜的驯养和繁殖使生产力得到了发展，产品开始有了少量剩余。于是在氏族部落之间出现了剩余产品的交换。这是最早发生的交换，这种交换是极其原始的偶然的物物交换。

随着生产力的继续发展，手工业从农业中分离出来，于是便出现了人类社会的第二次大分工。手工业出现后，产生了直接以交换为目的的商品生产。随着商品生产和商品交换的不断扩大，货币产生了，商品交换逐渐成为以货币为媒介的商品流通。随着商品货币关系的发展，产生了专门从事贸易的商人，于是出现了第三次社会大分工。

生产力的发展，交换关系的扩大，加速了私有制的产生，直至国家出现。国家出现后，商品交换超出国界，便产生了国际贸易。

国际贸易可分为有形贸易（visible trade）和无形贸易（invisible trade）。

有形贸易指商品的进出口贸易。由于商品是可以看得见的有形实物，故商品的进出口被称为有形进出口，即有形贸易。国际贸易中的有形商品种类繁多，为便于统计，联合国秘书处于 1950 年起草了《联合国国际贸易标准分类》，是目前为止世界各国政府普遍采纳的商品贸易分类体系。《联合国国际贸易标准分类》历经四次修订，第四次修订版于 2006 年 3 月获联合国统计委员会批准。该修订版将国际贸易商品共分为 10 大类、67 章、262 组、1023 个分组和 2970 个基本项目。这 10 类商品分别如下：(0) 食品及主要供食用的活动物；(1) 饮料及烟草；(2) 燃料以外的非食用粗原料；(3) 矿物燃料、润滑油及有关原料；(4) 动植物油脂、油脂和蜡；(5) 未另列名的化学品及有关产品；(6) 主要按原料分类的制成品；(7) 机械及运输设备；(8) 杂项制品；(9) 未另分类的其他商品和交易。在国际贸易中，一般把 0 到 4 类商品称为初级产品，把 5 到 8 类商品称为制成品。

无形贸易指因劳务或其他非实物商品的进出口而发生的收入与支出。主要包括：

1. 和商品进出口有关的一切从属费用的收支，如运输费、保险费、商品加工费、装卸费等；

2. 和商品进出口无关的其他收支，如国际旅游费用、外交人员费用、侨民汇款、使用专利特许权的费用、国外投资汇回的股息和红利、公司或个人在国外服务的收支等。以上各项中的收入，称为"无形出口"；以上各项中的支出，称为"无形进口"。

有形贸易因要结关，故其金额显示在一国的海关统计上；无形贸易不经过海关办理手续，其金额不反映在海关统计上，但显示在一国的国际收支表上。

按照是否有第三国参加，国际贸易还可分为：

1. 直接贸易（direct trade），指商品生产国与商品消费国不通过第三国进行买卖商品的行为。贸易的出口国方面称为直接出口，进口国方面称为直接进口。

2. 间接贸易（indirect trade）和转口贸易（transit trade），指商品生产国与商品消费国通过第三国进行买卖商品的行为。间接贸易中的生产国称为间接出口国，消费国称为间接进口国，而第三国则是转口贸易国，第三国所从事的就是转口贸易。

翻译练习

I. 思考题

1. 从翻译角度而言，英汉语言差异一般可以分为哪几个层次？
2. 从"International Trade"中找出相应实例说明不同层次的英汉语言差异对英汉翻译的影响。

II. 从"International Trade"中摘录给你深刻印象的句子或词组。

1. _____
2. _____
3. _____
4. _____
5. _____

III. 商务术语翻译

arbitration	
Asia-Pacific Economic Cooperation (APEC)	
bargain	
bonded area	
brochure	
business line	
capital market	
catalog	
census	
commodity	
consumer price index (CPI)	
counter-offer	
documents against acceptance (D/A)	
documents against payment (D/P)	
draft	
dumping	
duration	
economic entity	
entrepreneur	
equity value	
exchange rate	
exporter	
fixed asset	
force majeure	
foreign direct investment (FDI)	
foreign exchange	

freight	
hedging fund	
holding company	
human resource	
joint venture	
know-how	
license	
life insurance	
margin	
market access	
mass production	
micro economy	
multinational company	
packaging	
parent company	
partial shipment	
preferential policy	
price list	
promotion	
quote	
registered capital	
royalty	
secondary industry	
shareholder	
state-owned enterprise (SOE)	
terms of delivery	
terms of payment	

trademark	
underwriter	

IV. 句子翻译

1. The 2022 Luohu Investment Promotion Conference kicked off on November 24 in Luohu District, Shenzhen. Twelve of the world's top 500 enterprises and 10 foreign businesses attended the conference. At the conference, investment deals worth 102.4 billion yuan ($14 billion) among 60 projects were inked.
2. In 2022, China sold about 6.89 million new energy vehicles (NEVs), up more than 93% year-on-year. NEV production also soared nearly 97% to about 7.06 million units, according to data from the China Association of Automobile Manufacturers.
3. Over the past years, Hong Kong's economy has been thriving. Its status as an international financial, shipping, and trading center has been maintained, and its innovative science and technology industries have been booming.
4. We welcome progress on voluntary channeling of Special Drawing Rights from countries with strong external positions to support countries most in need, as well as the IMF's decision to establish the Resilience and Sustainability Trust.
5. We endorse BRICS Statement on Strengthening the Multilateral Trading System and Reforming the WTO.
6. We reaffirm our commitment to continuing to enhance macroeconomic policy coordination, deepen economic practical cooperation, and work to realize strong, sustainable, balanced, and inclusive post-COVID economic recovery.
7. We should support the WTO-centered multilateral trading regime, ensure security and stability of the global industrial and supply chains, and make the "pie" of cooperation bigger to allow development gains to better trickle down to people of all countries.
8. Despite short-term headwinds or challenges, the fundamentals of a resilient, high-potential, and prosperous economy in China remain intact. The business environment for foreign enterprises has steadily improved in China over the last 10 years.
9. The goods are cleared by the customs authorities in Yinchuan, the capital of northwest China's Ningxia Hui Autonomous Region, and then loaded into containers entrusted to X Company by international shippers.
10. The bonded logistics system in Ningxia offers a "one-stamp" clearance service with customs to send goods abroad through shipping and railway without any transit.

V. 篇章翻译

Economists are debating whether recent supply chain turmoil and geopolitical conflicts will result in a reversal or reconfiguration of global production, in which factories that were sent offshore move back to the United States and other countries that pose less of a political risk. If that happens, a decades-long decline in the prices of many goods could come to an end or even begin to go in the other direction, potentially boosting overall inflation. Since around 1995, durable goods like cars and equipment have tamped down inflation, and prices for nondurable goods like clothing and toys have often grown only slowly.

Those trends began to change after the onset of the pandemic, as shipping costs soared and shortages collided with strong demand to push car, furniture, and equipment prices higher. While few economists expect the past year's breakneck price increases to continue, the question is whether the trend toward at least slightly pricier goods will last.

The answer could hinge on whether a shift away from globalization takes hold. "It would certainly be a different world—it might be a world of perhaps higher inflation, perhaps lower productivity, but more resilient, more robust supply chains," a Federal Reserve representative said at an event last month when asked about a possible move away from globalization.

翻译名家

朱光潜（1897—1986），著名美学家、文艺理论家、教育家和翻译家。他不仅在美学研究上具有突出的贡献，在翻译理论上也颇有建树，翻译了大量的西方经典美学名著，为我国的翻译事业作出了卓越的贡献，留下了宝贵的翻译艺术资源。

朱光潜翻译的美学作品有克罗齐的《美学原理》、哈拉普的《艺术的社会根源》、黑格尔的《美学》、莱辛的《拉奥孔》、维柯的《新科学》，翻译的文学及文艺学著作有柏地耶的《愁斯丹和绮瑟》、萧伯纳的剧本《英国佬的另一个岛》、柏拉图的《文艺对话录》、爱克曼辑录的《歌德谈话录》以及一部分单篇译文。

朱光潜精通美学、诗学、文论和心理学，有着良好的语言学背景和深厚的国学背景。他在长期的翻译实践活动中积累了丰富的翻译经验，基于这些经验，他从语言学角度入手，在词汇、句法、语义甚至语用学以及诗学等方面，提出了自己的翻译思想和观点。朱光潜主张翻译应忠实于原文，在翻译方法上，他既反对直译，也反对意译，主张采取二者取中的方法。他认为，译者需具备三个条件：精通外国文，精通本国文，具有文学修养。至于如何学好外语，他建议多听、多读、多写、多背诵，用外语进行思考，除此之外还要多做翻译、勤翻字典。他认为翻译是学好外语的最好途径。

第 3 章　商务词汇的翻译

> 字义了解的确是句义了解的根基，但是所谓字义，不能看做死的、固定的、分立的，须当做活的、有连贯的、不可强为分裂的东西。
>
> ——林语堂

问题导入

1. 翻译下面的句子。

   We shall write and ask for their ceiling for the advertising project and then we can budget accordingly. The syndicate tried to corner the market in silver.

   译文 _____
   _____
   _____

2. 说明你在翻译上句时遇到的困难，并和同学们讨论解决困难的方法。

   难点：_____

   解决方法：_____

翻译知识讲座

商务英语词汇的特点与翻译

1. 商务英语词汇的特点

商务的范围很广，涉及国际贸易、经济、金融、营销、物流、保险和法律等多个领域。商务英语是国际商务活动中使用的英语，具有非常明显的实践性和实用性。《朗文语言教学与应用语言学词典》把商务英语归为专门用途英语（ESP: English for Specific

Purposes）。商务英语作为专门用途英语，有其独特的语言特征。商务英语词汇是商务背景下具有特定商务语义的词汇。词语的选用与文体密切相关，不同的文体要求使用不同的词汇。从根本上来说，商务英语来源于通用英语（EGP: English for General Purposes），是普通英语与商务领域专业知识的结合，因而商务英语词汇主要由两类词汇构成：一是普通英语中的常见词汇，这些词汇在商务英语语境中具有特殊含义，要根据上下文对其意义作出准确理解；二是商务背景下国际贸易、经济、金融、营销、物流、保险和法律等不同领域特有的专用词汇。具体而言，商务英语词汇主要具有如下特点：

（1）措辞专业

具体表现为以下两个方面：

a）大量的专业词汇

如前文所述，商务活动涵盖多个领域，每个领域都有自己的专业术语，词义比较单一、专业性强。如国际贸易领域术语：anti-dumping measure（反倾销措施）、partial shipment（分批装运）、trade surplus（贸易顺差）；经济领域术语：holding company（控股公司）、checking account（支票账户）、ready money（现金）；金融领域术语：acceptance method（承兑方式）、account current（往来账户）、advance-decline theory（涨跌理论）；营销领域术语：adoption process（采购过程）、cost analysis（成本分析）、distribution channel（分销渠道）；物流领域术语：logistics management（物流管理）、field warehouse（现场仓库）、bulk storage product（大宗散装存储产品）；保险领域术语：risk of clashing（碰损险）、event limit（事件限额）、cover（承保）；法律领域术语：property tenancy（财产租赁）、company listing（公司上市）、legal opinion（法律意见书）。

b）普通词汇专业化

商务英语中不仅包含大量词义单一的专业词汇，还有许多准专业词汇，这些词在普通英语里是日常生活中常用的意义，但在商务活动背景下，往往被赋予了特定的专业含义。如 kitty 通常指"小猫"，在金融领域指"筹集的资金、共同资金"；option 通常意为"选择"，而在金融语境中则特指"期权"；average 通常表示"平均水平"，在保险领域中，average 指"海损、海损费用"，with average 指"水渍险"；在商务语境中，down-payment 指"（分期付款的）首付款，定金"；documentary credit 中文对应"跟单信用证"，而非"记录信用证"；trade discount 不能译为"贸易折扣"，而应为"同业折扣"等。这些准专业词汇在不同的场合、不同的语境中有不同的含义，只有仔细推敲才能准确翻译。例如，同样使用 cover 一词，open policy cover 是指"预约保险"，而 under separate cover 则指"另邮"。

另一种需要注意的现象是，同一词汇在不同商务主题中也会有不同意义。例如同样使用 clean 一词，clean bill of lading 是"清洁提单"，而 clean draft 则是"光票"；liability 一词在 legal liability 中表示"法律责任"，而在 asset and liability 中则为"资产负债"；claim 在 lay claim to 中意思为"要求"，而在 claim for damage 中则表示"索赔"；同样一个"单"字，在商务英语中对应的表达方式各不相同：在"海运提单"中是 marine bill of lading，在"保险单"中是 insurance policy，而在"投保通知单"中则是 cover note。

（2）用语简洁

随着现代商务交往日益频繁，商务用语除了必须确保准确、清晰、缜密外，还要求用词简洁,例如 documents against payment 表示"付款交单",freight forward 表示"运费到付",extension of L/C 表示"信用证延期",All sales are final 表示"货物售出,概不退换"。

在激烈的商务竞争环境中,传达信息的效率很重要,因此,商务英语往往倾向于简约的风格,其显著特征是频繁使用缩略词。缩略词以其语言简练、使用方便、信息丰富的特性,成为商务交流中的有力工具。缩略词主要分为四类:首字母缩写词(initialism,即按字母一一拼读的缩略词)、首字母拼音词(acronym,即按完整单词发音的缩略语)、拼缀词(blending)和截短词(clipping)。在实际商务英语应用中,首字母缩写词和截短词尤为常见。一般来讲,重要的国际组织、国际公约、国际协会等大多以首字母缩写词的形式出现;此外,商业术语、计量单位和常用词汇等则通常采用截短词的形式。举例如下表:

缩略词	全称	译文
WTO	World Trade Organization	世界贸易组织
ADB	Asian Development Bank	亚洲开发银行
IMF	International Monetary Fund	国际货币基金组织
L/C	Letter of Credit	信用证
CIF	Cost, Insurance, and Freight	成本、保险加运费(到岸价)
FOB	Free on Board	装运港船上交货价(离岸价)
A/R	All Risks	全险;一切险
Co., Ltd.	Company Limited	有限责任公司
ad	advertisement	广告
min	minimum	最小值
memo	memorandum	备忘录

(3) 用词正式

商务英语的总体特征是准确、规范、得体、简洁,在词汇的选择和使用上严格规范、专业性强。主要体现在以下四个方面:

a) 复合副词的使用

商务英语可以分为普通商务英语(English for General Business Purposes)和特殊商务英语(English for Specific Business Purposes)。在普通商务英语中,词汇选择和应用方面讲求得体规范、平实易懂、简短达意。而在特殊商务英语,如商务合同、确认书、正式信函、法律文书中,由于文本本身具有的特殊性质和法律约束力等因素,倾向于使用正式、书面化、专业的词汇。此类词汇运用偏好包括由 here-、there- 和 where- 等开头,与一个或几个介词组成的复合副词,旨在凸显文本的典雅庄重、严格规范,以及此类文本的传承性和权威性。例如 therein 表示"在其中",用来指代文中特定内容;thereafter 表示"其后、此后",用来指示时间顺序;hereinafter 表示"在下文中",用来指代后续提到的内容；thereby 表示"因此"，用来表达因果关系；hereby 表示"特此"，用于正式声明。

  b）逻辑性语法词的使用

  商务类文本中包含大量的推理和论证，因此，它们经常借助逻辑性语法词来有效组织思考与表达，一般主要体现在使用一些连词、副词、介词、介词词组等。例如，表原因类的有 because、because of、due to、owing to、as a result of、caused by、for；表限制类的有 only、if only、except、apart from、unless；表条件或假设类的有 suppose、supposing、assuming、provided、providing；表语气转折类的有 but、however、nevertheless、yet、otherwise 等。

  c）同义词（近义词）并列的使用

  同义词（近义词）并列是同义词（近义词）或相关词汇由 and 或 or 连接并列使用。这种结构的使用克服了由于英语一词多义可能产生的语义不明，能有效避免商务双方按各自的意图来理解文本，体现了商务语言的庄重和严谨。根据词性分类，有名词叠用（如 power and authority）、动词叠用（如 alter and change）、形容词叠用（如 sole and exclusive）、连词叠用（如 when and as）和介词叠用（如 from and after）等。国际商务合同和文件力求正式而准确，避免可能出现的误解或分歧，所以同义词（近义词）并列的现象十分普遍。例如，在合同文档中，terms 通常指付款或费用（如手续费、佣金等有关金钱的）条件，conditions 则指其他条件，但是 terms and conditions 常常作为固定模式出现在合同中，通常直接合译为"条款"。类似例子还有 null and void 译为"无效、失效"，stipulations and provisions 译为"法律条文"，costs and expenses 译为"各种费用"，insufficiency and inadequacy 译为"不足"，use and wont 译为"习惯、惯例"等。同义词（近义词）并列已被视为习惯用语，表示固定的含义，在商务合同翻译时不能随意拆分。

  d）情态动词的使用

  商务英语中有大量文件，特别是合同，为明确双方当事人的权利、义务和责任，以避免产生法律纠纷，会经常使用到 shall、may、must、shall not、may not 等情态动词来描述双方"允许做的事情""必须做的事情"和"禁止做的事情"。商务英语合同中的情态表达大多属于指令性或义务性的范畴，而不是传统意义上表示可能性的情态范畴。限定性情态动词的使用简洁明了，能够避免因合同条款产生歧义而引起纠纷。这些词除了在普通语境中表示将来的行为或意图外，在商务英语和法律语境下，更具有其特殊的意义，需要特别留意。

  除了上述四个方面，商务英语用词正式的特点还体现在一些约定俗成的语言习惯用法上，比如通常偏好使用 upon 而不是 on，选用 for the purpose of 代替简单的 for，以及使用 concerning/with reference to/with regard to 来取代 about。此外，在商务英语中，purchase 比 buy 更为正式，utilize 也被视为是 use 的更正式表达。

2. 商务英语词汇的翻译方法

  商务英语翻译的基本原则可以用两个词语来概括：忠实、得体。这一标准体现了原文和译文之间的功能对等，忠实是指译文信息与原文相一致，而得体则是指译文的语言形式、文体风格与原文相适应。根据商务英语词汇的特点，翻译中可相应采用如下方法：

（1）直译法

一般认为，译文形式与内容都与原文一致谓之直译（方梦之，2019）。商务英语中的术语词汇都是固定的，都有其特定的、精确的含义。换言之，在商务英语学科领域内，一个术语只表达一个概念，同一个概念只用同一个术语来表达。如"备用信用证"只能用英语 standby credit 来表示，不能用 spare credit 来代替。由于这些专业词汇意义比较单一，一词多义的现象较少，且大多不带有感情色彩，所以往往借助商务专业词典就能译出，无须依赖上下文来理解。因此，在处理商务英语术语时，应采用直译的方式。

（2）意译法

方梦之（2019）认为，译文内容一致而形式不同谓之意译，即以原文形式为标准，译文表达形式上另辟蹊径。商务英语的一个词组可以表达一个中文句子或数个中文词组所表达的内容。为了保持简洁凝练的文体特点，汉译时不必逐字逐句译出，也不必拘泥于英语文本的句型结构，可适当采用四字格的词语和某些文言文句式。例如：Work on small profit margins cannot grant open account facilities 可译为"薄利经营，无法赊账"；Thank you for your kind consideration 可译为"承蒙垂询，谨致谢意"。

综上，鉴于商务英语词汇具有专业性强、覆盖面广、用词严谨准确等特点，处理商务英语词汇时应依据专业知识，从专业角度深入分析词义，并根据具体语境理解词义，避免误译。商务英语译者需要不断学习、扩大知识面，博闻强记，磨炼专业能力，在商务英语翻译中，措辞力求恰当、得体、准确，避免不必要的误解和纠纷。

商务语篇翻译与解析

Multinational Corporation

A multinational corporation (MNC) is a corporation or enterprise that manages production (1) <u>establishments or delivers</u> services in at least two countries. Multinational corporations can also be termed as multinational enterprises or transnational corporations. Multinational corporations are often divided into three broad groups according to the configuration of their production facilities: Horizontally integrated multinational corporations manage production establishments located in different countries to produce the same or similar products; vertically integrated multinational corporations manage production establishments in certain country/countries to produce products that serve as input to its production establishments in other country/countries; diversified multinational corporations manage production establishments located in different countries that are either horizontally or vertically integrated.

Although multinational corporations existed before the twentieth century, only since the 1960s have they become a major force on the world scene. In 1900, only European corporations were major transnational (2) <u>players</u>, but by 1930, American MNCs had begun to (2) <u>make their presence felt</u>. The year 1960 marks the beginning of a new era in corporate transnationalization. In each of the decades from 1960 to the present, world foreign direct investment stock has more than tripled, whereas it only doubled during the first half of the century. (3) <u>The phenomenal increase in transnational corporate activity in the latter part of the twentieth century can be accounted for in large part by technological innovations in transportation, communication, and information processing that have permitted corporations to establish profitable worldwide operations while maintaining effective and timely organizational control</u>. Taking advantage of rapidly improving communications and transportation, MNCs have been a powerful force in hurdling national boundaries and restrictions, so that trade, commerce, goods, services, and ideas can flow more freely, to the benefit of all mankind.

(4) <u>There are four reasons why the above strongly affirmative statements emphasizing the importance and potential of MNCs can be made</u>. First, to some extent the multinational corporation is a powerful force for peace. In its own interests it seeks to further a uniformity of tax, patent and copyright laws, trade practices, and all the rules of the economic game worldwide, so it can reach out under common rules to serve the mass market. Second, the internationalization of production and services carried out by MNCs is a powerful element in generating the levels of electronic growth necessary to global progress. Third, most of the technology that is desperately needed in the developing world if growth is to take place has been developed, and is owned and controlled by the private sector. It is proprietary, created at great cost, and considered very valuable property by the companies that own it. Fourth, international companies have a special capacity to deliver technology. (5) <u>This</u> goes beyond what is commonly called high technology, to include management capacity and marketing know-how. (6) <u>The distinctive aspect of the role that MNCs can play most effectively is not so much the transfer of resources as such, but the impact of moving those resources—whether they be capital, technology, or management skills—as a finely honed combination of productive factors, tailored to the needs of a given opportunity or project</u>.

Multinational companies today play a vital role on the world economic scene. The activities of multinational enterprises drive the economic globalization process to a very large degree. Much of the technology, management talent, and private capital needed to solve the world's economic problems is controlled by MNCs.

(7) <u>Nearly all major multinationals are either American, Japanese, or Western European</u>. Advocates of multinationals say they create jobs and wealth and improve technology in countries that are in need of such development. On the other hand,

critics say multinationals can have undue political influence over governments, exploit developing nations as well as create job losses in their own home countries. (8) <u>Unsuccessful efforts were made</u> in 1992, through the UN, to negotiate a voluntary code of conduct for multinationals, but governments and corporations alike were hostile to the idea. In June 2000, the Organization for Economic Cooperation and Development issued guidelines for multinational enterprises. The guidelines, drawn up with the aid of non-governmental organizations and trade unions, aimed to promote better relationships between multinational companies and the societies within which they worked.

难点解析

（1）英语词汇一词多义现象本就普遍，不少词汇在一般语篇和商务语篇中所表达的词义并不相同，甚至在不同的商务领域里也有不同的词义。establishment 在一般语篇中的含义为"确立、建立；机构、当局"，此处引申为"企业或公司"，deliver 一词通常表示"递送、交付"等意思，但此处如翻译成"递送服务"则令人费解，应译成"提供服务"。

（2）在翻译时首先要了解英语原文中词语的基本意义，并吃透词汇在特定上下文中的引申意义，再选择恰当的汉语对应词。player 这个词的原意是"游戏者；选手；运动员"，在本文语境中，该词引申为"跨国商务活动的参与者"，即"跨国经营者"。另外，英语中的被动语态多数情况下可转换成汉语中的主动句，本句中 make their presence felt 的字面意思是"使他们的出现被别人感觉到"，这种直译方式显然不符合汉语表达习惯，不妨转换角度，译为"崭露头角"，这样既体现了原文的意义，又避免了翻译腔。下文中的 can be accounted for 也可采用同样的处理方法。

（3）phenomenal increase 是名词短语，翻译成汉语时，将其转换成动词结构更为自然些，更加符合汉语中多用动词的特点。此外，本句中包含多个名词并列结构，还有 that 引导的定语从句以及 while 连接的非谓语动词结构，体现了不同于汉语的语言结构和思维方式，翻译时注意进行拆句处理，并根据句间的关系增加衔接手段，使句子间的关系更清晰。

（4）原句中 why 引导同位语从句，对 reasons 作补充说明，从句中的 emphasizing 为后置分词短语修饰 statements。环环相套的句式需要用分句法对原句的结构进行分解。考虑到汉语的行文习惯，译文可将同位语从句和后置分词短语从主句中拆分出来，形成两个新的分句，使译文更加流畅，并增强语言表达效果。

（5）这里的代词 this 指代的是前面一句话中提到的 technology，为使译文读者明白这一点，翻译时可以考虑对 this 进行增词解释，译为"这里所说的技术"。

（6）这句话很长，高度概括了跨国公司的作用，the distinctive aspect of the role...is not...but... 是主干部分，中间套嵌若干修饰成分。翻译时要将原句拆分，尤其最后 as 引导的介词短语要再次细分，并进行语序调整，以保证译文流畅。另外在处理 the role that MNCs can play most effectively 这部分时，不要直接译成"跨国公司所扮演的最有效的角色"，而应将其翻成"跨国公司所能发挥的最有效的作用"。

（7）此处画线部分表示跨国公司的国家属性，以 be 动词加上表示国家属性的形容词这种结构来表示，若直译为"几乎所有主要的跨国公司都是美国的，日本的，或西欧的"，这种译文语句松散，不太符合汉语的表达习惯，因此可用"来自"这个动词解决这个问题。
（8）英语和汉语中都有含否定词的否定说法和不含否定词的否定说法，例如本句中的 unsuccessful（不成功的）。对这类表达进行翻译时需稍作调整。画线部分若直译为"作出不成功的努力"不符合汉语表达规范，译为"作出努力……却并未成功"更好。

商务知识讲座

跨国公司概述

19 世纪末 20 世纪初，在垄断统治形成和巨额资本输出的基础上，主要资本主义国家的一些垄断企业就开始在国外投资进行生产，发展成为早期的跨国公司。现代意义上的跨国公司于 19 世纪在欧美主要经济发达国家出现，这些跨国公司沿袭了自大航海时代以来的垄断传统，同时大力参与全球并购、投资、合作，形成了现代意义上的"跨国公司"。

进入 20 世纪 90 年代后，在世界市场趋于统一、贸易自由化和金融自由化进一步发展以及信息技术进步的综合作用下，借助经济全球化浪潮，跨国公司得到了前所未有的大发展。同时，作为推动经济全球化的主要力量，跨国公司在世界经济中的地位和作用日益重要。在此期间，跨国公司有以下特点：

1. 跨国并购成为跨国公司对外直接投资的主要方式。20 世纪 90 年代以来，跨国公司之间的竞争异常激烈，跨国公司为了分摊创新成本，获取技术资产的所有权，提高企业国际竞争力，抢占全球市场份额并取得规模经济，在全球范围内掀起了新一轮的跨国并购浪潮，其发展速度之快和规模之大前所未有。

2. 跨国公司战略联盟成为跨国公司的重要发展模式。跨国公司战略联盟是指两个或两个以上的跨国公司为实现某一战略目标而建立的互相协作、互为补充的合作关系。跨国联盟是世界经济全球化高度发展的产物，是各国经济活动国际化的表现。

3. 研发国际化成为跨国公司增强持续竞争力的重要工具。当代激烈的国际市场竞争实质上是新产品和新技术的竞争。谁拥有了先进的新技术，谁就能缩短产品生命周期，不断推出个性化产品，从而占领和扩大市场份额。因此，跨国公司往往把新技术的研发作为取胜的重要策略和企业持续发展的举措。

4. 本土化战略成为跨国公司在东道国立足的重要基础。跨国公司在国外建立分支机构时，必须充分考虑各地的具体条件并加以比较、选择，以保证子公司在最有利的条件下和最适宜的环境中得到更好的发展。

5. 发展中国家的跨国公司取得长足进步。进入 20 世纪 90 年代以来，随着发展中国家经济实力不断增强，尤其是东南亚、拉丁美洲一批新型工业化国家的兴起，发展中国家的跨国公司也取得了长足的进步，它们日益成为世界经济领域不容忽视的重要竞争力量。

跨国公司由于规模巨大、资金雄厚、技术先进，以及其遍布世界的生产、销售和科研机构,对世界经济的发展产生了深刻的影响。它促进了国际分工的深化与细化,构筑起全球生产体系,促进了国际贸易特别是公司内贸易的发展,促进了资本的国际流动,也促进了技术创新与技术转让。

跨国公司的发展对发达国家的对外贸易起到了极大的推动作用,使发达国家的产品能够通过对外直接投资的方式在东道国生产并销售,绕过贸易壁垒,提高了产品的竞争力,减少了发达国家对发展中国家在原材料和能源方面的依赖。这样,发达国家的产品较顺利地进入并利用东道国的对外贸易渠道,更易于获得商业情报信息。

跨国公司对于发展中国家的对外贸易在某种意义上也产生了积极影响,它在发展中国家的直接投资客观上补充了该国进口资金的短缺;跨国公司的资本流入加速了发展中国家对外贸易商品结构的变化,促进了发展中国家工业化模式和与其相适应的贸易模式的形成和发展。

但是,由于跨国公司从本身的利益出发,以追逐最大利润为目标来安排总公司和各分支机构的经营活动,从而不可避免地使公司的利益与其本国的公众利益和所在国的民族利益发生各种矛盾和冲突。在本国,主要是导致国内投资减少,引起生产停滞和工人失业等后果。至于与所在国民族利益的矛盾冲突,其范围则广泛得多,主要表现在:(1)跨国公司的投资规模、资本有机构成、经营方针和工业区位都未必符合所在国经济发展的需要。(2)跨国公司凭借其强大的经济实力,很容易控制所在国的某些关键工业部门,使这些国家的经济发展受到牵制。(3)跨国公司将大量资金在各国间频繁转移,经常使所在国国际收支的平衡和汇率的稳定遭到破坏。(4)跨国公司按照自定的"全球战略"安排进出口贸易,以及为了逃税和避免其他风险在公司内部实行转移定价,经常使所在国蒙受各种经济损失。(5)跨国公司把那些劳动密集型、能源消耗多、污染严重的产品或零部件转移到发展中国家进行生产或加工,在这些国家造成了一系列不良后果。

翻译练习

I. 思考题

1. 商务英语词汇具有哪些特征?
2. 根据商务英语词汇的特点,在翻译时可采用怎样的技巧?

II. 从"Multinational Corporation"中摘录给你深刻印象的句子或词组。

1. _____
2. _____
3. _____
4. _____
5. _____

III. 商务术语翻译

accidental disequilibrium	
acquisition	
arbitration tribunal	
bear	
bull	
compulsory license	
delivered at place (DAP)	
delivery date	
eurocurrency	
exchange dumping	
foreign exchange control	
foreign trade multiplier	
franchisee	
free carrier (FCA)	
gold reserve	
head office/headquarters	
hedging transaction	
limit order	
merger	
monopoly position	
non-governmental body	
official reserve asset	
open outcry	
opening	
option price	
partnership	

party to the dispute	
patent protection	
pirated copyright goods	
portfolio investment	
pricing	
takeover	
trade balance	
trustee	

IV. 句子翻译

1. Due to the pandemic, the world economic recovery lacks drive, and commodity prices remain high and are prone to fluctuation. All of this is making our external environment increasingly volatile, grave, and uncertain.

2. Multinationals can also move their operations from one country to another depending on which location offers more favorable economic conditions.

3. China will expand high-standard opening up, fully implement the negative list for foreign investment, expand the encouraged catalog for FDI, improve services for investment promotion, and add more cities to the comprehensive pilot program for service sector opening.

4. It is projected that fiscal revenue will continue to grow this year. In addition, we also have available to us the surplus profits of state-owned financial institutions and state monopoly business operations from recent years turned over in accordance with the law and funds transferred from the Central Budget Stabilization Fund. This will make it possible for government to increase expenditures by more than two trillion yuan over last year, putting significantly greater fiscal resources at our disposal.

5. Some analysts suggest that this is because of the lack of competition; others suggest that it is because merchant banking is still something of a novelty in Jakarta; and still others suggest that it is because business in most sectors of the Indonesian economy is booming.

6. Multinational corporations have several advantages. First, they can sidestep restrictive trade and licensing restrictions because they frequently have headquarters in more than one country.

7. China will take a series of concrete actions under the framework of the Global Development Initiative as deliverables of this Dialogue (list attached), including upgrading China's

South-South Cooperation Assistance Fund into the Global Development and South-South Cooperation Fund, with an additional input of $1 billion on top of the existing $3 billion.

8. National fiscal revenue exceeded 20 trillion yuan, growing 10.7%. A total of 12.69 million urban jobs were added, and the average surveyed unemployment rate stood at 5.1%. The consumer price index rose by 0.9%.
9. We recognize the crucial role that MSMEs play in the BRICS economies and reaffirm the importance of their participation in production networks and value chains.
10. The fundamentals of the Chinese economy—its strong resilience, enormous potential, vast room for maneuver and long-term sustainability—remain unchanged.

V. 篇章翻译

As long as price stability is a long-run, but not short-run, goal, central banks can focus on reducing output fluctuations by allowing inflation to deviate from the long-run goal for short periods and, therefore, can operate under a dual mandate. However, if a dual mandate leads a central bank to pursue short-run expansionary policies that increase output and employment without worrying about the long-run consequences for inflation, the time-inconsistency problem may recur. Concerns that a dual mandate might lead to overly expansionary policy are a key reason why central bankers often favor hierarchical mandates in which the pursuit of price stability takes precedence.

Hierarchical mandates can also be a problem if they lead to a central bank behaving as an "inflation nutter"—that is, a central bank that focuses solely on inflation control, even in the short run, and so undertakes policies that lead to large output fluctuations. The choice of which type of mandate is better for a central bank ultimately depends on the subtleties of how it will work in practice. Either type of mandate is acceptable as long as it operates to make price stability the primary goal in the long run, but not in the short run.

翻译名家

林语堂（1895—1976），著名作家、学者、翻译家、语言学家，以地道的英文向西方读者介绍中国传统文化和智慧，为中国文化传播海外作出了巨大贡献，享誉海内外。

1935 年，林语堂以英文讲述中国现实的作品 *My Country and My People*（《吾国与吾民》）为西方了解中国文化和中华民族打开了新的大门；1939 年出版的英文长篇小说 *Moment in Peking*（《京华烟云》）为他赢得了 1975 年诺贝尔文学奖提名。他还翻译了《卖花女》《女子与知识》《易卜生评传及其情书》等西方名著，编译了《老子的智慧》《孔子的智慧》等一系列中国经典古籍，以及《浮生六记》《兰亭集序》等散文名篇。

林语堂是中国译学史上第一位明确将现代语言学和心理学作为翻译理论基础的学者，著有长篇译论《论翻译》，提出翻译受到译者的个人心理和社会心理的影响，并以语言文字心理的剖析为立论根基。他认为，翻译是一门艺术，以"忠实""通顺"和"美"为标准。要成为合格的翻译工作者，不仅需要有语言天赋，还需要进行翻译艺术的训练。要翻译好一部作品，译者首先需要透彻了解原文文字及内容，其次需要具备相当的语言能力，能够清楚畅达地表述，最后需要承担对原作者、读者和艺术的三重责任，需要对翻译标准和翻译技巧了然于心，并常加操练。

第 4 章　句子的翻译

> Nothing is more common than for men to think that because they are familiar with words they understand the ideas they stand for.
> ——John H. Newman

问题导入

1. 翻译下面的句子，并总结你在翻译时遇到的难点及其解决方法。

   It has typically been assumed that firms from such markets, faced with slackening rates of growth and increased foreign competition in their domestic markets, will try to sell their products and services in less developed markets, leveraging their domestic competitive advantage internationally.

   译文_____
   _____
   _____

   难点：_____
   _____

   解决方法：_____
   _____

2. 对比上面的原文和你自己的译文，找出英汉语言句式结构上的差异。
   _____
   _____

翻译知识讲座

句子的翻译

句子是语言运用的基本单位，它由词、词组（短语）构成，能表达一个完整的意思，也是段落和语篇的组成部分。如前面章节所述，要做好翻译，就要养成自上而下理解、自下而上转换的习惯，即要从大处着眼，小处着手。因此，在翻译实践中，句子翻译成功与否在很大程度上影响着语篇翻译的质量。了解英汉两种语言句式结构方面的异同之处，找出句子翻译的某些规律，是做好语篇翻译的基础。

在第2章，我们已经就英汉两种语言的特点进行了对比，本章我们将在此基础上阐述在句子的翻译方面应该注意的一些问题。

1. 被动语态的翻译

与汉语相比，英语中被动语态使用更普遍，尤其在科技、新闻、公文等信息类文体中，被动语态使用频率更高。因此，在英汉翻译过程中，应考虑到两种语言在被动意义表达方式上的差异，采取灵活的处理方法进行转换，使译文符合汉语的表达方式。英语被动结构汉译方法可概括如下：

（1）译为汉语被动句

例 1 This organization is highly valued within the company for its ability to drive revenue. It is considered as important as other major departments, such as finance and sales.

参考译文：该部门因能提高公司收入而备受重视，其重要性不亚于财务部和销售部等其他主要部门。

（2）译为汉语主动句

例 2 Often, firms in this phase have been involved in international markets for a long period of time.

参考译文：处于这个阶段的公司通常已经参与到国际市场上很长一段时间了。

例 3 The enhanced product can be positioned to attract a smaller segment of the existing market.

参考译文：改进的产品可用于吸引现有市场上的一小部分顾客。

（3）译为汉语无主句，尤其是原文无法说出或无须说明动作执行者，或某些表明观点、态度、要求、呼吁、号召等的被动结构，都可用汉语无主句进行处理，这种情况下，原文主语往往可译为宾语。如：

例 4 The marketing department must be reinvented.

参考译文：必须重组市场部。

（4）"It + be + 过去分词 + that 从句"等由 it 引导的句型通常可译为泛指主语句或无主句

例 5 However, it can also be considered that marketing so many new products leads to economic resources being wasted.

参考译文：然而也可能有人认为，对这么多新产品进行营销导致了经济资源的浪费。

例 6 This is good advice in general, but often it's assumed that the goal of any marketing is to drive sales.

参考译文：总体而言，这个建议很好，但通常认为，任何一种营销都是为了促进销售。

2. 定语从句的翻译

英语中定语从句运用十分广泛，而汉语则缺少相应的表达形式，汉语习惯上把定语放在被修饰词之前，句子扩展方向一般是从右向左。定语从句的翻译是英译汉中的一个难点，需要译者根据上下文语境、句子结构等具体情况灵活变通。定语从句的翻译方法大致归纳为以下四种：

（1）前置法

如定语从句比较简单，可按照汉语表达习惯将其处理为汉语前置定语，这样可避免译文冗长啰唆。

例 7 Developing varieties that suit local tastes is not the only challenge that the company faces.

参考译文：开发出适合当地口味的各种产品并非该公司所面临的唯一挑战。

例 8 In the UK, where frozen foods are popular, consumers want units with 60% freezer space.

参考译文：在冷冻食品普遍的英国，消费者希望冰箱能拥有 60% 的冷冻空间。

（2）拆分法

如果定语从句结构比较复杂，无法译为汉语前置定语，可尝试将主句和定语从句拆分成独立的分句。根据不同的句子结构和语境，定语从句先行词既可保留，也可省略。因衔接上的需要，将定语从句处理为独立分句后，往往需要借助替代、重复等衔接手段，以使译文更加流畅连贯。

例 9 Companies have begun to evolve organizational structures that will allow them to compete effectively in the twenty-first century.

参考译文：很多公司均已开始调整组织结构，以提升其在 21 世纪的竞争力。

例 10 In Poland, where soup consumption is three times higher than in the US, they have developed varieties of condensed soup.

参考译文：波兰的汤类食品消费量比美国要高出两倍，他们已经在该国推出了不同品种的浓缩汤料。

（3）整合法

如果主句结构比较简单，且与定语从句关系紧密，翻译时可将定语从句与主句整合为一个句子。

例 11 The chief cultural officer must create incentives that eliminate these counterproductive mindsets.

参考译文：首席文化官必须制定激励措施来消除这些导致反作用的思维模式。

例 12 To succeed, the company would need a marketing engine that drove more-direct collaboration with customers and led to new markets.

参考译文：为获得成功，该公司营销模式需要推动与顾客更为直接的合作，从而形成新的市场。

当然我们也可以用前置法来翻译例 11，用拆分法来处理例 12，译文分别如下：

例 11：首席文化官必须制定消除这些产生反作用的思维模式的激励方式。

例 12：为了取得成功，该公司需要一种营销模式，这种模式推动与顾客更为直接的合作，从而形成新的市场。

（4）译为偏正复句

某些定语从句实际上承担状语从句的功能，用来说明原因、结果、目的、让步、转折、时间等关系，翻译时可根据上下文推断主从句之间的逻辑关系，适当添加衔接词，将定语从句处理为汉语偏正复句。

1）译为表示原因的偏正复句。如果定语从句用于解释主句的原因，翻译时可加上表示因果关系的连词，如"由于""因为"等。

例 13 In Poland, where 98% of the soup is homemade, the company has targeted working mothers while stressing the convenience of its product.

参考译文： 在波兰，由于 98% 的汤类食品都是在家中烹制的，该公司在强调其产品便利性的同时，还将目标顾客锁定为职场母亲。

2）译为表示结果的偏正复句。必要时可添加表示结果的连词，如"因此""因而""所以"等。

例 14 Consumers are unable to physically feel or try on the product, which can be a limitation for certain goods.

参考译文： 顾客无法亲身感受和试用产品，这对某些商品来说是一种限制。

3）译为表示目的的偏正复句。可在译文中增加表示目的的连词，如"为了""以便"等。

例 15 There are requirements that a company will meet to participate in mobile marketing.

参考译文： 为了参与移动营销，公司需要满足一些要求。

4）译为表示转折的偏正复句。可在译文中增加表示转折的连词，如"然而""却""但是"等。

例 16 Over the years I've found that most entrepreneurs spend too much time and money on promotions that don't generate new business.

参考译文： 这些年来，我发现大部分企业家在促销上花费了大量的时间和金钱，然而那些促销却并没有带来新的业务。

3. 状语从句的翻译

英语状语从句用来表示时间、地点、条件、原因、方式、目的、让步、结果、比较等关系，其功能与汉语偏正复句大致相当，翻译时一般没有太大困难。需要指出的是，英语状语从句与汉语偏正复句毕竟不尽相同，某些方面的差异还是应该引起译者的注意。

如前所述，英语为形合语言，各类状语从句都需要由表示逻辑关系的连接词加以引导，汉语则偏向于意合，尽管不排斥关联词语的运用，但分句之间的逻辑关系通常会隐含在字里行间。另外，英语状语从句与汉语偏正复句语序上也存在差异。英语状语从句位置较为灵活，除方式、比较和结果从句多为后置外，其他状语从句的位置既可位于主句前，也可放在主句之后，而汉语偏正复句的从句一般位于主句之前。鉴于上述差异，在翻译英语状语从句时，译者应注意以下两点：一是要避免字字对应，应在正确理解主从句逻辑关系的基础上进行灵活处理，必要时也可省略原文中的连接词；二是要尊重汉语表达习惯，灵活调整主句和从句的位置。

例17 The company must expand its exports well above this level if it is to become a major international player in the car industry.

参考译文： 要成为国际汽车行业的主要参与者，该公司必须进一步扩大出口。

在原文中，条件状语从句的主语与主句的主语一致，译文不必再次重复主语。此外，译文也没有使用表示假设关系的"如果"，因为这种关系已隐含在上下文中。最后，译文调整了语序，采用先因后果的表达方式，更符合汉语表达习惯。英语状语从句汉译应注意如下几个方面的问题：

（1）表示原因、条件、目的等的英语状语从句翻译时可调整到主句之前。

例18 Most online businesses use dropshipping method of marketing because it requires only minimum budget.

参考译文： 由于所需预算最少，大多数网络商户使用代发货营销模式。

例19 We will use an integrated marketing communications plan in order that the message we send to our target audience is consistently delivered through various communication channels.

参考译文： 为使信息能通过各种传播渠道源源不断地输送至目标客户，我们将采用整合营销传播模式。

需要指出的是，由于受翻译文体的影响，现代汉语有时也会把从句置于主句之后，且这种欧化句式也逐渐得到了认可。据此，上述两句也可译为：

例18：大多数网络商户将采用代发货营销模式，因为这种模式所需预算最少。

例19：我们将采用整合营销传播模式，通过各种传播渠道把信息源源不断地输送至目标客户。

（2）避免将 before 一概译为"在……之前"，应根据表达内容需要，灵活采用其他表述方式。

例20 You need a solid definition of marketing before you can increase sales.

参考译文： 要先彻底弄清什么是营销，才能提高销售量。

（3）when 既可表达一段时间，也可表示某个时间节点，转换时不宜一概采用"当……的时候"。译为汉语时，可根据上下文及 when 所表达的逻辑关系进行灵活处理。

例21 When the relationship ended in 1971, the company continued to manufacture scooters, retaining much of the original design.

参考译文： 合作关系于1971年终止后，该公司继续生产摩托车，并保留了大部分原有设计。

例22 Why should I consider inbound marketing when I'm already using social media?

参考译文： 我已经在使用社交媒体了，为何还要去进行集客式营销呢？

例23 When a product is more about clever engineering than customer needs, sales can suffer.

参考译文： 如果一种产品只是设计巧妙而不考虑顾客的需求，销售量就会受影响。

（4）在 until 引导的状语从句中，主句如使用肯定形式，其动词必须是延续性的，主句如使用否定形式，动词为延续性或非延续性均可。在这两种情况下，until 不宜一概译为"直到……",而应根据情况灵活处理。

例24 Don't spend money on marketing until you know this.

参考译文： 不明白这一点，就不要把钱花在营销上。

例25 It was not until the 1930s that companies began to place a greater emphasis on advertising.

参考译文： 直到20世纪30年代，企业才开始更加重视广告宣传。

例26 You can't master Internet marketing until you become a good communicator.

参考译文： 只有成为一名好的沟通者，你才能掌握网络营销的窍门。

4. 长句的翻译

英语中长句的出现频率远高于汉语，在书面语体及某些特殊文体中尤其如此。在英汉翻译中，长句翻译往往是个难点，需要引起学习者的注意和重视。在翻译长句时，首先要分析原文，理清句子的主谓结构；然后分析其他成分，理清各成分之间的逻辑关系，再根据汉语习惯将这些内容重新安排，用符合汉语表达习惯的方式把原文意义表达出来。英语长句的翻译方法大致可归纳为以下四种：

（1）顺译法：如英语长句叙述层次和逻辑关系与汉语相似，可按照原文顺序依次组织译文。

例27 In order to compete effectively against established competitors, these firms need to determine how to leverage resources and capabilities from their domestic market to differentiate themselves clearly from competitors and provide themselves with a competitive edge in international markets.

参考译文： 为有效抗衡那些地位稳固的竞争者，这些公司应确定如何利用其本土市场的资源和力量，将自己与竞争者区别开来，并为自身带来国际市场上的竞争优势。

（2）重组法：某些英语长句语序与汉语表达习惯不同，翻译时可按照汉语行文习惯重组语序。一般情况下，英语句子重心在前，汉语句子重心在后，故而重组语序时往往可以从后往前进行翻译。

例28 This famous automobile manufacturer plans to become a global player in the automobile market by targeting price-sensitive market segments in the US with low-priced compact cars and four-wheel-drive vehicles, leveraging its experience in manufacturing auto components.

参考译文： 这家著名的汽车制造商计划凭借其汽车零部件生产的经验进军全球汽车市场，它选择了低价的紧凑车型和四轮驱动车型，并将目标顾客锁定在美国消费者中对价格敏感的消费群体。

（3）拆分法：如英语长句的主干和修饰语关系不甚密切，在翻译时可将主干与修饰成分拆分成独立的句子。

例29 For example, if toys are found to contain dangerous paints, some Western media will hostilely brand them as "Chinese toys" or "cheap imports from China," giving the impression that the whole country and its billion inhabitants are somehow to blame for a failure in quality control by a multinational manufacturer.

giving 引导的分词短语实际上是另一个意群的开始，因而可以考虑进行拆分，只是拆分后需要添加必要的衔接成分才能使译文流畅自然。在本句中，为了使上下文之间在意义上更加连贯，可增加"这种做法"。

参考译文： 举例来说，如果玩具被检测出有害的涂料，一些西方媒体会充满敌意地将其称为"中国玩具"，或者是"从中国进口的廉价品"。这种做法给人的印象是，整个中国及其十几亿民众要莫名其妙地为某个跨国生产商的劣质产品而遭受指责。

（4）综合法：翻译过程中，往往不能使用单一的技巧来处理英语长句，而需要根据语境综合运用多种技巧。

例30 W Company's aggressive move into world markets was prompted in part by the actions of a major competitor, the Swedish firm E Company, which had made acquisitions in Europe and gained access to the US market by acquiring a major American company.

参考译文： 作为 W 公司的主要竞争对手，瑞典的 E 公司已在欧洲收购了多家公司，且通过收购一家大型美国公司而进入美国市场。正是 E 公司的这种做法，才在某种程度上促使 W 公司作出大举进军国际市场的举动。

例31 The company's development of sodium batteries, which was born of the need for new technology to power hybrid locomotives and grew into a stand-alone business that serves telecom and other industries, was an "imagination breakthrough."

参考译文： 该公司需要新的技术来为混合动力机车提供动力，因此研发出了钠电池。该项目随后逐渐发展成为独立的业务，为通信及其他产业提供服务。钠电池开发可谓是一项"创想突破"。

上述两例均综合利用了拆分、重组等长句翻译技巧。例 30 先重组原文语序，然后把原文拆分成两个句子。例 31 则先运用顺译法处理原文中的定语从句，然后再进行拆分。

英语和汉语句子结构存在着诸多差异，翻译过程中，译者如不充分了解这些差异，就很容易被原文牵着鼻子走，笔下译文也摆脱不了翻译腔。鉴于此，英语长句汉译过程中，至少应遵循两个基本原则：一是要了解英语和汉语句式上的差异，分析并理解原文结构，而后用合乎汉语习惯的表述方式组织译文；二是要灵活运用各种翻译技巧，这是提高翻译质量不可或缺的方面。

商务语篇翻译与解析

Developing Strategies for Global Markets

(1) Developing a global marketing strategy to compete effectively in world markets is one of the most critical challenges facing firms today. Whether the firm concentrates

on a few markets close to home or targets many markets throughout the world, a long-run dynamic strategy must be formulated to provide the firm with a sustainable competitive advantage. This strategy must, at the same time, enable the firm to anticipate, respond, and adapt to the growing complexity and rapid pace of change in the global marketplace.

However, depending on the extent of the firm's involvement and experience in international markets, the specific issues that a firm faces in designing an effective global strategy will vary. Here, three stages or phases of involvement are (2) <u>identified</u>: 1) initial entry, 2) local market expansion, and 3) global rationalization. When entering international markets for the first time, a firm's primary concern is to assess and select the countries which provide the most attractive opportunities for its products and services, and to devise competitive market entry strategies to take advantage of these opportunities. Once a foothold has been successfully established in international markets, management attention typically turns to expanding local market presence. Early on, this entails broadening the product line, adding new (3) <u>variants</u>, developing new products, and adapting marketing (3) <u>tactics</u> to compete more effectively in local markets. Later, as the firm's role in local markets expands, mechanisms to coordinate and control operations across national markets need to be established. As the firm's international operations develop and evolve over time, pressures arise to rationalize and consolidate operations across national boundaries (4) <u>so as to improve global efficiency and facilitate the transfer of knowledge and skills within the firm</u>. A strategy has to be developed to (5) <u>leverage</u> the firm's competitive position in global markets and take advantage of potential synergies arising from global market operations.

The (6) <u>directions</u> pursued by firms in global markets are highly diverse, as a result of their different backgrounds, resources, capabilities, and competitive strengths. Most previous discussion and research relating to the global strategy has, however, focused on large multinationals, particularly those from the Industrial Triad. (7) <u>It has typically been assumed that</u> firms from such markets, faced with slackening rates of growth and increased foreign competition in their domestic markets, will try to sell their products and services in less developed markets, leveraging their domestic competitive advantage internationally. Later, they will try to consolidate their position in these markets and, eventually, establish a dominant position worldwide.

The global (8) <u>landscape</u> is, however, no longer the sole domain of multinational behemoths originating from the Industrial Triad. It is now populated by an array of companies, including a growing number of small and medium-sized companies. Domestic market leaders from (9) <u>emerging economies</u> are venturing into international markets as once-protected home markets open up to foreign competition. State monopolies are also becoming privatized and taking on the competition.

(10) <u>Such firms do not benefit from the same resources and capabilities as a large multinational. Nor do they have the same market position and power on which to</u>

base global strategies. While large multinationals benefit from their size and extensive networks of resources, small firms need to be nimble and focused in developing strategies. Large emerging market firms and former state-owned enterprises need to consider how to leverage their domestic advantage in international markets. Furthermore, these firms are often at an earlier stage of involvement in international markets. Multinationals from industrialized countries often have a long history of involvement in international markets, and are either in Phase 2 or 3. More recent (11) <u>entrants</u>, on the other hand, are still in Phase 1, seeking to establish their position in international markets, and determining which markets or regions to target, and which competitors to confront. As a result, the challenges these firms face, the nature of the competitive threat, the key decisions and strategic imperatives all differ, as do the functional goals to be emphasized.

  Regardless of the stage of international market development, the task facing managers is the same—crafting a strategy that will allow the firm to win in global markets. However, winning takes on a very different meaning and requires different actions depending on the extent of the firm's involvement in international markets. Early on, a winning strategy is (12) <u>simply</u> one that works in a few markets and achieves modest sales goals; later on, winning may imply confronting major competitors worldwide, requiring a (12) <u>massive deployment</u> of resources and (12) <u>continued vigilance</u> on multiple fronts in different parts of the world.

  (13) <u>Underlying any strategy are key imperatives that establish broad parameters for success in a particular phase and the trajectory that the firm will follow into the next phase</u>. In Phase 1 (initial entry), in addition to devising an entry strategy, a firm must develop mechanisms for learning (and an ongoing commitment to learning) about international markets and how to operate successfully in specific country markets. Firms in Phase 2 (local market expansion) have successfully entered the international fray and are beginning to establish a presence in a number of markets. As they seek to expand further appropriate strategies will differ depending on the industry and the underlying strategic parameters, as well as a firm's willingness to broaden its base of operations. While firms continue to learn, the main focus in this phase is on building a presence in each market. As this is accomplished, the focus will gradually shift to improving coordination and control across country markets. Firms in Phase 3 (global rationalization), have already established themselves in international markets and are now attempting to rationalize operations worldwide in order to achieve synergies from operating on a global scale. At this stage, while learning and building continue, consolidation of the firm's market position to establish global leadership (14) <u>takes precedence</u>.

难点解析

（1）本句主语较长，是一个现在分词短语，翻译时我们可以将句子的主谓部分进行拆分，翻译成各自独立的分句。

（2）identify 一词的翻译不能简单照搬词典的解释来处理，可将其引申为"划分"。可在译文中为其增加主语，将其处理为汉语的主动句，也可以翻译为汉语的无主句。另外本篇包含较多被动语态，翻译时应根据情况灵活处理。

（3）根据上下文，variants 一词在此指产品的系列，翻译时可在译文中增加必要的词汇，使该词的意义更为明确。对 tactics 一词的翻译要体现出与 strategy 的不同。

（4）本句较长，翻译时可根据汉语句式特点适当调整原句的语序，把 so as to 这个目的状语提前，使译文更为通顺。

（5）leverage 是商务语篇中常见的词，它作动词用时可理解为：a）利用……的优势，充分利用。如 How do you best leverage your limited marketing resources? 你如何最充分地利用有限的市场资源？ b）使……举债经营，使发挥杠杆作用。如 A public corporation may leverage its equity by borrowing money. 上市公司可通过借债使其资产增值。在本句中该词作第一种理解，和后半句的 take advantage of 同义，故而采用合句法，译为"充分利用……和……"即可。

（6）directions 一词在此可译为"方向"，在其前增添"发展"一词，可将原文的含义表达得更加清楚。

（7）在翻译 It + be + v-ed + that-clause 句型时，我们往往为其添加一个泛指的人称主语，将其转变为汉语的主动句。翻译本句时，还要注意处理好句中的过去分词和现在分词短语。

（8）landscape 一词在此显然不能直接翻译为"风景"，需要结合上下文将其意义具体化。根据文章的语境，可译为"商业市场"。

（9）emerging 一词指"正在兴起的"，economies 一词在此处不是我们通常理解的"经济"，而是对某个区域的经济组成的统称，一般译为"经济体"。如：China is now the second largest economy in the world. 中国现在是世界上第二大经济体。

（10）这两个句子如果译为"这类企业并没有……，或它们也没有……"，会显得比较累赘，更为妥当的处理方法是将两个句子合为一句。另外在翻译本段的两个 benefit from 时，要结合上下文进行处理。第一个 benefit from 的含义是指这类企业没有大型跨国企业所拥有的资源和实力，自然无法受益于这些资源和实力。应注意选择恰当的措辞来体现出这一层的含义。

（11）英汉语篇的词汇衔接手段侧重点不一样。重复在汉语语篇中的使用频率要高于其他词汇衔接手段，而英语语篇的一个明显趋势是更多地使用同义词。这里的 entrants 一词，不能将其简单地译为"新加入者"。结合语境我们可以发现，这个词是上文提到的 these firms are often at an earlier stage of involvement in international markets 中 these firms 的同义词，在翻译这个词时，我们可以使用重复这种衔接手段，使译文更符合汉语的表达习惯。

（12）本段中有几个词汇在翻译时要予以高度注意。simply 一词在这里用于强调，不能想当然地把它理解为"简单地"，翻译时要选择适当的表达体现出强调的意义。massive deployment 和 continued vigilance 是名词结构，但表示的是动态概念，在翻译时可转换为汉语中的动词结构。

（13）本句为倒装句，underlying any strategy 为句子的表语部分，系动词 are 后的部分均为主语。为了保持句子结构的平衡，避免头重脚轻，原文使用倒装结构。翻译时，不必拘泥于原文的语序，而应根据句子的意思和逻辑关系，灵活调整译文的语序。另外这个长句的结构也较为复杂，包含了两个定语从句，第一个 that 引导的定语从句先行词为 key imperatives，这个定语从句还包含了以 trajectory 为先行词的另一定语从句，而 trajectory 又作为第一个定语从句中谓语动词 establish 的宾语，与 parameters 一起构成并列宾语。翻译前要搞清楚这些逻辑关系，才能恰当地安排译文的语序。

（14） take precedence 是固定用法，意为"优先于、比……更重要"。如：The needs of the community must take precedence over individual requirements. 公众的利益高于个人的利益。

商务知识讲座

市场营销基础理论

市场营销又称为市场学、市场行销或行销学，简称"营销"。市场营销是企业的一种功能，是企业一系列创造、交流并将价值观传递给顾客的过程，它通过管理客户关系来让企业及其股东获利。

市场营销包含两种含义，一种是指企业的具体活动或行为，这时称之为市场营销或市场经营，是企业对产品及服务制定设计、定价、促销及分销的方案并实施的过程；另一种是指研究企业的市场营销活动或行为的学科，称之为市场营销学、营销学或市场学等。市场营销学的研究对象是市场营销活动及其规律，即研究企业如何识别、分析评价、选择和利用市场机会，从满足目标市场顾客需求出发，有计划地组织企业的整体活动，通过交换，将产品从生产者手中转向消费者手中，以实现企业营销目标。

从营销组合（marketing mix）的角度讲，市场营销理念经历 4P → 4C → 4R 三个发展阶段：

1. 4P 市场营销理念

4P 指的是 Product（产品）、Price（价格）、Place（地点，即分销或渠道）和 Promotion（促销）。这一理论认为，如果一个营销组合中包括合适的产品、合适的价格、合适的分销策略和合适的促销策略，那么这将是一个成功的营销组合，企业的营销目标也可以实现。

4P 营销理念自 20 世纪 60 年代末提出以来，对市场营销理论和实践产生了深刻的影响，被营销经理们奉为营销理论中的经典。如何在 4P 理论指导下实现营销组合，实际上是公司市场营销的基本操作方法。

2. 4C 市场营销理念

随着市场竞争日趋激烈，媒介传播速度越来越快，4P 理念受到挑战。4C 营销理念于 20 世纪 90 年代提出，4C 分别指代 Customer（顾客）、Cost（成本）、Convenience（便利）和 Communication（沟通）。该理论认为，企业应通过同顾客进行积极有效的双向沟通，建立基于共同利益的新型企业/顾客关系。这不再是企业单向的促销和劝导顾客，而是在双方的沟通中找到能同时实现各自目标的途径。

3. 4R 市场营销理念

　　4R 营销是 21 世纪初出现的一种营销理念。4R 分别指：Relevancy（关联），即认为企业与顾客是一个命运共同体，建立并发展与顾客之间的长期关系是企业经营的核心理念和最重要的内容；Respond（反应），在相互影响的市场中，对经营者来说最现实的问题不在于如何控制、制定和实施计划，而在于如何站在顾客的角度及时地倾听，并从推测性商业模式转变成为高度回应实际市场需求的商业模式；Relation（关系），在企业与客户的关系发生了本质性变化的市场环境中，抢占市场的关键已转变为与顾客建立长期而稳固的关系；Return（回报），任何交易与合作关系的巩固和发展，都是经济利益问题。因此，一定的合理回报既是正确处理营销活动中各种矛盾的出发点，也是营销的落脚点。

　　4R 营销理论的最大特点是以竞争为导向，在新的层次上概括了营销的新框架。它根据市场不断成熟和竞争日趋激烈的形势，着眼于企业与顾客的互动与双赢，不仅积极地适应顾客的需求，而且主动地创造需求，运用优化和系统的思想去整合营销，通过关联、关系、反应等形式与客户形成独特的关系，把企业与客户联系在一起，形成竞争优势。

　　根据活动范围，市场营销可分为国内市场营销（domestic marketing）和全球市场营销（global marketing）。全球市场营销也称为国际市场营销（international marketing），是一种跨越国界的营销活动，指对商品和劳务流入两个或两个以上国家的消费者或用户手中的过程进行计划、定价、促销和引导，创造产品和价值并在国际市场上进行交换，以满足多国消费者的需要并获取利润。

翻译练习

I. 思考题

1. 英汉句式上的差异有哪些？
2. 结合自己的翻译实践，总结一下在翻译英语句子时应该注意的问题。

II. 从 "Developing Strategies for Global Markets" 中摘录给你深刻印象的句子或词组。

1. _____
2. _____
3. _____
4. _____
5. _____

III. 商务术语翻译

aggressive export pricing	
application positioning	
benefit segmentation	
brand awareness research	
brand name counterfeiting	
brand name generation and testing	
buyer behavior research	
competitive pricing analysis	
concentrated targeting	
consumer segmentation study	
controlled test marketing	
core product strategy	
Delphi method	
differentiated targeting	
direct mail retailing	
direct selling	
geocentric orientation	
geographic segmentation	
global marketing	
global standardization	
gray market	
idea generation	
image advertising	
integrated marketing communication (IMC)	
international market potential study	
international marketing research	

international product life cycle (IPLC)	
international promotional mix	
international public relation	
multinational marketing	
penetration pricing strategy	
predatory pricing	
product user positioning	
product-country stereotype	
purchase behavior study	
relationship marketing	
simulated test marketing	
skimming pricing strategy	
standardizing pricing	
undifferentiated targeting	
usage segmentation	
use positioning	
user status segmentation	

IV. 句子翻译

1. Today's strategic planners, having created as much value as they could by cutting costs, are now looking to grow domestic markets, as well as build new markets and revenues in such countries as Brazil, China, India, Malaysia, and Mexico.
2. Whether a late entrant or a pioneer seeking to foil newcomers, it helps to have a thorough understanding of the entry and defensive strategies available, a good sense of timing, and a game plan for decision-making.
3. Studies show that in most cases, being first to the market provides a significant and sustained market-share advantage over later entrants. Still, later entrants can succeed by adopting distinctive positioning and marketing strategies.
4. Reduced price can induce the pioneer's current customers to switch. Still, this strategy is likely to result in reduced margins for the new entrant compared with other players in

the market, unless the new entrant's cost of production is relatively lower.

5. This service could both complement and replace options available to current customers, but most of the potential players in the marketplace are targeting either traveling professionals who need to be in constant touch or the rural market, in which the cost-to-provision telecommunications infrastructure is very high and satellite-based options help governments offer ubiquitous telecommunications services.

6. Faced with intense competition and maturation in the local markets in the United States, regional telecommunication companies are expanding into emerging markets such as Brazil.

7. Going global is not the only solution. Sometimes the risk and the investment required to penetrate international markets may not be worth the return. Focusing on existing markets, where your company has a good understanding of the environment, can prove less risky and bring quicker success.

8. In addition to choosing the appropriate marketing strategy, it is crucial to determine the timing of the introduction of any new product. This is especially true in high-tech industries, in which product life cycles are short and it is difficult for late entrants to catch up and extract reasonable returns.

V. 篇章翻译

Marketing is one of the areas of business operations where it is widely predicted that artificial intelligence (AI) will drive enormous change. In fact, a McKinsey study found that, along with sales, it is the single business function where it will have the most financial impact. This means that if you're a marketer and you're not using AI, you're missing out on the benefits of what is possibly the most transformational technology.

Actually, the chances that there are people out there doing marketing today and not using AI in any shape or form are somewhat unlikely. This is simply because there are so many tools with AI features that we are used to using without even thinking about it. The most frequently used social and search engine advertising solutions, email marketing platforms, e-commerce solutions, and tools designed to assist with content creation all provide functionality that taps into what we refer to as "AI" in business today. To be clear, this isn't what we think of as "general" AI—machines that have the capability to think and communicate like us and turn their hands to just about any task. In business today (and in marketing in particular), AI refers to software that helps us carry out one particular job—such as identifying where to place advertising in order to maximize efficiency or how to personalize an email to increase the likelihood of receiving a reply—and get better and better as it is exposed to more data.

However, while there may be many tools out there and most marketers are increasingly comfortable with using them on a day-to-day basis, it's often done in an ad hoc manner. Many marketing departments still lack a coordinated, strategy-focused approach to implementing bigger projects. Just as importantly, many are lagging when it comes to fostering an AI-friendly, data-first culture as well as developing competencies and upskilling in order to meet the skills demand.

翻译名家

杨绛（1911—2016），著名作家、文学翻译家和外国文学研究家。她先任教于上海震旦女子文理学院和清华大学，后在中国社会科学院文学研究所、外国文学研究所等工作，曾获"资深翻译家"称号。

杨绛一生译作不多，但翻译界赞其"每译一书，必为佳作"。杨绛翻译的《堂·吉诃德》是第一部从西班牙语译入汉语的译本，广受好评，她因此获得西班牙政府颁发的勋章。1999年，88岁的杨绛翻译出版了柏拉图对话录中最难翻译的《斐多》篇，被称为"迄今为止最感人至深的哲学译本"。

杨绛认为翻译包括三件事：选字、造句和成章，其中关键是造句，因为需得造成句子，才能选定文字，连句成章。她主张在译句时，译者须把句子融会于心，以原文句子作为翻译单位，但原文一句不一定等于译文一句。由于西语多复句、长句，中文多单句、短句，断句是免不了的。断句的方法是分清原句里的主句、分句以及各种词组，并认明以上各部分的从属关系，在此基础上，将原句断成几句，按照汉语语言习惯重新组合句子。她还指出，最大的困难不在断句，而在重新组合，因为译者难免受到原文顺序的影响。她建议译者在重新组合时要摆脱原文顺序，并将这个过程称为"冷却"。她引用孟德斯鸠讨论翻译拉丁文时所说的"先得精通拉丁文，然后把拉丁文忘掉"，将"冷却"类比为"把拉丁文忘掉"。"冷却"后，译者再读译文，对照原文，就容易发现翻译不妥的地方。

杨绛专注于学问，曾说最想"隐于世事喧哗之外，陶陶然专心治学"。她潜心治学、严谨认真的翻译态度，堪称译者学习的楷模。

第 5 章　主语和谓语的翻译

> The golden rule for good grammar is not a rule of grammar. It is true that there are rules of grammar, as in music there are rules of harmony, and that they are important, but one can no more write good English merely by keeping those rules than one can compose good music.
>
> —The Anonymous

问题导入

1. 翻译下面的句子。

   From the individual's point of view, the purchase of an adequate amount of insurance on a house eliminates the uncertainty regarding a financial loss in the event that the house should burn down.

   译文：_____

   _____

   _____

2. 说明翻译上句时遇到的困难及其解决方法，并特别关注原文中主语和谓语的翻译方法。

   难点：_____

   解决方法：_____

翻译知识讲座

主语和谓语的翻译

第 2 章中指出英语句子多采用主谓结构，汉语则多采用话题—评述结构。正是因为这些差异，主语和谓语对英语和汉语而言在句子结构上有着不同的重要性，学习者应关注这些差异并在翻译中进行相应的调整。

1. 英语主语的翻译

人类在思维方式上存在一定的差异性，这在一定程度上造成了英汉两种语言在主语方面的不同。汉语句式多选择有生命的名词或代词作为主语，此类句式常被称为有灵主语句。而英语中常将无生命的名词或代词用作主语，这种句式被称为无灵主语句。

在构句过程中，英语主语是非常重要的句子成分。概括起来，英语主语具有以下特点：

(1) 除了祈使句、省略句及某些惯用语，主语是句子必不可少的组成部分，在全句中起主导作用，是整个句子的灵魂；
(2) 主语与谓语关系密切，对谓语动词的形态变化产生一定的制约作用；
(3) 主语通常由名词性短语或代词充当，其他词类若要充当主语，需进行形态变化；
(4) 既有人称主语，也不乏物称或非人称主语；
(5) 出于句式平衡等方面的需要，经常用 it 作形式主语。

比较而言，汉语主语的特点表现如下：

(1) 主语不是必要的句子结构成分，在特定语境下，常可以省略或干脆不用主语，从而构成所谓的无主句；
(2) 与谓语的关系松散，不像英语主语那样对谓语有很大的牵制作用；
(3) 不仅名词性词语可以充当主语，不少其他词类也可充当主语；
(4) 常以人称作主语，物称主语不甚常见。

关于英汉主语各自的特点及相互之间的差异性，我们可借助下面两例加以分析说明：

例 1 But restricting the ability of insurers to reflect risks in setting premiums causes problems. Insurance firms argue that removing sex as a rating factor will add an uncertainty premium to everyone's bill. Using more detail on individuals' characteristics will also add to costs.

参考译文： 但是不允许保险公司将风险作为保费确定的依据也会引发一些问题。保险公司认为，如果不将性别作为设定保费的因素，将会给每位投保人增加一笔无法确定的保险金额。过分细致地考虑个人特点也会增加成本。

例 1 选自一篇讨论欧洲法院的文章。由于汉语无须考虑主谓一致问题，第一个分句中主谓之间数的一致性无须在汉语中体现出来。此外，译为汉语时，上例中充当主语的动名词 restricting 和 using 都可处理为动词，这也体现了汉语主语的使用特征，即汉语动词可直接充当主语。

例 2 《论语》一书是中国古代文化的经典著作。在孔子以后几千年的中国历史上，没有哪一位思想家、文学家、政治家不受《论语》这本书的影响。不研究《论语》，就不能真正把握中国几千年的传统文化，也不能深刻理解古代中国人内在的心境。

参考译文： An enduring classic of Chinese culture, *The Analects* has influenced all thinkers, writers, and politicians throughout thousands of years of Chinese history after Confucius. No scholar could truly understand this long-standing culture or the inner world of the ancient Chinese without this book.

英语句子的主语必须由名词或代词充当，所以在例 2 中，汉语原文中的动词性主语

"没有哪一位思想家、文学家、政治家"和"不研究《论语》"就无法直译为英语句子的主语，需要进行转换。根据上下文和英语的表达习惯，参考译文对第一个动词性主语所在的分句进行调整，将原文的动词性主语转换为名词性主语 The Analects。而第二个动词性主语所在的分句为典型的汉语无主句，翻译时可添加适当的主语。

在翻译实践中，英汉主语使用上的差异要求译者应根据汉语特点进行必要的调整，切忌对原文结构亦步亦趋，否则会导致字对字的硬译或死译。概括起来，在翻译中对英语主语的处理应注意以下几个方面：

（1）根据上下文语义和汉语的表达习惯，将英语无灵主语句转换为汉语有灵主语句。英语物称主语运用比较普遍，而汉语则更多地使用人称主语，这种情况下，应该考虑对主语进行转换。

例 3 The annual review of the insurance sector saw 20 life insurers, 24 general insurers, four life reinsurers, and two general reinsurers in the top 50 list.

参考译文： 在保险行业年度评审中，20家人寿保险公司、24家综合保险公司、4家人寿再保险公司和2家综合再保险公司进入前50名。

例 4 It was in that moment that a question came to my mind: How do you know if you're in need of a life insurance policy?

参考译文： 正是在那一刻我想到了一个问题：如何确定自己是否需要一份人寿保险？

例 5 Past experience has taught us that insurers will have to process billions of dollars in claims when a disaster strikes.

参考译文： 根据以往的经验，保险公司在灾难性事件发生时要处理数十亿美元的保险理赔。

例 3 中 the annual review of the insurance sector、例 4 中 a question 和例 5 中的 past experience 均为无灵主语，翻译时要根据汉语习惯灵活处理。

（2）英语句子多采用主谓结构，汉语则多采用话题—评述结构，因而处理原文主语时，应酌情进行主语与话题之间的转换，使译文符合汉语表达习惯。

例 6 The number of people who claim that insurance is something you cannot take a step outside without seems to be equal to the number of people who disregard the opportunities insurance offers and call it a mere waste of money.

参考译文： 有人声称没有保险寸步难行，有人则对保险所带来的机遇不屑一顾，认为保险不过是浪费钱财。这两种人在数量上似乎不相上下。

比较例 6 中的原文和参考译文，可以发现原文中的主谓结构在翻译时被处理为话题结构，如 the number of people 译为汉语中的话题结构"有人"，that 从句后的主谓结构也转换为汉语中的话题—评述结构，"寸步难行"是对"没有保险"这一话题的说明。同样的处理方法也用于句子的主干部分 the number of people seems to be equal to the number of people，"这两种人在数量上"是话题结构，而"不相上下"则对话题进行说明。这样的转换使得参考译文流畅自然，更符合汉语表达习惯。

（3）翻译形式主语 it 时，可酌情增添泛指性人称，也可把原文中的逻辑主语补充出来。

例7 It isn't clear that regulators and banks would be more adept at judging such risks.
参考译文： 监管机构和银行是否更加擅长判断出此类风险，这一点尚不清楚。

2. 英语谓语的翻译

英汉谓语也存在着明显的差异性。英语结构严密，主语和谓语是句子的主轴，共同构成句子的主干成分；汉语主谓关系较为松散，整体结构在形式上不如英语句子严谨。

汉语谓语选择范围比英语要广泛得多。英语谓语只能由动词充当，而汉语中可以充当谓语的成分多种多样，这就使得汉语主谓搭配形式更为复杂。英语谓语的特点可概括如下：

(1) 与主语关系密切，独立性弱，在人称、数等方面与主语保持一致；
(2) 以动词充当谓语；
(3) 在时态、语态、语气等方面具有形态变化。

汉语谓语特点也可概括为如下三点：

(1) 与主语关系松散，独立性强，可单独成句，构成非主谓句；
(2) 除动词性词语外，形容词、名词等均可直接充当谓语；
(3) 无形态变化，主要通过词汇手段表示时态、语态等语法意义。

英汉谓语之间存在着极大差异，在英汉翻译实践中，译者要注意谓语形式的选择与表达，从而使译文更符合汉语表达习惯。英语谓语汉译应注意以下两个方面的问题：

(1) 汉语动词无时态、语态、语气等方面的形态变化，在翻译过程中，需要通过必要的词汇手段来表现原文谓语的形态变化，以再现原文的时态、语态或语气。例如：

例8 For years entertainment insurance has been a small but profitable niche.
参考译文： 多年来，娱乐保险始终是规模小而利润高的利基市场。

(2) 英语谓语均由动词充当，汉语谓语则要灵活得多，除动词外，形容词、名词性短语等都可充当谓语。翻译过程中，应根据上下文将英语谓语灵活地处理为形容词、名词、主谓短语等汉语谓语结构。请看例句：

例9 Insurance that covers losses if a film or television show is leaked online is becoming more common.
参考译文： 为防止电影或电视节目在网上遭到泄露而蒙受损失的保险业务越来越普遍。

例10 The global group health insurance market remained largely stable over the last year, despite the prevailing uncertainties.
参考译文： 虽然存在普遍的不确定性，但去年全球团体健康险市场总体保持稳定。

例9中原文谓语部分的 is becoming more common 在参考译文中翻译成形容词性谓语，例10中原文谓语部分的 remained largely stable 则转换成主谓结构。

主语和谓语是英语句子的核心，应作为英汉翻译中重点关注的对象。可以这样说，无论原文结构如何复杂，只要摆正了主语和谓语两个棋子，就可以盘活整个句子。因此，翻译学习者要注意培养语言差异意识，在翻译过程中根据汉语的特点来处理语言差异，使译文符合汉语的表达习惯。

Nature of Insurance

Insurance is a complicated and intricate mechanism, and it is consequently difficult to define. However, in its simplest aspect, it has two fundamental characteristics:
- Transferring or shifting risk from one individual to a group;
- Sharing losses, on some equitable basis, by all members of the group.

We may define insurance from the individual's viewpoint as follows: (1) <u>From an individual point of view, insurance is an economic device whereby the individual substitutes a small certain cost (the premium) for a large uncertain financial loss (the contingency insured against) that would exist if it were not for the insurance.</u>

The primary function of insurance is the creation of the counterpart of risk, which is security. Insurance does not decrease the uncertainty for the individual as to whether the event will occur, nor does it alter the probability of occurrence, but it does reduce the probability of financial loss connected with the event. (2) <u>From the individual's point of view, the purchase of an adequate amount of insurance on a house eliminates the uncertainty regarding a financial loss in the event that the house should burn down.</u>

Some people seem to believe that they have somehow wasted their money in purchasing insurance if a loss does not occur and indemnity is not received. Some even feel that if they have not had a loss during the policy term, their premium should be returned. Both viewpoints constitute the essence of ignorance. Relative to the first, we already know that the insurance contract (3) <u>provides a valuable feature in the freedom from the burden of uncertainty</u>. Even if a loss is not sustained during the policy term, the insured has received something for the premium: the promise of indemnification if a loss had occurred.

(4) <u>With respect to the second, one must appreciate the fact that the operation of the insurance principle is based on the contributions of the many paying the losses of the unfortunate few.</u> If the premiums were returned to the many who did not have losses, there would be no funds available to pay for the losses of the few who did. Basically then, the insurance device is a method of loss distribution. What would be a devastating loss to an individual is spread in an equitable manner to all members of the group, and it is on this basis that insurance can exist.

In addition to eliminating risk for the individual through transfer, the insurance device reduces the aggregate amount of risk in the economy by substituting certain costs for uncertain losses. These costs are assessed on the basis of the predictions made through the use of (5) <u>the law of large numbers</u>. We may now formulate a second definition of insurance: From the social point of view, insurance is an economic device (6) <u>for reducing and eliminating risk through the process of combining a sufficient number of homogeneous exposures into a group to make the losses predictable for the group as a whole</u>.

Insurance does not prevent losses, nor does (7) <u>it</u> reduce the cost of losses to the economy as a whole. In fact, it may very well have the opposite effect of causing losses and increasing the cost of losses for the economy as a whole. (8) <u>The existence of insurance encourages some losses for the purpose of defrauding the insurer, and, in addition, people are less careful and may exert less effort to prevent losses than they might if the insurance did not exist</u>. Also, the economy incurs certain additional costs in the operation of the insurance mechanism. It must bear not only the cost of the losses but also the additional expense of distributing the losses on some equitable basis.

Perhaps we should make one final distinction regarding the nature of insurance. (9) <u>It is often claimed that insurance is a form of gambling</u>. "You bet that you will die and the insurance company bets that you won't." Or "I bet the insurance company $300 against $100,000 that my house will burn." The fallacy of these statements should be obvious. In the case of a wager, there is no chance of loss, and hence no risk, before the wager. In the case of insurance, the chance of loss exists whether or not there is an insurance contract in effect. In other words, the basic distinction between insurance and gambling is that gambling creates a risk, while insurance provides for the transfer of an existing risk.

难点解析

（1）本句是一个比较典型的英语长句，包含了一个主句和两个从句，第一个从句由 whereby 引导，whereby 是个常用于正式文体的关系副词，相当于 by which；这个从句中又包含了一个由 that 引导的定语从句，其先行词为 financial loss。在上一章中，我们谈到了英语长句和定语从句的处理方法。请参照这些处理方法，先试着进行翻译，然后和参考译文进行对照。

（2）本句在翻译时有三个地方需要关注。本句的主语由 the purchase of an adequate amount of insurance on a house 这个名词性短语来充当，根据汉语的语言特点，可译成包含动词的结构"为房屋购买适当金额的保险"。本句的谓语部分 eliminates the uncertainty regarding a financial loss，如果翻译成"消除与经济损失相关的不确定性"，意义不够明确，可变换一种说法，"消除了某事的不确定性"，也就是指"消除蒙受经济损失的风险"，这样意义更具体明确。本句中最后一部分 in the event that the house should burn down 为条件从句，should 是虚拟语气，翻译时需选择相应的汉语表达来传递这一意义。

（3）本句中 provides a valuable feature 这个谓语结构如果照直翻译为"（保险合同）提供了一个很有价值的特征"，其意义比较模糊，翻译时应将其意义进行引申和具体化。the freedom from the burden of uncertainty 这一词组也体现了英语倾向于使用名词表现动作的特点，翻译时可处理为动词短语。

（4）本句中 the fact 后接同位语从句，其中 the operation of the insurance principle 这个抽象名

词短语作从句的主语，paying the losses of the unfortunate few 是 the many 的逻辑谓语，这两处都体现了英语句子信息容量大的特点，翻译时需要根据汉语的特点进行处理。另外，one 是英语泛指人称，翻译时可转换为汉语中表复数的泛指人称"我们"。

（5）the law of large numbers，"大数法则"（又称"大数定律"或"平均法则"），原本是经济学或统计学的概念。大数法则来源于统计数字所表现出来的规律性，英国17世纪经济学家约翰·戈劳特揭示了这样一条统计学原理："通过大量充分的统计数字可以看出，各种现象（其中单个现象是偶然的）在整体上受着某种严格的规律性的支配。"尽管单一事件没有意义，但如果该事件多次重复，实际结果的分布就会呈现出一定的规律，这就是大数定律。

（6）本句中介词 for 和 through 使很多信息穿插在一起，结构比较复杂，给理解也带来一定困难。翻译前先要理清句子各成分之间的逻辑关系，然后按照汉语的习惯对内容要点进行重组。本句中，reducing and eliminating risk 是最终目标，其实现手段是 the process of combining a sufficient number of homogeneous exposures into a group，通过该手段实现 to make the losses predictable for the group as a whole 这一目标。翻译时应当适当调整原文语序。此处，exposures 一词是指"受影响的状态"，可以引申译为"风险"。

（7）本句中的 it 是指前面的 insurance，且不能省略，这是英语句子结构的要求，但是在翻译成汉语时则可以省略，不必使用"它"来指代上文中提到的"保险"。

（8）翻译本句时，要关注以下三点：a）抽象名词 existence 不宜直接翻译成"存在"，需要根据上下文进行引申；b）encourages 一词也不能按照通常理解译为具有褒义色彩的"鼓励"，这里和下一句中的 incurs 为同义词，需要根据上下文灵活变通；c）比较级和虚拟语气看似简单，在转换成汉语表达时也会有一定难度。

（9）这个句子可以翻译为"人们常说保险是一种赌博"，也可将其译为"保险经常被认为是一种赌博"。试比较一下这两种译法各自的优势。

商务知识讲座

保险概述

作为一种互助机制，保险有着悠久的历史，它是商业文明发展的产物。在与大自然抗争的过程中，古代人们就萌生了对付灾害事故的保险思想，并产生了原始形态的保险方法。据史料记载，公元前2000年，在西亚两河（底格里斯河和幼发拉底河）流域的古巴比伦王国，国王曾下令僧侣、法官等对他们所辖境内的居民收取税金，用以救济遭受火灾及其他天灾的人们。在古埃及石匠中曾有一种互助基金组织，向每位成员收取会费以支付个别成员死亡后的丧葬费。保险从萌芽时期的互助形式逐渐发展成为冒险借贷，发展为海上保险合约，再发展为海上保险、火灾保险、人寿保险和其他保险类型，并最终演变成为现代保险。它体现了人类的科学理性精神和道德良知。今天保险不仅仅是保障风险的代名词，更是促进社会进步的安全机制，成为现代社会体系中最具有活力的组成部分。

　　海上保险在各类保险中起源最早，正是海上保险的发展，带动了整个保险业的繁荣与发展。在海上保险的产生和发展过程中，一度包括人身保险。15世纪后期，欧洲的奴隶贩子把运往美洲的非洲奴隶当作货物进行投保，后来船上的船员也可投保。如遇到意外伤害，由保险人给予经济补偿，这些应该是人身保险的早期形式。

　　在法律和经济学意义上，保险是一种风险管理方式，主要用于会带来经济损失的风险。保险通过缴纳一定的费用，将一个实体潜在损失的风险平均转嫁给一个实体集合，是以货币形式平摊的社会风险转嫁机制。通俗地讲，就是一旦加入某个团体，就"一人有难，大家平摊"。

　　从本质上讲，保险体现的是一种经济关系，表现在：
　　(1) 保险人与被保险人之间的商品交换关系；
　　(2) 保险人与被保险人之间的收入再分配关系。

　　从经济角度来看，保险是一种损失分摊方法，以多数单位和个人缴纳保费建立保险基金，使少数成员的损失由全体被保险人分担。从法律意义上说，保险是一种合同行为，即通过签订保险合同，明确双方当事人的权利与义务，被保险人缴纳保费以获取保险合同规定范围内的赔偿，保险人则有收受保费的权利和提供赔偿的义务。因此保险乃是经济关系与法律关系的统一。

　　上述所说的保险一般指商业保险，而保险还有另外一种形式，即社会保险。社会保险是指在既定的社会政策的指导下，由国家通过立法手段对公民强制征收保险费，形成保险基金，用以对其中因年老、疾病、生育、伤残、死亡和失业而导致丧失劳动能力或失去工作机会的成员提供基本生活保障的一种社会保障制度。社会保险不以营利为目的，运行中若出现赤字，国家财政将会给予支持。与社会保险不同，商业保险按商业原则经营，以营利为目的，由专门的保险企业经营。所谓商业原则，就是保险公司的经济补偿以投保人交付保险费为前提，并力图在损失补偿后有一定的盈余，具有有偿性、公开性和自愿性。两者比较，社会保险具有强制性，商业保险具有自愿性；社会保险的经办者以财政支持作为后盾，商业保险的经办者要进行独立核算、自主经营、自负盈亏；商业保险保障范围比社会保险更为广泛。

翻译练习

I. 思考题

1. 英汉两种语言在主语和谓语上有哪些差异？
2. 结合翻译实例，简述英汉主谓差异对翻译的影响。

II. 从"Nature of Insurance"中摘录给你深刻印象的句子或词组。

1. _____
2. _____
3. _____
4. _____
5. _____

III. 商务术语翻译

accident insurance	
accidental death and dismemberment insurance	
(enrolled) actuary	
air cargo insurance	
all risks insurance	
annuity	
beneficiary	
business insurance	
casualty insurance	
catastrophic health insurance/critical illness insurance	
claim	
claim adjuster	
claimant	
commercial insurance	
compulsory automobile liability insurance	
consignment insurance	
contract of insurance	
contributing insurance	
coverage	
endowment insurance	

exposure	
insurance agent	
insurance broker	
insurance carrier	
insurance solicitor	
insurer	
life insurance	
personal injury insurance	
(insurance) policy	
policyholder	
premium	
reinsurance	
renewal	
risk	
risk avoidance	
settlement	
tertiary beneficiary	
the insured	
travel (accident) insurance	
underwriter	
underwriting cycle	
whole/permanent life insurance	
wrap-up insurance	
written business	

IV. 句子翻译

1. There were howls of protest from the insurance industry when the European Court of Justice ruled on March 1 that a person's gender should not be used to set insurance policies.
2. A person called an actuary constantly crunches demographic data to estimate the life of a person. This is why characteristics such as age, sex, smoker, etc. all affect the premium that a policyholder must pay.
3. Insurance can have various effects on society through the way that it changes who bears the cost of losses and damage. On the one hand, it can increase fraud; on the other hand, it can help society and individuals prepare for catastrophes and mitigate the effects of catastrophes on both households and communities.
4. If the damages related to climate change mount in the coming decades, insurance companies may face the prospect of paying larger disaster claims and being dragged into global warming lawsuits. But many firms, especially in the US, have barely begun to confront the risks.
5. The company which specializes in commercial insurance and reinsurance saw renewal rates increase due to the high number of disasters last year, up 9.6% in the US and 16.2% in the rest of the world.
6. Consumers are increasingly becoming aware of the quality of services being offered to them, making it essential for the services industry to implement quality improvement techniques for conforming to customer expectations. This is especially true for the insurance industry where the relationship between the insurer and the insured is still largely governed by sustained personal contact.
7. An organization that is deemed to have poor cybersecurity or has a history of falling victim to hackers or data breaches would likely get charged more for a cyber insurance policy than one that has a good reputation for keeping itself secure.
8. Insurers that succeed in the coming years will be those that recognize talent strategy has the same importance as core business strategy.
9. In 1666 the Great Fire of London finally and forcibly demonstrated the need for fire insurance. The primitive fire-fighting methods of the day were virtually helpless against the hungry flames that roared unchecked through narrow streets reducing timbered dwellings to ashes.
10. Close to 30 leading companies from the insurance industry, worth over $5 trillion in total assets and representing over 10% of world premium volume, together with insurance associations from different regions around the world, have joined a UN-backed process to promote a set of Principles for Sustainable Insurance that aims to green the sector and provide insurance tools for risk management in support of environmental, social, and economic sustainability.

V. 篇章翻译

The global financial crisis has spared few industries, not least those that live by the wits of their risk managers and survive at the whim of capital markets. So it is perhaps surprising that insurers have fared as well as they have. Barring those that acted like banks, American International Group (AIG) being the most glaring example, and those that owned banks, such as some Dutch insurers, the insurance industry has needed hardly any bail-outs.

The industry reckons that of the $11 trillion in direct and indirect support that governments gave to the financial sector as a result of the crisis, only $10 billion or so went to insurers other than AIG. Yet the next few years may be far tougher on insurers, partly as a result of actions taken to mitigate this crisis.

Insurers survived this shock with few failures for two main reasons. The first is that, unlike banks, they are funded by premiums rather than flightier forms of debt. The only way many of their clients can get their money back is if they suffer misfortune. As it happens, mishaps such as warehouse fires have a tendency to rise suspiciously in economic downturns, but not enough to strain the balance-sheets of big insurers.

The second reason is that insurers had already been tested by the bursting of the dot-com bubble, which sent the values of their share portfolios plunging and left many close to being unable to meet their commitments. Since then, most have brushed up on risk management and cut back on their equity holdings.

翻译名家

杨宪益（1915—2009），著名翻译家、外国文学研究专家和诗人，被誉为"翻译了整个中国的人"。他一生中翻译了百余部（篇）体裁多样、题材丰富的中国传统典籍和现当代作品，中国译界鲜有人企及。杨宪益倾毕生精力向世界译介中国文学，充分体现了老一辈翻译家的爱国情怀和责任担当。

杨宪益认为，翻译的首要原则是忠实原文，但这种忠实不是简单的语言符号的忠实，而是"把原文的意义用另一种语言表达出来"，是动态的、意义上的忠实。在英译汉中，他采取归化为主的翻译策略，以减少译文读者对源语文化的陌生感。而在汉译英时，他则采取异化为主、意译为辅的翻译策略，"向外国人如实介绍中国文化"，表现了他保存民族文化独立性的文化自觉意识。在翻译《红旗谱》时，他把书名译为 Keep the Red Flag Flying（让红旗飘扬下去），从而保留了"红旗"的文化意象，也传达出原文中"把革命传统传下去"的信息。翻译的忠实原则尤其体现在杨宪益的代表译作《红楼梦》的英译本中，他尽量保留这部文学经典中的各种传统文化信息，使外国读者充分了解中国的物质和精神文化遗产。在众多红楼译本中，他的译本被认为还原度最高，被美国汉学家倪豪士赞誉为"完整而准确"的译本。在中国文化走出去的过程中，翻译的作用举足轻重，杨宪益在汉译英实践中采取的翻译策略，为中国文化的传播提供了有益的借鉴。

第 6 章　翻译中的转换

> Translation is the paradigm, the exemplar of all writing. It is translation that demonstrates most vividly the yearning for transformation that underlies every act involving speech, that supremely human gift.
>
> —Harry Mathews

问题导入

1. 仔细阅读并翻译下面的句子。

   To the extent that the parent allocates managerial bonuses or investment capital to its subsidiaries on the basis of profitability, the unit managers have incentives to squabble over the transfer price because they care about how the MNC's accounting system reports their unit's performance.

   译文 _____
   _____
   _____

2. 将自己的译文与下面的参考译文进行比较，与同学讨论并记下疑问与心得。

   参考译文： 鉴于母公司视子公司收益率的高低向其派发管理奖金或投入资金，子公司经理非常重视本单位在母公司账面上的表现，因此在转让价格上锱铢必较，各不相让。
   _____
   _____

3. 查阅词典中对短语 to the extent that 的解释，并翻译以下例句。

   To the extent that he encouraged their bad behavior, he's to blame for it.

   译文 _____
   _____

翻译知识讲座

翻译中的转换

翻译的过程就是语际转换的过程，但这一过程并不简单，语言符号、语法结构、思维方式、社会文化等多种因素使其错综复杂。为了更好地理解这一过程，我们将在本章借用语言学研究中的转换生成语法对其加以探讨。

转换生成语法认为，语言包括两个层次：深层结构和表层结构。深层结构是语言的核心语义关系，是说话人的心理认知，是存在于思维中的观念；表层结构是语言的外部形式，是观念的外化，是所闻与所见。表层结构是深层结构的映射与衍生。表层结构和深层结构未必统一，同样的表层结构可能有着不同的深层结构，反之亦然。深层结构与表层结构之间可以通过一系列规则进行转换。转换生成语法还认为，虽然不同语言的表层结构差异很大，但其深层结构有着普遍的相似性。这种相似性为语际转换提供了基础。

在翻译实践中，句子表层结构的转换一般涉及词类转换、句式转换、视角转换等。下面将举例予以说明。

1. 词类转换

所谓词类转换，是指在翻译过程中将源语中的某类词译为目的语中的另一类词。当目的语中不存在对应的词类，或用对应词类无法生成符合目的语语法要求或语言习惯的表层结构时，则需要进行词类转换。英汉翻译中常涉及以下几类转换。

（1）转换为动词

英语偏静态，多用名词，而汉语偏动态，多用动词。在英汉翻译中，将名词转为动词可使译文更地道。

例 1 In the **absence** of this restriction, US firms could escape federal corporate income taxes.

参考译文： 如果**没有**这种限制，美国公司就有可能避缴联邦企业所得税。

将前半句译为"这种限制的**缺失**"也能达意，但不够自然。前半句还可译为"**离开**了这种限制"，所用方法一致，都是将名词转成动词。

例 2 In 2021, China's GDP was 114.4 trillion yuan, an **increase** of 8.1% year-on-year, and the growth rate ranked at the forefront among the world's major economies.

参考译文： 2021 年，中国国内生产总值达 114.4 万亿元，同比**增长** 8.1%，增速位居世界主要经济体前列。

本例中，an increase of 8.1% year-on-year 是一个名词短语，用来描述数字变化幅度。英语为了表达方便，常常将数字增幅用名词短语来呈现，并将其作为插入成分，这种表达法在财经新闻中非常常见，但在翻译时如果把 increase 处理为名词，则可能导致汉语表达不那么自然与流畅，因此参考译文将其转换为动词。

（2）转换为名词

由于思维和语言习惯上的差异，英语中某些非名词性表达形式在翻译成汉语的过程中往往需要转换为名词或名词短语。

例 3 The amendment to the tax law **aims** at granting international firms the same tax treatment as domestic firms.

参考译文： 修订税法的**目的**在于使跨国公司与国内企业享有同样的税收政策。

aim at 的意义是"瞄准……"或"以……为目的"，参考译文对其本义进行了引申，转成了"……的目的"这样的名词性结构，从而使译文在开头部分就揭示主题，使原句意义表达更明确。

例 4 We recognize the critical need for expanding the scope of regulation and supervision and making it more **effective**.

参考译文： 我们认识到，迫切需要扩大监管和监督范围并提高其**效力**。

make sth more effective 字面理解是"使……更有效"，但这种表达在文体上不太符合原句的风格，为了使译文更加郑重，将形容词 effective 转换为名词"效力"。

例 5 The relationship between a US parent and its foreign subsidiaries, in its totality, is akin to **that** of a franchisor and franchisee.

参考译文： 整体而言，美国母公司与其外国子公司的关系大致相当于特约经销授权方与特约经销商之间的**关系**。

that 指代前面的 relationship，以避免重复，而汉语中词语的重复是形成连贯语篇的重要手段。因此可以把指示代词 that 转换为名词"关系"。

（3）转换为形容词

出于表达习惯的需要，英语中的某些词类有时也可转换为汉语中的形容词。例如：

例 6 The market, the center for trade **in its many manifestations**, has long been at the center of the city.

参考译文： 集市是**形形色色**贸易的中心，也一直是城市的中心。

原文中介词短语 in its many manifestations 用来修饰 trade，意为"以其多种表现形式"，参考译文中直接转换为形容词"形形色色"，并改作前置修饰，表达更加符合汉语习惯。

例 7 The marketing strategy of the company is **perfectly** adaptive.

参考译文： 该公司的营销策略有着**极强的**适应性。

由于原文中的形容词 adaptive 转换成名词"适应性"，故其修饰词 perfectly 也随之而转换，由副词变成形容词"极强的"。

（4）转为副词

词类转换还可以出现在其他词类与副词之间。例如：

例 8 All these have been leading to a **continuous** growth of Austria's mobile advertising market.

参考译文： 所有这些都使得奥地利的移动广告市场**不断扩大**。

由于原文中的名词 growth 需要转换成动词"扩大"，其修饰词 continuous 也随之转换为副词"不断"。

例 9 There is an idea that an increase in tax rates tends to function as an incentive for taxpayers to **try** to increase their pretax incomes.

参考译文： 有人认为，提高税率能够刺激纳税人**努力**提高其税前收入。

短语 to try to increase 包含了两个动词，就深层结构而言，原句意义更侧重 to increase，因此可以将其处理为动词偏正结构"努力提高"，以副词"努力"来修饰动词"提高"。

2. 句式转换

鉴于英汉语句法结构各自的特点，在翻译过程中，应尽量按照汉语的语法要求、思维习惯和逻辑顺序生成译文，而不必拘泥于英语原文的表层结构。

例10 The company's **adaptability and profitability** make it a good choice for investors.

参考译文： 该公司**适应性强**，**盈利能力突出**，成为投资者的理想选择。

原句的表层结构句式紧凑，其深层结构包含了较强的因果关系，勉强将其译为"该公司的适应性和盈利能力使得它成为投资者的理想选择"也能说得过去，但因为没有具体阐明其适应性和盈利能力如何，逻辑不够透彻，不符合汉语的表达习惯。参考译文分别增加了"强"和"突出"来说明适应性和盈利能力，因果关系更加凸显，且句子主题唯一，更符合汉语表达习惯。

例11 People are, **not surprisingly**, turning to gold as a store of value at a time when no one is very clear where exchange rates are going.

参考译文： 由于汇率走势不明，人们纷纷选购黄金以求保值，**这也在意料之中**。

原句深层结构中包含"不足为奇"之意，只要按照汉语语法和思维习惯在汉语表层结构中对其加以表述即可，不必拘泥于 not surprisingly 出现的位置和表述的视角。

例12 One disadvantage is that managers of the buying and selling units may waste time and energy arguing over the appropriate transfer price because it will affect their reported profits, **even though** it will have no overall impact on the parent's consolidated before-tax income.

参考译文： 其缺点之一在于，**虽然**转让定价对母公司总的税前收入没有影响，但却会影响买卖双方上报的利润，从而使双方管理人员为转让定价争论不休，造成时间和精力的浪费。

原句的深层结构既包含因果关系，又包含让步关系。在汉语中寻找对应的表层结构时，一方面要符合汉语因果句、让步句的表达习惯，另一方面还要把握原句中因果与让步之间的逻辑关系，作出相应调整。

3. 视角转换

视角转换是指改变原文的叙述角度，换一种角度来表述，从而使语义更清楚，表达更顺畅。视角包括相反视角和相异视角，视角相反时可在肯定与否定之间进行正反转换，视角相异时则需要根据时空顺序、人物关系、逻辑关系、语言习惯等灵活处理。

例13 It's **not uncommon** for department managers to get fed up with delays in software development by IT departments and simply hire their own coders to get a program written.

参考译文： 部门经理**常常**因为受够了信息技术部屡屡拖延的软件开发进度而自行招聘程序员开发软件。

此例为否定转化为肯定。鉴于汉语中偶有"也不是不常见"的说法，因此不进行视角转换也能说得过去，但"常常"这种表述更为普遍。另外，此句包含因果关系，且原因部分较长，故将原句打散重排是一种方法。

例14 Media companies have **tried in vain** to be allowed to push these advertisements to mobile phones.

参考译文： 媒体公司**力图**获得在手机上发布这些广告的许可，但一直**未能如愿**。

此例为肯定转为否定。与上例不同的是，在汉语中，"努力但徒劳地做某事"这样的表达非常少见，也不符合语法规则，因此有必要加以调整。

例15 Because of these deficiencies, as noted earlier, a full exemption method of relieving double taxation **is difficult to justify** and is used by few countries.

参考译文： 由于存在上述缺陷，完全免税法在消除双重征税时**理据不足**，使用者寥寥无几。

justify 这个动词颇具代表性，它不是一个单纯的动作，而是携带附加信息（条件、程度、结果等）的动作。英汉双解词典将其解释为 show that (sb/sth) is right, reasonable, or just，相应的汉语解释是"表明或证明（某人/某事）是正当的、有理的或公正的"。因此 is difficult to justify 可译成"很难证明……是合理的"，只是稍显拖沓。换个视角，从正面来描述的话，则可译成"理据不足"，从而使译文更简洁。

例16 The organization of cities and the pursuit of trade share a common fabric, man's desire to reach out to others, socially and commercially.

参考译文： 城市的组织和对贸易的追求，一脉相承，即人们都有与他人交往的欲望，不论从社会还是商业角度，莫不如此。

还有一种类型的视角转换是抽象和具体之间的转换，即源语中的抽象表达在译入语中采用具体表达，或者源语中的具体表达翻译为抽象表达。本例中 fabric 原义为"布料、织物"，share a fabric 是一个形象表达，喻指两物具有相同的结构或组成部分，所以参考译文采用了抽象化的表达"一脉相承"。

语言现象千变万化，需要转换的情形绝不限于上述几种。然而万变不离其宗，只要把握好原句的深层结构，根据汉语的语法要求、思维习惯和逻辑顺序对其重新加以组织，即可生成具有规范的表层结构的译文。

商务语篇翻译与解析

Transfer Pricing

Like domestic firms, international firms seek to (1) <u>maximize</u> their after-tax income. However, they are also challenged to meet the tax requirements (which unfortunately are often in conflict) of all the countries in which they operate. International businesses typically must navigate a (2) <u>careful path</u> between taking advantage of tax incentives and sidestepping punitive taxes.

(3) Two common means international businesses adopt to reduce their overall tax burden are transfer pricing and tax havens. Transfer pricing refers to the prices one branch or subsidiary of a parent charges a second branch or subsidiary for goods or services. Transfer pricing is important to international business for several reasons. Intracorporate transfers of goods, technology, and other resources are common between subsidiaries located in different countries. On one estimate intracorporate shipments account for 40% of US international trade in goods. Transfer prices also affect an MNC's ability to monitor the performance of individual corporate units and to reward (or punish) managers responsible for a unit's performance. Further, transfer prices affect the taxes an MNC pays both to its home country and to the various host countries in which it operates.

In practice, transfer prices are calculated in one of two ways: the market-based method and non-market-based method.

The market-based method utilizes prices determined in the open market to transfer goods between units of the same corporate parent. (4) Suppose a tech company wants to export memory chips from the ROK for use in assembling personal computers at one of its US subsidiaries. It can establish the transfer price for the memory chips between its US and the ROK subsidiaries by using the open-market price for such chips.

This market-based approach has two main benefits. First, it reduces conflict between the two units over the appropriate price. The higher the price charged in the intracorporate transfer, the better the selling subsidiary's performance appears and the poorer the buying subsidiary's performance appears. (5) To the extent that the parent allocates managerial bonuses or investment capital to its subsidiaries on the basis of profitability, the unit managers have incentives to squabble over the transfer price because they care about how the MNC's accounting system reports their unit's performance. From the parent's perspective, however, such arguments waste firm resources. Once the firm's accounting records are consolidated, its overall before-tax profits will remain the same regardless of whether the transfer price overstates unit A's profitability and understates unit B's, or vice versa. Assuming both subsidiaries recognize the basic fairness of the market-based price, such intracorporate conflict will be reduced.

Second, the market-based approach promotes the MNC's overall profitability by encouraging the efficiency of the selling unit. (6) If the price the unit can charge for intracorporate sales is limited to the market price, its managers know the unit's profitability depends on their ability to control its costs. Moreover, they recognize that if they successfully produce the product in question more cheaply than their international competitors can, the parent's market-based transfer pricing will acknowledge their efforts in full. Motivated by the prospects of bonuses and lucrative promotions, unit managers have every incentive to improve the efficiency and profitability of their operations.

Transfer prices also may be established using non-market-based methods. Prices may be set by negotiations between the buying and selling units or on the basis of cost-based rules of thumb, such as production costs plus a fixed markup. (7) <u>Some services of the corporate parent may be assessed as a percentage of the subsidiary's sales, such as charges for general corporate overhead or for the right to use technology or intellectual property owned by the parent.</u>

(8) <u>MNCs commonly use non-market-based prices partly because, for some goods and services, no real market exists outside the firm.</u> For example, the sole market for an engine produced in a famous automobile factory in Spain may consist of its automobile assembly plants in Belgium, Germany, and the United Kingdom. Because no external market exists for this engine, the automobile company may establish a transfer price for the engine based on production costs plus an allowance for overhead and profit.

The use of non-market-based prices has both disadvantages and advantages. One disadvantage is that managers of the buying and selling units may waste time and energy arguing over the appropriate transfer price because it will affect their reported profits, even though it will have no overall impact on the parent's consolidated before-tax income. Non-market-based transfer prices also may reduce the selling unit's efficiency. A transfer price based on the seller's costs plus some markup may reduce the seller's incentive to keep its costs low because it can pass along any cost increases to other members of the corporate family through the non-market-based price.

However, strategic use of non-market-based transfer prices may benefit an international business. Creative rearranging of intracorporate prices may allow the parent to lower its overall tax bill. For example, an MNC can lessen the burden of an ad valorem import tariff by reducing the price the selling unit charges the buying unit, thereby lowering the basis on which the tariff is calculated. Further, such pricing may enable a firm to slash its total income taxes. Suppose an MNC operates in two countries, one with high corporate income tax rates and the other with low rates. The firm can raise the transfer prices charged to the subsidiary in the high-tax country and lower those charged to the subsidiary in the low-tax country. (9) <u>Doing this will reduce the profitability of the first subsidiary, as measured by its accounting records, while increasing the profitability of the second.</u> (10) <u>The net effect is to shift the location of the MNC's profits from the high-tax country (which would tax them more) to the low-tax country (which taxes them less)</u>, thereby reducing the firm's overall tax burden.

难点解析

（1）maximize，"使……最大化"，根据汉语表达习惯，这里可将动词转换为名词，将其译为"……的最大化"。

（2）careful 为 path 的修饰语，但是这对修饰关系在汉语中无法找到对应的表达形式，因此有必要将 careful 转换为副词来修饰 navigate。

（3）如果照搬原句结构，本句可译为：跨国公司采用的以降低总体税负为目的的两种常见方法是转让定价和避税港。这样的译文不够地道，可读性也不强。可依据汉语思维和表达习惯对原句句式进行转换，将其改译为：跨国公司经常借助转让定价和避税港这两种手段来降低总体税负。如此一来，原译文定语过长的问题得以解决，全句主语也由属物的概念"方式"变成了属人的概念"跨国公司"，更符合汉语的表达习惯。

（4）这两句之间存在紧密的逻辑关系，前句为后句的前提，翻译时可合并为一句，用逗号代替原来的句号。

（5）本句涉及长句的顺序调整与从句简化问题。如长句句式复杂，成分较多，可首先理顺主要信息点之间的逻辑关系，继而用符合汉语表达习惯的顺序将其重新组合。本句中有三个信息点：a）公司视业绩给予奖励；b）子公司为价格而争吵（或子公司重视价格）；c）子公司重视业绩。其逻辑关系是：a 导致 c，c 导致 b（因为价格会影响业绩）。因此，翻译时可按照汉语因在前、果在后的表达习惯将原文 a→b→c 表达顺序调整为 a→c→b 顺序，使译文条理清晰。在 because 从句中，如将 how 引导的从句直接译作"他们对跨国公司的财会系统将如何报告他们单位的表现非常重视"也说得过去，但译为"他们非常看重自己在母公司账面上的表现"，可使表述更清晰。

（6）本句中的 depends on 部分除了可以译成 A 依赖 B 的结构，还可以译成"要……，就必须……"。由此可见，译文并非唯一的，关键在于哪一种更容易为受众所接受，更接近原文的表达意图。

（7）在本句中，general corporate overhead 容易误译，主要原因有两点：一是望文生义，二是就近联系。overhead 通常可理解为 above one's head，考虑到母公司与子公司之间"上下级"关系，有人可能将其译为"其上级总公司"，而在商务英语中，overhead 可指"经营、管理等各方面的费用"。此外，general 并非修饰 corporate，而是修饰 overhead，故不可译为"总公司"。在商务文本翻译中，译者应时刻保持警惕，切勿忽视词语的专业意义，也不可仅凭词语在句子中的位置来判断其关系的远近亲疏。类似的例子还有本段中出现的 parent 和 markup，前者原义为"父母"，而此处表示"母公司"；后者原义为"作了标记的东西"，而此处为"加价"。

（8）本句的翻译涉及肯定与否定的转换。首先，non-market-based 可译为"不以市场为基础"，但也可以换个视角，采用肯定译法，如"脱离市场"。同样，no real market exists outside the firm 既可译成"在公司外部并不存在真正的市场"，也可换个视角，译为肯定语气，"其市场仅限于公司内部"。

（9）翻译本句时应考虑如何使译文更为简洁。原句要表达的是：这样做将会降低第一个子公司的收益率（收益率通过财会记录来体现），并提高第二个子公司的收益率。但这样的译文显然比较啰嗦，试将"这样做将会"变成"这样一来"，将"第一个子公司"和"第二个子公司"分别改为"前者"和"后者"（依托上文），将"收益率通过财会记录来体现"译为"表现在财会记录中的收益率"，再转化为"账面收益率"，即"这样一来，前者的账面收益率降低了，而后者的却提高了"，表达显然更为简洁。

（10）本句涉及插入式附加信息的翻译。一般而言，"以括号译括号"并无不妥，但某些情况下，如能将括号中的内容融入上下文中，则可使译文更为流畅，从而获得更好的表达效果。此句不宜"以括号译括号"，原因还在于其中的两个 them 容易引起混淆。如果将 them 用其所指内容代替，则译文会显得拖沓。鉴于括号内外的内容有契合之处（都涉及"国家"），可将括号内的成分作为定语来修饰括号外的成分，译文就成了"由征税较多的高税率国家转移到了征税较少的低税率国家"。本文还有类似的例子，如 to reward (or punish) 可以合译为"奖惩"。

商务知识讲座

国际税收与避税

国际税收是指两个或两个以上的国家政府凭借其政治权力，对跨国纳税人的跨国所得或财产进行重叠交叉课税，以及由此所形成的国家之间的税收分配关系。

跨国纳税人面对激烈竞争的国际市场，在利益的驱使下，往往会精心研究有关国家的税收法规制度，利用各国税收上的种种差异减轻税负，以谋求利润最大化。除此主观原因外，国际避税之所以能够实现，还有其客观原因。首先，各国税收制度不同，其课税对象、征税标准、税率水平、征收方法等存在差别。其次，各国避免国际双重征税办法不同，常见的有免税法、抵免法以及饶让抵免法等，不同的征税方法可导致纳税人税负失衡。第三，各国征管水平及其他非税因素存在差异。各国税务当局及其官员的征收管理水平不一，也会导致纳税人的税负不同，产生国际避税。第四，各国对国际避税的认识不同。并非所有国家都认为国际避税是需要打击的行为。避税在一些国家等同于逃税，而在另一些国家则是合法的行为。

一些跨国纳税人主要通过借用或滥用有关国家税法或国际税收协定，利用其差别、漏洞、特例和缺陷来规避纳税义务，以实现少纳税或不纳税的目的。其主要方式包括转让定价、利用国际避税地、滥用国际税收协定、利用电子商务等。

转让定价方式避税是指跨国纳税人通过人为压低境内公司向境外关联公司销售货物、贷款、服务、租赁和转让无形资产等业务的收入或费用分配标准，或有意提高境外公司向境内关联公司销货、贷款、服务等收入或费用分配标准，使境内公司的利润减少，使利润集中到低税国家（地区）的关联公司的避税方法。

国际避税地也称避税港或避税天堂，是指为吸引外国资本流入，繁荣本国（本地）经济，弥补自身资本不足和改善国际收支情况，或为引进外国先进技术以提高本国（本地）技术水平，而允许外国人在本国（本地）或确定范围内投资或从事各种经济活动，取得的收入或拥有的财产可以不纳税或只需支付很少税收的国家和地区。避税最常见的手法就是跨国公司在国际避税地虚设经营机构或场所来转移收入和利润。

国际税收协定是指两个或两个以上的国家或地区为了协调相互间在处理跨国纳税人征纳事务方面的税收关系，依照平等原则，通过谈判所缔结的在国际税收分配关系方面具有法律效力的书面税收协议。为达到消除国际双重征税的目的，缔约方之间应彼此约束与让步，形成缔约方居民适用的优惠条款。然而国际避税活动无孔不入，一些原本无资格享受某一特定税收协定优惠的非缔约方居民，会采取种种手法，如通过开设导管公司、利用双边关系开设低股权控股公司而享受税收协定待遇，以规避其纳税义务。

电子商务在实现了书写电子化、信息传递数据化、交易无纸化、支付现代化的同时，也引起了审计环境、审计线索、审计信息的储存介质、审计技术方法、审计方式等一系列的重大变化。这些使得国际税收中传统的居民定义、常设机构、属地管辖权等概念无法进行有效约束，无法准确区分是销售货物、提供劳务或是转让特许权，因而电子商务的迅速发展在推动世界经济发展的同时也给世界各国政府提出了国际反避税的新课题。

  为防范和制止国际避税，许多国家或地区采取了积极措施进行反避税。反避税的主要内容从广义上讲包括财务管理、纳税检查、审计以及发票管理，从狭义上讲就是通过加强税收稽查，堵塞税法漏洞。反避税的主要措施有：一、从纳税义务上制定具体措施，如在税法中规定与纳税人有关的第三者必须提供税收有关信息，或纳税人某些交易的价格必须得到政府部门的认可和同意等。二、不断调整和完善税法，如取消延期纳税，限制关联企业之间通过转让价格进行避税，避免子公司海外经营利润长期滞留在避税地等。三、强化征收管理，如成立专业的反避税机构，加强对纳税人银行账户的审查等。四、加强国际税收合作。

翻译练习

I. 思考题

1. 翻译中常见的转换有哪些？
2. 结合实例说明翻译中进行转换的原因和必要性。

II. 从"Transfer Pricing"中摘录给你深刻印象的句子或词组。

1. _____
2. _____
3. _____
4. _____
5. _____

III. 商务术语翻译

advance pricing agreement	
advance tax	
arm's length method	
basic exemption	
capital-export neutrality	
check-the-box rule	
comparable profit method	

correlative adjustment	
cost contribution arrangement	
credit method	
deduction method	
double-dip lease	
dual-resident taxpayer	
earnings stripping	
entity approach	
excise tax	
exemption method	
exemption with progression	
foreign tax credit	
formulary apportionment	
global approach	
grace period	
harmful tax competition	
imputation system	
international double taxation	
participation exemption	
place-of-incorporation test	
place-of-management test	
profit-split method	
residence country	
residence jurisdiction	
soak-up tax	
source country	
source jurisdiction	

tax avoidance	
tax base	
tax break	
tax deferral	
tax evasion	
tax haven	
tax incentive	
tax shelter	
tax sparing	
thin capitalization rule	
tie-breaker rule	
transfer pricing rule	
unitary approach	
withholding tax	

IV. 句子翻译

1. Government agencies, such as the State Taxation Administration, are well aware of these opportunities to play accounting games.
2. The deduction method may be justified from the viewpoint of national self-interest.
3. Clever structuring of transfer prices can even allow a firm to evade host country restrictions on repatriation of profits.
4. As a result, both home and host countries scrutinize the transfer pricing policies of MNCs operating within their borders to ensure the firms do not evade their tax obligations and the governments receive their "fair share" of taxes from the firms.
5. Further, the exemption method is often restricted to income that has been subject to tax or subject to a minimum rate of tax by the foreign country.
6. No international consensus has been reached on the appropriate method for granting relief from international double taxation.
7. Such a tax increase would not discourage investment from abroad, but would result in a shift of tax revenues from the country of residence to the source country.
8. Foreign-source income earned by residents of a country that uses the deduction method

generally is taxable at a higher effective rate than it would be under either the credit method or the exemption method.

9. A closer look at the revenue structure of these countries in a global context confirms a relatively high reliance on trade taxes, but it also indicates strong revenue performance in the area of consumption taxes.

10. In view of the relatively high expenditure ratios built into these countries' fiscal systems, failure to reduce spending or improve the tax effort points to a potential revenue shortfall and an increased risk of fiscal deterioration in the future.

V. 篇章翻译

MNCs can save millions of dollars in income and other taxes through the use of tax havens and transfer prices. For example, by manipulating transfer prices, an MNC can shift profits from high-tax countries to low-tax countries. But is such behavior ethical?

Skillful utilization of tax havens and transfer prices obviously benefits the MNC and its shareholders. However, such techniques reduce the revenues available to the home or host country government to solve important social problems such as poverty, homelessness, and drug addiction. An MNC's failure to pay its "fair share" of taxes in the countries in which it operates means that either the resources needed to solve these problems will be unavailable or that other taxpayers will be forced to pick up the tab. Because an MNC benefits from various services the local governments provide, such as transportation infrastructure, educational facilities, and police protection, many people claim it is unethical for the MNC to shirk paying for its share of these services.

Others argue that as long as an MNC is engaging in tax avoidance, its use of transfer prices and tax havens to reduce its tax burden is ethical. (Experts distinguish between tax avoidance, whereby a firm uses legal tax code loopholes to minimize its tax burden, and tax evasion, whereby a firm engages in illegal activities to lessen its tax payments.) Many accountants argue that an MNC's officers are bound by their fiduciary duties to their shareholders to take advantage of tax avoidance opportunities provided by various national tax codes. Indeed, from this perspective a manager's failure to do so could be viewed as unethical.

翻译名家

沈苏儒（1919—2009），中国外文局资深翻译家，中国对外传播学的开拓者。他1945年毕业于中央大学外文系，1953年从《上海新闻》（新中国第一份英文日报）调往北京外文出版社（外文局的前身），之后长期在外文局及《中国建设》杂志社（后更名为《今日中国》）工作。其主要译著有《宋庆龄：二十世纪的伟大女性》《突破封锁访延安》《见证中国：爱泼斯坦回忆录》等。沈苏儒编著的《对外传播教程》《对外报道教程》《对外传播概要》和《对外传播的理论和实践》等著作丰富和发展了我国的外宣理论，对我国的对外传播理论研究作出了重大的贡献。

沈苏儒认为，对外传播翻译是一种特殊的翻译，是在外文层面的再创造。译者除将中文译成外文外，还要发挥主动性和创造性，去掉翻译腔，使译文读起来像用外文直接写成，从而更易于为外国受众理解和接受。沈苏儒继承发展了严复的"信达雅"学说，他认为，"信"是要了解原文，忠实于原文；"达"是要把原文信息尽可能充分地用另一种语言表达出来；"雅"是要使译文符合译入语规律，为译文受众所理解、接受和欣赏。他还将"信达雅"作为鉴别对外传播译文质量的总标准和总指导原则，并据此提出了外宣翻译的原则：从实际出发，区别对待。"从实际出发"是区分不同类型的稿件及其不同的目的、对象和要求；"区别对待"是根据不同稿件、不同对象和预期效果，采取不同的翻译策略和技巧。

第 7 章　信息的拆分与融合

> To translate, one must have a style of his own, for otherwise the translation will have no rhythm or nuance, which come from the process of artistically thinking through and molding the sentences; they cannot be reconstituted by piecemeal imitation. The problem of translation is to retreat to a simpler tenor of one's own style and creatively adjust this to one's author.
>
> —Paul Goodman

问题导入

1. 翻译下面的句子。

   Given the disadvantages and failures of existing and proposed legal mechanisms to cover information products, it is not surprising that commentators have embraced the task of either proposing new solutions or, if not providing a solution, at least discussing the factors of a successful proposal.

   译文 _____
   _____
   _____

2. 比较以下两个译文，并结合自己的体会分析造成二者差异的原因。

   （1）鉴于现有的和提议的法律机制在保护信息产品方面的缺陷和不足，评论者更推崇要么提出新的解决方案，要么即使拿不出方案，至少探讨一下成功的提议的必备要素这一任务也就不足为奇了。

   （2）现有的法律机制在信息产品保护方面存在诸多缺陷与不足，而新提案亦是如此。眼下能提出新的解决方案当然最好，即使不能，至少也应探讨一下理想的方案应具备什么样的要素。评论者普遍赞成以此作为当务之急，也是理所当然。

翻译知识讲座

信息的拆分与融合

除了交流文化、沟通情感，翻译最重要的目的就在于传播信息。人类语言多种多样，不同语言、不同类型文本中的信息存在形式也千差万别。在翻译过程中，译者需要对原文中的信息进行整理、重构，最终使信息以新的形态出现在目的语中。由于英汉语在词法、句法、思维等方面具有明显差异，同一个信息在两种语言中往往采用不同的表达形式，照抄照搬势必会造成信息耗散或扭曲，导致信息传播的失败。要对蕴藏在商务英语文本中的信息进行准确、完整、富有逻辑的再现，往往需要在顺应汉语表达习惯、考虑商务文本语言特征的基础上，运用适当的手法对其进行重构。商务翻译中的信息重构手法不一而足，比较常用的是信息的拆分与融合。本章将从词、短语和句子层面对其加以探讨。

1. 信息的拆分

在翻译中，当原文所含信息较为密集而难以用同样的结构或形式加以转换时，或原文信息结构与目的语迥异，整体照搬有悖于目的语行文习惯时，应考虑将这些结构拆分为两个或两个以上的句子或短语。信息拆分的目的主要是为了避免原文信息在转换过程中因语言结构差异而发生耗散或扭曲。拆分后的译文有时会偏离原文的形式，但如果能更好地再现原文的内容信息和逻辑关系，也未尝不可。

（1）以词为单位的信息拆分

商务文本翻译中，信息的拆分并非只限于长句或短语。英汉词法的差异在词类、词序、词义、搭配等方面均有体现，因而翻译时也会涉及信息拆分问题。

例 1 Justifiably, governments fear changing systems that have a direct impact on their revenue collection, with unknown results and inadequate tools to protect against fraud and revenue loss.

原译 面对未知的结果，缺乏有效防止舞弊、避免收入流失的手段，政府害怕体制的变化直接影响收入，这是合理的。

在原文中，政府担心体制变化以及这种担心情有可原这两部分论述都在前面，而具体解释却在后文，这一点有别于汉语前因后果的信息排列习惯。另外，就信息点之间的逻辑关系而言，体制变化影响收入是导致政府担心的最主要原因，而结果难料、缺乏手段只是加剧政府担心的额外因素。因此，翻译时可将主要信息拆分出来，单独放在前面，并用句号将其与后文中的额外因素及最终造成的结果分隔开来。

参考译文： 体制的变化会直接影响政府收入。在结果难料且又无法有效防止舞弊、避免收入流失的情况下，政府的担心并非没有道理。

例 2 Ideally, the fragmented and often incomplete law of the WTO would rather call for a larger scope of interpretation in order to achieve full coherence with the system.

原译 理想地，为与该体系充分衔接，世贸组织支离破碎、残缺不全的法律规则需要在更大范围内进行解释。

参考译文： 要与世贸体系充分衔接，就得在更大范围内对世贸组织支离破碎、残缺不全的法律规则进行解释，这才是比较理想的办法。

将 ideally 译为"理想地"并放在句首不符合汉语习惯。调整后的参考译文在提高了可读性的同时，还将由 ideally 拆分出的译文单独放在句尾，辅以"才"字修饰，再现了原句中 ideally 的独特位置所蕴含的强调之意。

通常情况下，对整个句子进行解释和说明，表达说话人对本句话的看法或态度的评注性状语（如 appropriately、pardonably、justifiably），仅修饰句子的部分内容且难以按原语序进行转换的词语（如 undeservedly），以及搭配形式无法在目的语中延续的词组（如 quietly brilliant），在翻译时往往需要进行信息拆分。

（2）以短语为单位的信息拆分

在商务英语文本中，尤其是商务英语合同或契约文本中，介词短语和分词短语不仅使用数量多，而且含义丰富、位置灵活，在翻译时稍有不慎就可能造成译文佶屈聱牙、繁冗拖沓，妨碍信息的有效传达。

例 3 During the last session of Congress, two bills aiming to implement the WTO ruling were introduced without avail.

参考译文： 国会上次会议提出了两个旨在执行世贸组织裁定的议案，但并未获得通过。

介词短语 without avail 虽只有两个词，且位居句末，但从所承载信息的重要程度上来看，并不亚于句中其他单词或短语。本句包含的主要信息有两条：一是"有提议"，二是"未通过"。虽然两条信息英文字数多寡不同，但重要程度相当，因此宜将 without avail 单独译出，使之成句，与前文并列。

例 4 There are now countries such as Brazil and India which, given their growing contribution to world trade, are less susceptible to pressure and more able to represent the interests of the developing world.

参考译文： 现如今，随着巴西、印度等国对世界贸易的贡献与日俱增，它们已不再轻易屈从于外部压力，与此同时，它们为发展中国家利益代言的能力也已今非昔比。

从形式上看，句中的 given... 为分词短语，以插入语的形式存在，并非主干，但实际上，它所承载的信息是本句中国际贸易形势发生变化的原因，是后文的前提。其信息内容独立而重要，因此在翻译时宜独立成句，并按汉语的思维习惯放在句首，为后文提供逻辑基础。

（3）以句子为单位的信息拆分

在涉及经贸、法律信息的商务合同类文本中，长句、从句使用非常普遍，句式结构多样，逻辑关系复杂，在翻译中很难亦步亦趋地在译文中再现出来。这时就有必要在把握原文信息内容与逻辑关系的基础上，将其中所包含的信息融会贯通，以符合汉语表达习惯的方式进行重构。

例 5 In particular, multilateral retaliation might be infeasible if countries that are not involved in a dispute are unwilling to raise their trade barriers, and selling the rights to retaliate is incompatible with the central premise of the WTO that protection is undesirable and therefore not something a country should be willing to pay for.

原译 值得注意的是，如果未卷入争端的国家不愿提高贸易壁垒，多边报复就有可能行不通；并且出卖报复权有悖世贸组织认为贸易保护令人反感、因此不值得某国出资购买的核心原则。

上例中，原译虽然也大致说得通，但信息表达过于集中，使某些句子成分（如"核心原则"的定语）过长过重，不易理解。另外，原文信息点之间的关系较为隐蔽，需要分析句子语法结构并辅以一定的专业知识才能更好地理解。比如，要理解前面的 trade barriers（贸易壁垒）与后面的 protection（贸易保护）之间的关系，译者需要知道贸易壁垒是贸易保护主义的表现形式之一。在理解了本句包含的各信息点，以及这些点之间的逻辑关系后，就可以将信息拆分，形成相对独立的分句或短语，然后再根据其逻辑关系和目的语的表达习惯进行重组。

参考译文： 值得注意的是，如果未卷入争端的国家不愿提高贸易壁垒，多边报复就有可能沦为空谈；如转卖报复权，则又有悖于世贸组织的核心原则，即贸易保护令人反感，不可能作为一项权利由成员随意购买。贸易保护并非其所愿，因而不是某个国家愿意花钱购买的。

例 6 Many developing countries have surplus labor; it is possible to expand exports without adversely affecting existing allocation of resources.

原译 许多发展中国家存在剩余劳动力，扩大出口而不给当前的资源分配带来负面影响是有可能的。

原文由两个存在因果关系的句子并列而成，第二句包含了两个有可能彼此矛盾的情况：一是"扩大出口"，二是"维护现有的资源分配格局"。此时可依照汉语相对松散的信息表达习惯，将其拆成两个分句，各含一条信息，再用关系词衔接，从而使信息排列重点突出，层次分明。

参考译文： 许多发展中国家劳动力过剩，有可能做到既扩大出口，又不影响现有资源的分配。

2. 信息的融合

所谓信息的融合，是指当原文中的多个信息内在关系紧密而外在结构松散时，借助翻译手段将信息集中表达，从而增强信息的整体性和逻辑性。信息融合有利于读者从整体上对相关信息予以把握，也有利于提高信息容量，使译文更简洁。

例 7 Naturally, the system has not been able to solve all the disputes that have arisen. But it has at least been able to contain the effects of these disputes.

原译 当然，该体系无法解决一切争端。但是，它至少可以限制这些争端的消极影响。

原文前后两句构成了转折，所含信息密切相关，加之句子较短，信息内容单一，因而在翻译时可将其整合成一句，使信息表达更集中，逻辑关系更突出。

参考译文： 当然，该体系无法解决一切争端，但至少可以限制其消极影响。

例 8 Just as the US did not fulfill its expected role as the defender of free trade during the Uruguay Round, developing countries did not play their accustomed role as opponents of the multilateral trading regime.

第 7 章 信息的拆分与融合 91

原译 在乌拉圭回合谈判中，正如美国没有像人们预期的那样去捍卫自由贸易一样，发展中国家也没有扮演其作为多边贸易体系的反对者的一贯角色。

原句主要包括两点信息：人们预期美国会扮演某种角色，但它却没有；发展中国家一贯扮演某角色，但这次也没有。由于信息内容存在交叉，在翻译过程中可将两个信息加以融合，从而使行文更简洁，逻辑更清晰。

参考译文： 在乌拉圭回合谈判中，人们原以为美国会继续捍卫自由贸易，发展中国家也会继续反对多边贸易体系，但事实并非如此。

信息的拆分与融合是为了更有效地传达原文信息，虽手法不同，但基本思路一致，即传递信息内容，改善表现形式。所谓传递信息内容，是指对原文实质信息不增、不减、不变；所谓改善表现形式，是指以最适合目的语的表达方式来承载信息，当拆则拆，当合则合，不拘泥于原文结构。

商务语篇翻译与解析

The Dispute Settlement System of WTO

(1) According to the Dispute Settlement Understanding (DSU), the agreement establishing the dispute settlement system that was negotiated as part of the Uruguay Round of 1995, WTO members may seek to resolve conflicts through the good offices of the organization's director-general or by agreeing to arbitration; they may also invoke the formal dispute settlement mechanism. To pursue this last option, the parties in the dispute are first required to engage in consultation. If these consultations are unsatisfactory, a complainant can, within sixty days, request the establishment of (2) a panel of three members to hear the case. The panel issues an interim report and then a final one. If it finds that a member has failed to comply, and that member does not appeal, the body can make a recommendation as to how the member could come into compliance. If it is impractical to comply immediately, the member is given "a reasonable period of time in which to do so." (3) The finding can also be appealed to a second panel of three members of a permanent seven-person Appellate Body, which operates like the supreme court of the organization.

If the member loses the appeal and fails to act within a reasonable period of time, (4) the rules call for the parties to negotiate compensation, "pending full implementation." (5) "Compensation" is generally understood to require the defendant to provide additional concessions, typically in the form of reducing other trade barriers of interest to the plaintiff. Compensation is, however, "voluntary" and rare. If after twenty days, compensation cannot be agreed upon, the complainant may request authorization to suspend equivalent concessions. In particular, "the level of the suspension of concession...shall be equivalent to the level of nullification and impairment." When, for example, the WTO found that the EU had cost the United States $116.8 million worth of exports by illegally banning hormone-fed beef, the United States was authorized to impose punitive tariffs on $116.8 million worth of EU exports.

The dispute settlement system has generally been successful in helping members resolve disputes and in obtaining compliance where violations have been found. Many cases have been settled in the consultation stage. While there are delays, particularly when legislative action is required, and a few cases in which compliance has been lacking, the evidence suggests that by and large many countries eventually come into compliance. Nations appear to comply less because of retaliation, (6) <u>which has rarely been used</u>, but rather because they believe it is in their interest to do so. This is because on balance they benefit from the rules and care about their reputations in a system in which there are ongoing negotiations. They also care about their relationships with significant trading partners.

Although the very least developed countries do experience difficulties in using the system, there is evidence that it is being widely used by both developed and developing countries (7) <u>in rough proportion to their shares in world trade</u>. Between 1995 and 2000, for example, high-income countries filed 70.2% of disputes, while developing countries represented 29.8% of submitted cases. In the next five years (2001–2006), by contrast, developing countries filed a majority of the cases (52.1%). While these numbers reflect mainly developing countries with large export shares, such as India and Brazil, there are also cases of small developing countries that have (8) <u>leveraged the system effectively</u> to challenge large trading partners. Another noticeable development is the increase in South-South disputes. All in all, recent trends attest to developing countries' increased knowledge of and confidence in the WTO dispute resolution process.

Several features of the system merit emphasis. First, the WTO itself does not conduct investigations and instigate proceedings. Although the WTO does review its members' trade policies, there is no central policing mechanism—(9) <u>enforcement is carried out entirely as a result of member initiatives</u>. While the respondents cannot block the case from going forward, the claimant may withdraw the case at any time, even if the defendant has not come into compliance.

Second, the operation of the system reflects the nature of the WTO as an intergovernmental organization. (10) <u>Although private counsel can be employed to make arguments, and amicus briefs by non-governmental entities have been allowed on occasion, only governments have standing to bring cases</u>. There is no private right of action. Violations of the agreements may have damaged private parties, but they have no recourse on their own and must operate through their governments. Similarly, retaliation is undertaken against the defendant country, and it could inflict damage on the incomes of exporting firms that had nothing to do with the infraction and whose only error was being located in the defending country—a reason why some believe that only compensation should be allowed.

Third, the DSU does not ordain a common-law system with binding precedents. Technically, there is no stare decisis. Each panel ruling is thus in principle unique—only the members themselves can adopt rules that "add to or diminish the rights and obligations" in the agreement. In practice, however, precedents are actually given great weight, and panel and Appellate Body reports refer frequently and deferentially in many footnotes to the reasoning contained in other reports. The Appellate Body plays a particularly important oversight role in disciplining judgments and ensuring their consistency. Thus, de facto, the DSU has established something approaching a common-law system.

Fourth, WTO rulings are not (11) <u>automatically</u> implemented. In practice, even if not technically in law, members have discretion as to whether they will comply; they may refuse even though this may mean breaking the agreement and perhaps facing retaliation against their exports. De jure such retaliation is meant to be temporary and is not a substitute for compliance. But de facto retaliation can become the permanent outcome of a dispute. This means that the retaliation system may operate as a (12) <u>safety valve</u>.

Fifth, there is no attempt to compensate the winner for damages incurred during the period of noncompliance, (13) <u>a practice that stands in contrast to contract cases in common-law legal systems</u>. This has the advantage of not generating further disputes over the size and payment of such damages. But the downside is that parties expecting to lose have an incentive to delay the process as long as possible. Parties also may engage in rule-breaking behavior in the knowledge that the most that they will have to do is come into compliance at a later date.

In sum, the WTO dispute settlement mechanism is a distinctive form of arbitration combined with a variation of judicial review. The parties are required to submit to the process if one party launches a complaint. An arbitration panel investigates and reaches conclusions based on rules previously negotiated by the members. (14) <u>The resulting rulings are binding on the parties</u>. Failure to comply or provide compensation can result in the suspension of concessions. The rulings are also subject to appeal. However, the WTO system remains weaker than the arbitration processes common in domestic legal systems for four major reasons: Enforcement is not automatic, precedents are not strictly binding, standing of all injured parties is not assured—only governments bring cases—and remedies are limited.

难点解析

（1）汉语的信息单元一般容量不大，通过多个单元层层推进来表达复杂信息。而英语不同，它讲究以形统义，在符合语法的前提下，信息繁复多变，常有信息延迟与等待、前后部分相隔万里却又前后呼应的现象。本句即如此，the agreement...of 1995 将行为的依据与行为的内容分割开来，补充了依据的形成历史。译成汉语时，需按汉语的信息表达习惯，将句子拆分成两部分：前者讲行为的背景，后者讲行为的内容。这两部分相对完整，可各自成句。

（2）本句的末尾与下句的开头均提到专家组（panel），且后者是前者在信息上的延伸（成立专家组、听证、提交报告），构成信息内容上的交错，翻译时不妨将这两句合并，从而使表达更连贯、简洁。

（3）本句连用两个 of，后面又有 which，附加信息较多，且信息内容彼此交错，层次不明显，如沿用原文结构直译成汉语，容易造成信息芜杂凌乱，故宜梳理信息之间的关系，将背景信息置于前，实质信息在后。

（4）本句中的 the rules 为无灵主语，直接翻成"规则呼吁各方就补偿展开磋商"也能基本达意，但不符合汉语表达习惯。不妨移至句首，译为"按照规定"，后文译为"争端各方可先就补偿展开磋商"。

（5）本句中的被动语态可转换为主动，以符合汉语表达习惯。类似的例子还有下面的 compensation cannot be agreed upon 等。

（6）本句中逗号之间的 which has rarely been used 为补充信息，在翻译时无须拘泥于其原有形式与位置。可译为"（主要不是因为对）鲜有实施的（报复措施有所顾忌）"，以前置定语的形式来表达信息。

（7）本句中的 in rough proportion to their shares in world trade 虽然是作为状语的短语，但其所包含的信息相对独立，因此宜拆分出来，作为拥有独立谓语结构的句子来翻译，译为"与其在世界贸易中所占的份额大致成正比"。

（8）leverage 一词来自 lever（杠杆），有以小博大之意，引申后可指"融资；借助影响力来左右"等。在本句语境下，较小的发展中国家借助世贸组织争端解决机制向贸易大国挑战，有借助杠杆四两拨千斤之意。因此，在翻译时应充分挖掘其内在信息，结合后文的 effectively，将 leveraged 译为"巧妙而有效地利用"。

（9）翻译 enforcement is carried out entirely as a result of member initiatives 时宜进行语态转换，并按汉语语言习惯重新表达。如将 as a result of member initiatives 译成"作为成员主动性的结果"有僵化之嫌，不妨改为"（审查意见完全）靠成员主动（履行）"。

（10）本句与上下文关系紧密，构成对比。鉴于下文句子简短，信息单一，可合译为一句，以凸显"谁拥有诉讼权"这一关键信息。另外，amicus briefs 一词源于拉丁语，专业性强，涉及西方法律传统，翻译时需多查资料，遵循业内表达习惯。

（11）此处 automatically 强调的是在体制、成规的作用下必然随之发生，不宜翻译成"自动地"。例如：Employees who steal are dismissed automatically. 员工有偷盗行为者一律辞退。

（12）本句中的 safety valve（安全阀）原为机械专业技术词汇，不太常用，在汉语中表修辞的场合不多，容易造成语义模糊，因此翻译时有必要将其隐含信息补充完整。

（13）从形式上来看，本句中的 a practice that stands in contrast to contract cases in common-law legal systems 只是前半句的同位语，二者所指相同，但从信息内容的角度来看，二者所含信息存在差异，故应在译文中以相对独立的并列句式加以传达。为使前后部分有机衔接，可添加"这一点"等指代性的衔接词。
（14）本句与下句 Failure to... 在信息内容上紧密相关，且两个句子都比较短，所含信息较为单一，故翻译时可考虑合为一句，用逗号连接。

商务知识讲座

世界贸易组织

世界贸易组织（the World Trade Organization，WTO）简称世贸组织。它是根据乌拉圭回合多边贸易谈判达成的《建立世界贸易组织马拉喀什协定》（Marrakesh Agreement Establishing the World Trade Organization）于1995年1月1日建立的，取代了1947年的《关税与贸易总协定》（General Agreement on Tariffs and Trade，GATT），并按照乌拉圭回合多边谈判所达成的一整套协定和协议的条款为法律框架，对各成员之间在经济贸易关系方面的权利和义务进行监督、管理。

世贸组织的法律框架主要来自《1994年关税与贸易总协定》《服务贸易总协定》以及历次多边贸易谈判，特别是乌拉圭回合谈判所达成的一系列规定，同时还包括了世贸组织成立以后在一些新领域达成的一系列协议，如《基础电信协议》《金融服务协议》《信息技术协议》等。世贸组织的协议与规则大致可分为五部分：有关世贸组织本身的组织规则，有关货物贸易的法律规则，有关服务贸易的协议，有关知识产权保护的规则以及世贸组织的程序框架。

世贸组织的宗旨是创造自由开放的全球贸易环境，积极推动世界经济贸易自由化。世界贸易组织在《建立世界贸易组织马拉喀什协定》中明确规定了要实现的五项目标：第一，提高人民生活水平，保障充分就业，保证实际收入和有效需求的大幅稳定增长；第二，扩大货物、服务的生产和贸易；第三，坚定地走可持续发展之路；第四，积极努力确保发展中国家，尤其是最不发达国家在国际贸易增长中获得与其经济发展需要相当的份额和利益；第五，通过互惠互利的安排来实质性削减关税和其他贸易壁垒，消除国际贸易中的歧视待遇。

世贸组织的主要职能包括：第一，负责多边贸易协议的实施、管理和运作，促进世贸组织目标的实现；第二，为各成员就多边贸易关系进行谈判和部长级会议提供场所，并提供实施谈判结果的框架；第三，通过争端解决机制解决成员之间可能发生的贸易争端；第四，运用贸易政策审议机制定期审议成员的贸易政策及其对多边贸易体制运行产生的影响；第五，通过与其他国际经济组织（国际货币基金组织、世界银行及其附属机构等）的合作和政策协调，实现全球经济决策更大的一致性；第六，对发展中国家和最不发达国家提供技术援助及培训。在上述六项职能中，前两项是最主要的职能。

作为正式的国际组织，世贸组织具有法人资格，在行使有关职责时享有必要的特权和豁免权。世贸组织与世界银行和国际货币基金组织不同，它不是联合国专门机构，其成员不仅包括主权国家，也包括单独关税区。

作为一个永久性经济组织，世贸组织设有各种通用和专业组织机构。按协议规定，世贸组织设有向所有成员代表开放的部长级会议和总理事会。部长级会议是世贸组织的最高决策机构，由世贸组织的所有成员组成，也是各成员方最重要的谈判场所。总理事会负责世贸组织的日常领导与管理。总理事会下有货物贸易理事会、服务贸易理事会、与贸易有关的知识产权理事会及各专门委员会，此外还有争端解决机构、贸易政策审议机构、秘书处及总干事。总理事会任命总干事担任世贸组织秘书处的负责人，总干事根据由总理事会批准的规则任命秘书处的工作人员。

　　世贸组织的九大基本原则包括：无歧视待遇原则、最惠国待遇原则、国民待遇原则、透明度原则、贸易自由化原则、市场准入原则、互惠原则、对发展中国家和最不发达国家优惠待遇原则、公正平等处理贸易争端原则。

　　按照世贸组织的规定，世贸组织的决策应首先考虑适用协商一致原则，不能达成协商一致的实行多数票规则，但某些决策必须实行协商一致规则。在协商一致规则下，只要出席会议的成员方对拟通过的决议不正式提出反对就视为同意，沉默、弃权或进行一般的评论等均不能构成反对意见。对于实行多数票的决策，根据决策内容的不同分别适用简单多数、2/3 多数、3/4 多数或反向一致规则。

翻译练习

I. 思考题

1. 在翻译中对信息进行拆分与融合应注意哪些问题？
2. 结合实例说明翻译中进行信息拆分与融合的原因与方法。

II. 从 "The Dispute Settlement System of WTO" 中摘录给你深刻印象的句子或词组。

1. _____
2. _____
3. _____
4. _____
5. _____

III. 商务术语翻译

advisory group	
anti-dumping proceeding	
appellate report	

arbitration award	
challenge procedure	
complaining party	
conciliation	
consultation procedure	
contracting party	
counter-complaint	
deferential treatment	
dispute settlement mechanism	
enabling clause	
escalation clause	
established practice	
exemption or deferral	
expert review group	
final determination	
flexibility provision	
good offices	
implementing regulation	
initial commitment	
injury assessment	
institutional arrangement	
interim report	
margin of dumping	
mediation	
nullification or impairment	
panel	
permanent group of experts	

prima facie evidence	
privilege and immunity	
qualification procedure	
rectification or modification	
relief measure	
remedial measure	
remission or drawback	
retaliatory measure	
rule of non-discrimination	
schedule of concession	
secretariat	
specific subsidy	
spot check	
substantial interest	
substantive provision	
suspension of concession	
tie vote	
transitional safeguard mechanism	

IV. 句子翻译

1. The principal international agreement under which world trade has been regulated in the post-World War II period is the General Agreement on Tariffs and Trade dated October 30, 1947.
2. US negotiators are justifiably proud of these accomplishments but fear overloading the political circuits by adding to the ongoing adjustment burden of US industries and workers generated by recently concluded trade reforms.
3. This trust and dialog are prerequisites for the mutual exchange of questions and answers without which the work we do would be in vain.
4. Ideally, panel members have a knowledge of international trade and are either lawyers or trade specialists who have been active in the field.

5. Between meetings of the ministerial conference, which is responsible for carrying out the functions of the WTO, the organization is managed by the General Council at the level of diplomats.
6. It contrasts with the philosophy underlying the intellectual property laws of many other countries, which place greater emphasis on the "natural rights" that authors and other creators have in the product of their labor.
7. "Reciprocity" indicates that all WTO members are expected to satisfy their legal and trade obligations as a natural response to the multilateral trade concessions of other WTO members.
8. It helps the United States itself keep protectionist impulses at bay. It is also particularly useful for dealing with disputes with America's largest trading partners, such as the European Union, Japan, China, India, and Brazil, with which the United States has not signed free trade agreements.
9. Companies that have thrived despite recessions and crises in the past have tended to take care to ensure access to finance, and have a broad range of businesses to insulate them from downturns in particular sectors.
10. The ongoing crisis has highlighted the extent to which our economies are integrated, the indivisibility of our collective well-being, and the unsustainability of a narrow focus on short-term gains.

V. 篇章翻译

All WTO members, including those in the developing world, have reduced their trade tariffs since the Uruguay Round. In its Everything But Arms Agreement, the European Union has unilaterally lowered its trade barriers to the least developed countries. The United States adopted the African Growth and Opportunity Act. And in November 2001, the members of the WTO launched the Doha Development Agenda. In doing so, they acknowledged that to make progress in the fight against poverty, rich country markets should be more open to the goods of poor countries, and that developing countries should open their markets as well to address a range of institutional issues.

The advance at Doha presents a unique opportunity for development, but it will require substantive participation from all countries to succeed. In particular, each participating developing country will need a thorough understanding of how trade liberalization can contribute to its national objectives of economic growth and poverty reduction. Such strategic understanding will have to be supported by both trade negotiators and civil society; at times, the medium-term goal of poverty reduction requires governments to challenge the interests of some particular industries for short-term protection.

In addition, many countries will have to break new ground. Today's trade issues go beyond the traditional mechanisms of tariffs and quotas and include "behind-the-border" issues, such as the role of infrastructure and governance in supporting a well-functioning trading economy. Many poor countries have yet to create intellectual property regimes that make traditional knowledge or cultural products into negotiable and defensible assets, to identify options to upgrade and enforce national product, health, and safety standards, or to strengthen institutions for prudential and pro-competitive regulation of services. Developing countries will have to quickly acquire the needed expertise on these complex issues, so they can negotiate more effectively and ensure that agreements serve their objective of poverty reduction.

翻译名家

陈忠诚（1922—2013），著名法律翻译家和翻译批评家。他曾肄业于上海圣约翰大学经济系，后于 1947 年、1949 年分别获东吴大学法学学士、法学硕士学位。20 世纪 50 年代，陈忠诚曾翻译大量苏联法律和政治著作。他通晓英语、俄语和日语，曾担任法学专业英语、俄语和日语的同声传译。

陈忠诚对法律翻译的英译汉和汉译英都颇有研究，他认为汉译英是一种外向型翻译，其翻译效果会直接影响我国法律的国际形象。在现实层面，法律翻译中的汉译英相较于内向型的英译汉更为薄弱，所以他特别重视汉译英，这在他的《法窗译话》《法苑译谭》《〈民法通则〉AAA 译本评析》中都有集中体现。他的法律翻译作品内容上实践性较强，常常是以实例论证实例或者以实例批判实例。在翻译批评方法上，他首创了词典"比较评论法"，以表格形式排列出比较项目，列举各个词典对该项目的不同处理。他认为，作为法律翻译工作者，除了要精通外文之外，还需知法懂法，这样才能准确地抓住原文的脉搏。

陈忠诚治学严谨，一丝不苟，双语辞书批评是他最大的学术嗜好，他写的批评文章不仅针对中国的辞书，还包括国外一些知名辞书，内容以指人谬误为主，笔锋犀利，在双语辞书评论界被称为"指谬专家""义务校对第一人"。

第 8 章　翻译中的衔接与连贯

> 对一个有意义的可接受的语篇来说，它在语言各层次（如语义、词汇、句法、语音等）的成分都可表现出某种程度的衔接，从而使说话人在交际过程中所欲表达的意图贯通整个语篇，达到交际目的。但在特殊情况下，语言成分之间的衔接并不能保证语篇的交际意图总是取得连贯；另一方面，衔接不太明显的语篇有时却是内容连贯的。
>
> ——胡壮麟

问题导入

1. 指出下面这些句子的衔接手段。

(1) An ad valorem tariff is one that is calculated as a percentage of the value of the goods being imported or exported.

(2) Those who would argue against imposing trade barriers point to the possibility of retaliation by other nations, leading to a trade war.

(3) As a result, global resources are less efficiently allocated and the level of world income and production is reduced.

2. 试译上面的句子，并说明自己是如何在汉语中再现这些衔接手段的。

(1) _____

(2) _____

(3) _____

再现方法：_____

翻译知识讲座

翻译中的衔接与连贯

20 世纪 60 至 70 年代兴起的系统功能语言学和语篇语言学以语篇而非句子作为最大的语言研究单位。受此影响，一些翻译研究者提出应将语篇作为翻译的基本单位。尽管学界对此认识并不统一，但毫无疑问，翻译中译者不仅要考虑词、句的翻译，也要考虑如何按照译文的表达习惯将原文各个句子衔接成为一个连贯的语篇。因此，本章将重点讨论语篇研究中的两个重要问题——衔接与连贯——以及它们在翻译中的处理方法。

语篇通常由多个句子构成，这些句子并不是作者随意堆放在一起的，而是借助各种衔接手段构成语义连贯的语篇。衔接与连贯可以说是语篇研究的核心，是语篇特征的重要内容，但对于如何定义这两个概念以及如何看待两者之间的关系，语言学界尚未达成共识。为了讨论的方便，本书将衔接定义为将语句聚合在一起的语法及词汇手段的统称，即衔接手段；连贯则是这些衔接方法和手段所产生的效果，借助适当的衔接手段，就可以表达流畅连贯的语篇语义。了解原文语篇的衔接手段，在翻译过程中我们就可以采取适当的方式把这些衔接手段恰当地转换为目的语，形成连贯的语篇。

语篇衔接手段可大致分为语法衔接和词汇衔接两类，其中语法衔接主要包括照应、替代、省略和连接。词汇衔接手段主要包括重复、同义词、上下文语义关系和搭配。与语法衔接手段相比，英汉两种语言在词汇衔接手段上的差别不是很大，本章将重点讨论英汉翻译中语法衔接手段的处理问题。

1. 照应

在语篇中，如果两个语言成分之间存在指称意义上的解释关系，即产生了照应关系。照应是一种语义关系，有人称照应和指示照应两种形式。请看例句：

例 1 Farmers, just like any other businesspeople, will decide what to produce based on what they see the market to be. And if they don't see that the market is open, they won't produce as much.

例 2 Countries need to do things within their own borders to remove barriers to trade.

例 3 It is not clear how much time the Group of 20 will be able to devote to trade.

例 4 Who is hurt by tariffs? First there are those who buy a product upon which the tariff has been levied.

在例 1 中，可以看出 they 和 farmers 构成了照应关系，例 2 中的 their 和 countries 构成了照应关系。这两例均属于人称照应，也就是使用代词复指上下文出现的名词，所用指代手段一般包括人称代词、形容词性物主代词和名词性物主代词。例 3 中的 it 是形式主语，指代从句 how much time the Group of 20 will be able to devote to trade，避免从句直接作句子主语导致的句式笨重。此外，使用 it 作为形式主语的句式通过创建照应关系，即 it 与其所指代的从句之间的联系，增加了文本的连贯性和可读性。例 4 则属指示照应，用指示代词（如 this/these, that/those）、具有指代意义的时间和地点副词（如 now/

then, here/there）以及定冠词表达照应关系。

上述例句的参考译文如下：

参考译文 1： 一如其他从商人员，农民也会根据个人从市场上观察到的情况来决定生产何种产品。一旦发现市场不够开放，他们就会降低产量。

参考译文 2： 各国需要在本国范围内消除贸易障碍。

参考译文 3： 二十国集团能在贸易上投入多少时间还不清楚。

参考译文 4： 谁会受到关税的损害呢？首先是那些购买了被征收关税的产品的人。

比较而言，英语更为频繁地借助人称代词和指示代词来表达照应关系，汉语则通常运用零式指称和名词重复来表达照应关系。因此，英汉翻译过程中，不必把原文中所有的照应关系都一一译出，而应根据汉语表达习惯进行灵活处理，或用零式指称，或重复使用名词，或省略不译。

2. 替代

替代是另一种十分重要的语篇衔接手段，可分为名词性替代、动词性替代和小句性替代。请看例句：

例 5 An ad valorem tariff is one that is calculated as a percentage of the value of the goods being imported or exported.

例 6 Non-tariff trade barriers have replaced tariff ones as a main approach of trade protection.

例 7 The president renews his pledge that the US will abolish all trade barriers if other countries do the same.

例 8 In the past three decades, there have been reductions in the numerous barriers to international trade in goods, in some services, and in capital flows. Even so, many remain.

例 9 But the marrow must be a close genetic match to your own. If not, it will lash out at you and kill you.

上述各句中，前三例使用了名词性替代，以可充当名词词组中心词的替代词代替了另一名词词组；在这种结构中，常用的替代词语主要是 one 及其复数形式 ones，有时也会使用 the same。例 7 中还出现了动词性替代，即用替代性动词 do 去代替动词词组。例 8 和例 9 属小句性替代，即用替代词替代上文名词性小句所表达的意义，替代词分别为表达肯定意义的 so 和表示否定意义的 not。

在替代手段的使用上，英汉两种语言既有共性，更存在差异。其差异之处可概括如下：英语名词性替代词有单复数之分，动词性替代词有时态上的形态变化，而在汉语中，名词和动词都没有屈折变化；英语频繁使用替代手段来实现语篇衔接，同样情况下，汉语则更倾向于重复手段。

上述例句的参考译文如下：

参考译文 5： 从价关税是一种按进出口商品价值的百分比计算税额的税种。

参考译文 6： 非关税贸易壁垒已经取代关税贸易壁垒，成为贸易保护的主要方式。

参考译文 7： 总统再次呼吁，如果其他国家取消所有贸易壁垒的话，美国也将这么做。

参考译文 8： 过去三十年，国际贸易中商品、服务及资本流动方面不胜枚举的壁垒已有所减少。即便如此，仍然存在许多贸易壁垒。

参考译文 9： 但是移植的骨髓一定要和骨髓移植受者的基因匹配。如果不匹配，移植的骨髓就会向受者发起攻击，置受者于死地。

3. 省略

作为一种衔接手段，省略可避免重复，用较少的语言单位传达出更多的语言信息，使语篇简洁紧凑，符合语言使用的经济原则。请看例句：

例10 Why then does virtually every nation in the global economy impose trade barriers of one form or another?

例11 This South Korean car brand, which is currently the fastest-growing, if not yet the top-selling brand in the Philippines, is exploring ways to penetrate the luxury car market in the country.

例12 Not only are they really the way that food moves from places of supply to places of demand, but they also play a big role in the decisions that farmers make about how much they should produce and what they should produce and when.

例 10 省略了名词词组 another form 中的中心词 form，属名词性省略。例 11 省略了 if 从句中的主谓结构 it is，为动词性省略。在例 12 中，when 一词后面省略了小句 they should produce，属于小句性省略。

英汉两种语言都不乏名词性省略、动词性省略和小句性省略。值得注意的是，汉语多省略主语，一般不省略谓语，特殊情况（如祈使句等）除外，英语主语一般不能省略，因而英语没有汉语中所谓的无主句。英汉翻译过程中，应注意这方面的差异，根据译入语的习惯使用语言，这样才能使译文流畅自然。

上述例句的参考译文如下：

参考译文 10： 那么，在全球经济中，为何每一个国家都会使用这样或那样的贸易壁垒手段呢？

参考译文 11： 这家来自韩国的汽车品牌在菲律宾即使算不上最为畅销的汽车品牌，也是目前发展最快的，该品牌眼下正在寻求如何打入菲律宾豪华车型市场。

参考译文 12： 这不仅是把粮食从供应地运送至需求地的方式，也对农民决定生产何种产品、生产数量以及生产时间产生了极大影响。

例 10 译文也采用了省略的方法，其结构与原句类似。例 11 根据汉语习惯对句子结构进行了调整，将定语从句译为独立分句，并补齐了原句主干中表示转折关系的从句的主谓成分。原句的主语仍保留并译为"该品牌"。例 12 的译文也根据汉语习惯将原文 when 后面的 they should produce 补充出来，译为"生产时间"，这样显然更自然些，也更符合汉语表达习惯。

4. 连接

连接即通过连接词将句子衔接在一起，连接词主要包括连词、连接副词或介词短语。请看例句：

例13 When the food crisis began several years ago, with soaring prices and supply shortages, governments agreed to invest much more in agriculture. And with predictions of a global population of nine billion by 2050, the need for more food has become increasingly urgent. But some say food security cannot be achieved unless trade barriers are removed.

例14 Also injured are domestic firms that now sell fewer goods because Americans have to spend more to purchase the tariff-imposed products.

英汉语连接词具有类似或相同的功能，即通过句子或段落衔接，把句子或段落之间的语义及逻辑关系表达出来。但另一方面，两种语言在连接词使用上也存在着差异：英语多用显性连接，汉语则多用隐性连接。英汉翻译过程中，译者应注意将英语的显性连接恰当转换为汉语的隐性连接。例13 和 14 的参考译文分别为：

参考译文 13： 几年以前，食品危机出现时，粮食价格飞涨，粮食供应短缺，各国政府同意增加农业投入。此外根据预测，到 2050 年，世界人口将达到 90 亿，粮食需求已愈加紧迫。然而有人认为，只有消除贸易壁垒，才能获得粮食安全。

参考译文 14： 国内公司也受到了伤害，商品销售量目前已经下降，因为美国人不得不花更多的钱去购买被征收关税的产品。

上述译例表明，语篇衔接分析之于翻译实践具有重要的指导作用。词或句子本身的翻译固然会直接影响到表达效果，但译文整体效果的再现却需要从语篇角度对种种衔接手段以及与此相关的连贯问题加以考量，并在译文中进行灵活再现。衔接手段在译文中的再现主要取决于篇章语义表达的需要，而非机械的一一对应。所以，在翻译操作中要注意对语篇整体的把握。

商务语篇翻译与解析

Trade Barriers

Trade barriers may occur in international trade when goods have to cross political boundaries. A trade barrier is a restriction on what would otherwise be free trade. (1) The most common form of trade barriers are tariffs, or duties, which are usually imposed on imports. There is also a category of non-tariff barriers, also known as non-tariff measures, which also serve to restrict global trade.

There are several different types of duties or tariffs. (2) An export duty is a tax levied on goods leaving a country, while an import duty is charged on goods entering a country. A duty or tariff may be categorized according to how it is calculated. (3) An ad valorem tariff is one that is calculated as a percentage of the value of the goods being imported or exported. For example, a 20% ad valorem duty means that a duty equal to 20% of the value of the goods in question must be paid. Duties that are calculated in other ways include a specific duty, which is based on the quantity, weight, or volume of goods, and a compound duty (also known as a mixed tariff), which is calculated as a combination of an ad valorem duty and a specific duty.

Duties and tariffs are also categorized according to their function or purpose. An anti-dumping duty is imposed on imports that are priced below fair market value and that would damage domestic producers. Anti-dumping duties are also called punitive tariffs. (4) <u>A countervailing duty</u>, another type of punitive tariff, is levied after there has been substantial or material damage done to domestic producers. (4) <u>A countervailing duty</u> is specifically charged on imports that have been subsidized by the exporting country's government. The purpose of a countervailing duty is to offset the subsidy and increase the domestic price of the imported product.

(5) <u>A prohibitive tariff</u>, also known as an exclusionary tariff, is designed to substantially reduce or stop altogether the importation of a particular product or commodity. (5) <u>It</u> is typically used when the amount of imported goods exceeds a certain permitted level. (5) <u>It</u> may be used to protect domestic producers. Another type of tariff is the end-use tariff, which is based on the use of an imported product. For example, the same product may be charged a different duty if it is intended for educational use as opposed to commercial use.

In addition to duties and tariffs, there are also non-tariff barriers (NTBs) to international trade. These include quantitative restrictions, or quotas, that may be imposed by one country or as the result of agreements between two or more countries. Examples of quantitative restrictions include international commodity agreements, voluntary export restraints, and orderly marketing arrangements.

Administrative regulations constitute a second category of NTBs. These include a variety of requirements that must be met in order for trade to occur, including fees, licenses, permits, domestic content requirements, financial bonds and deposits, and government procurement practices. The third type of NTB covers technical regulations that apply to such areas as packaging, labeling, safety standards, and multilingual requirements.

In 1980 the Agreement on Technical Barriers to Trade, also known as the Standards Code, came into effect for the purpose of ensuring that administrative and technical practices do not act as trade barriers. Additional work on promoting unified standards to eliminate these NTBs was conducted by the General Agreement on Tariffs and Trade (GATT) Standards Committee, which in 1994 was succeeded by the newly created WTO. As a result more than 131 governments accepted the provisions of the Technical Barriers to Trade (TBT) Agreement enforced by the WTO.

(6) <u>Standards and testing practices can become technical barriers to trade when they are developed by national or regional interests and then imposed on the international trading</u>. The US Department of Commerce's 1998 report, "National Export Strategy,"

identified "the global manipulation of international standards and testing practices by governments and regional economic blocs" as a major threat to US competitiveness abroad. Under the TBT Agreement the WTO is supposed to guarantee due process and transparency in the establishment of international standards. The Department of Commerce, however, has presented examples where narrow regional or market interests have resulted in standards forced on international trade, and governments and regional economic blocs such as the European Union (EU) have openly used standards and related practices to achieve market domination. The United States was among those countries calling for technology and trade neutral standards, especially for markets in Latin America and Asia.

Other types of existing technical trade barriers include environmental, health, and safety certification requirements. In Europe such requirements range from banning imported beef from cattle raised with hormones to not allowing older airplanes to land because of noise pollution concerns.

Since the passage of the Omnibus Trade and Competitiveness Act of 1988, the US State Department periodically submits reports to Congress called "Country Reports on Economic Policy and Trade." These reports (7) <u>detail</u> significant barriers to US exports. Such barriers include not only tariffs, sanctions, embargoes, and technical regulations, they can also cover local conditions such as (8) <u>fuel shortages, lack of a modern telecommunications system, backward banking systems, and low purchasing power</u>.

Tariffs and other trade barriers have a definite effect on consumption and production. They serve to reduce consumption of the imported product, because the tariff raises the domestic price of the import. (9) <u>They also serve to stimulate domestic production of the product when that is possible, also because of the higher domestic price</u>. (10) <u>Proponents of tariffs argue that such an increase in domestic production is desirable, while opponents argue that it is inefficient from an economic standpoint</u>. The overall effect of tariffs and trade barriers on international trade is to reduce the volume of trade and to increase the prices of imports. Proponents of free trade argue that both of those results are undesirable, while proponents of protectionism argue that tariffs may be necessary for a variety of reasons.

难点解析
（1）which 替代的是 tariffs, or duties，由于汉语中没有关系代词，此处可运用重复手段加以处理。此外，英语非限制性定语从句往往对主句起补充说明作用，译成汉语时也可翻译为单独的句子。
（2）duty 和 tariff，levy 和 charge 为两对同义词，分别译为"关税"和"征收"即可。英语中多以同义词来避免重复，而汉语对重复容忍度较高，并且重复也是汉语中必要的衔接手段。
（3）one 是英语中常用的替代手段，翻译时可以隐去不译，也可以翻译成所替代词汇的同义词，此处可译为"从价关税是一种……税种"。
（4）两个句子的主语一致，是对同一概念进行解释说明，翻译时可考虑合并成一句，使译文更简洁。

（5）文中两次使用 it 指代首句的 a prohibitive tariff，将这三句衔接成篇，翻译时可采取合句法来处理这几个句子。本文中类似例子不少，在翻译时应注意。

（6）除表示时间关系外，when 所引导的从句也可表达其他逻辑关系，在本句中，when 引导的从句前后是假设关系。在翻译时应注意这一点，不可生硬地译成"当……的时候"。

（7）detail 此处为动词，意思是"详细列举"。

（8）fuel shortages, lack of a modern telecommunications system, backward banking systems, and low purchasing power 四个名词词组在此是并列关系，都是 local conditions 的具体内容。翻译时应该考虑对应译文的结构平行问题。如可译为"燃料短缺、现代通信系统匮乏、银行系统落后及购买力低下等"，注意不要译为"燃料短缺、缺乏现代通信系统、落后的银行系统及低下的购买力等"。

（9）本句中有两个 also：第一个 also 将两个 serve 并列，说明关税和其他贸易壁垒的作用；第二个 also 衔接两个 because，说明该项作用的原因。they 指代本段开始的 tariffs and other trade barriers。

（10）本句中的 proponents 和 opponents 为反义词，可分别译为"支持者"和"反对者"。本句中的 argue 一词也应该予以关注，其后接从句时，从句的内容是该动作发出者提出的观点、理由或原因。本句可译为：关税支持者认为，这种国内生产的增加是可取的，而反对者则认为，从经济角度而言，国内生产的增加不会带来效益。

商务知识讲座

国际贸易壁垒

在国际贸易中影响和制约商品自由流通的各种手段和措施，统称贸易障碍或贸易壁垒。广义而言，凡是使正常贸易受到阻碍以及市场竞争机制作用受到干扰的各种人为措施，均属贸易壁垒的范畴。

贸易壁垒一般分为关税壁垒和非关税壁垒两类。所谓关税壁垒，是指进出口商品经过一国国境时，由政府所设置的海关向进出口商征收关税所形成的一种贸易障碍。按征收关税的目的来划分，关税有两种：一是财政关税，其主要目的是为了增加国家财政收入；二是保护关税，其主要目的是为保护本国经济发展而对外国商品的进口征收高额关税。保护关税愈高，保护的作用就愈大，甚至实际上等于禁止进口。

非关税壁垒，是指除关税以外的一切限制进口的措施所形成的贸易障碍，又可分为直接限制和间接限制两类。直接限制是指进口国采取某些措施，直接限制进口商品的数量或金额，如进口配额制、进口许可证制、外汇管制、进口最低限价等。间接限制是通过对进口商品制定严格的条例、法规等间接地限制商品进口，如歧视性的政府采购政策，苛刻的技术标准、卫生安全法规、检查和包装、标签规定以及其他各种强制性的技术法规。

随着世贸组织等国际间贸易组织成员的不断增加以及各地区组织的建立，如北美自由贸易区等，对这两类组织的非成员方，关税壁垒还在起着作用。但值得注意的是，国际上非关税壁垒的作用正在增强，或有增强的趋势。一些发达国家利用其自身的技术优势对来自其他国家的产品提出认证要求，极大地阻碍了欠发达和发展中国家制成品的出口，导致它们只能出口一些资源性的初级产品，这加剧了南北之间的经济及贸易发展差距。另外，发达国家以及一些欠发达国家和发展中国家越来越多地采用的反倾销手段，也是非关税壁垒之一。

随着多种新贸易壁垒的出现和发展，贸易壁垒正在发生结构性变化。传统贸易壁垒逐渐走向分化，其中的关税、配额和许可证等壁垒逐渐弱化，而反倾销等传统贸易壁垒则在相当长的时间内继续存在并有升级强化的趋势。

相对于传统贸易壁垒，新贸易壁垒是指以技术壁垒为核心的，包括绿色壁垒和社会壁垒在内的，所有阻碍国际商品自由流动的新型非关税壁垒。它的根本特征是着眼于商品数量和价格等商业利益以外的东西，更多地考虑商品对于人类健康、安全以及环境的影响，体现的是社会利益和环境利益，采取的措施不仅仅是边境措施，还涉及国内政策和法规。

1. 绿色贸易壁垒

绿色贸易壁垒，是指环境（非关税）壁垒，是国际社会为保护人类、动植物及生态环境的健康和安全而采取的直接或间接限制甚至禁止某些商品进出口的法律、法规和政策措施。其实质是发达国家依赖其科学技术和环保水平，通过立法手段，制定严格的强制性技术标准，从而把来自发展中国家的产品拒之门外。

2. 技术性贸易壁垒

技术性贸易壁垒是非关税壁垒的主要表现形式，是指商品进口国制定的技术法规、标准以及合格评定程序对外国进口商品构成的贸易障碍。通过颁布法律、法规、技术标准、认证制度、检验制度等方式，在技术指标、卫生检疫、商品包装和标签等方面制定苛刻的规定，最终达到限制进口的目的或效果，这种限制或阻碍进口的技术性措施就是技术性贸易壁垒。以技术壁垒为核心的新贸易壁垒将长期存在并不断发展，将逐渐取代传统贸易壁垒，成为国际贸易壁垒中的主体。

3. 劳工标准壁垒

有些发达国家试图把劳工问题同贸易捆绑在一起，以期削弱发展中国家的劳动成本优势。常见的劳工标准有：废除强制劳动；严禁使用和剥削童工；非歧视的工资水平、同工同酬；实行最低工资标准，保证劳工的最低工资水平；工人有自由结社和集体议价的权利等。

解决贸易壁垒的方法主要包括双边磋商和谈判。通过交流和谈判，努力打破区域贸易壁垒，营造一个良好的国际贸易环境。同时要熟悉国际贸易有关法律，遭遇壁垒时及时调整自身产业结构，以更好地适应游戏规则，受到惩处时要据理力争，维护自身合法利益。

翻译练习

I. 思考题

1. 什么是衔接？衔接和连贯的关系是怎样的？
2. 结合实例概括主要的语篇衔接手段及其在翻译中的处理方法。

II. 从"Trade Barriers"中摘录给你深刻印象的句子或词组。

1. _____
2. _____
3. _____
4. _____
5. _____

III. 商务术语翻译

access restriction	
ad valorem duty	
anti-absorption	
anti-circumvention	
anti-dumping	
balance of trade	
conformity assessment	
countervailing duty	
customs union	
domestic content regulation	
environmental trade barrier	
fair trade	
fixed duty/specific duty	
green trade barrier	
laissez faire	

most-favored-nation tariff	
non-tariff barrier	
para-tariff measure	
reasonable departure clause	
refund of duty or tax	
retaliatory measure	
retaliatory subsidization	
retaliatory tariff	
simple license/non-exclusive license	
sporadic dumping	
sub-ceiling binding	
tariff concession	
tariff escalation	
tariff item number	
tariff level	
tariff peak	
tariff quota	
tariff-line basis	
technical barriers to trade	
technical regulation	
temporary duty	
terminal tariff rate	
threshold duty	
trade sanction	
voluntary export restraint	
Washington Consensus	
zero-sum game	

IV. 句子翻译

1. The real effects of protectionism are to reduce consumer choice, to raise the price of protected foreign products and domestic goods, to misallocate resources, and to lower worldwide production.
2. If a foreign country imposes a tariff on our products, our best response is not to retaliate at all. In fact, we should drop all tariffs and increase imports of the products of the offending nation. Foreigners in that country would then have a lot of paper dollars that they could use to purchase our products.
3. Certainly, if a tariff is removed, some workers in the protected industry may lose their jobs and some or all of the firms in the protected industry may be forced to close by the foreign competition.
4. The benefits to poor people in developing countries from removing rich countries' trade barriers would be more than twice the $50 billion in annual development aid that rich countries now provide.
5. After repeated pledges by world leaders to avoid erecting trade barriers, protectionism is on the march, provoking nasty trade disputes and undermining efforts to plot a coordinated response to the deepest global economic downturn since World War II.
6. Often, at the early stages of development where production and income are low, countries impose trade barriers to protect domestic infant industries. These trade barriers are reduced or removed at later stages of development. If not, domestic industries remain "infants" relying on continual government support and protection and unable to compete internationally.
7. The WTO has had a significant impact on reducing trade barriers among its members. Even so, entrepreneurs need to do careful research about barriers to trade with WTO members as some countries protect their domestic markets and industries through the creative use of trade barriers.
8. The sluggish economy makes it more important that governments and the international community remove obstacles to creating new jobs and opportunities for poor people in developing countries. Trade barriers and other impediments to investment top the list.
9. Even without protectionism, the synchronized global downturn is likely to result in the largest annual decline in world trade in 80 years, according to the World Bank. While the bank said it was difficult to quantify the effects of the new barriers, they could aggravate that decline.
10. Some trade skeptics caution against making too much of the link between the economic crisis and protectionism. Some people noted that many countries had not raised tariffs to the highest levels permissible under trade laws.

V. 篇章翻译

At root, the issue of tariffs and other trade barriers is a moral concern. To place such restrictions on the exchange of property is an infringement on the natural right to own and exchange property. Protectionism threatens the consumers' rights to choose from among goods and services. Protectionism is the policy of using coercion to restrict imports of foreign goods.

To argue for tariffs and other trade restrictions is the same as arguing against technological change and human progress. Trade barriers decrease the advantages gained through the international division of labor. The argument for protectionism is the argument for higher prices, lower quality goods, economic stagnation, and coercive monopoly.

Protectionists maintain that permitting consumers to purchase foreign-made products causes unemployment at home. We are told that jobs are lost when we are invaded by cheap foreign goods. Protectionists argue that tariffs and quotas keep domestic wages from being reduced to the wage levels in countries from which we import. When firms within certain industries call for protection to allegedly protect consumers from poor quality products and to ensure their employees' jobs, their real goal is to gain security through the removal of competition.

翻译名家

杨苡（1919—2023），翻译家和作家，代表译作《呼啸山庄》被誉为"不可撼动的经典译本"。杨苡认为"文学翻译决不能一挥而就，更不是人云亦云的依样画葫芦"。她形容自己的翻译过程是"极其繁琐的"，包括"泛读、精读、构思、写草稿、修改、重抄、再整理润色、再重抄"等阶段。

受巴金鼓励，杨苡决心翻译《呼啸山庄》，她谨记巴金对她的教诲："要好好翻译一本书……不要急……慢是好的，唯其慢才可细心去了解，去传达原意。"她首创了《呼啸山庄》（*Wuthering Heights*）的译名，此前这部文学巨作曾被翻译为《狭路冤家》《魂归离恨天》《咆哮山庄》。杨苡希望找到一个既能译出原书名的意义，又能基本上接近书名字音的译名。直到十二年后，在一个疾风呼啸的雨夜，雨点敲在窗上，宛如小说主人公凯瑟琳在窗外哭叫着开窗。杨苡所住的房子外正好是一片荒凉的花园，这使她获得灵感，将书名译为《呼啸山庄》。这一译名的形成充分体现了杨苡的翻译观：翻译实际上也是创作，而且比创作更艰苦累人。

杨苡一直抱着严谨谦虚的翻译态度，自谦为"永远处于'翻译习作'阶段的人"。她与兄长杨宪益、丈夫赵瑞蕻（《红与黑》的译者）共同推动中文与世界对话，使文学经典如种子般在不同文明的土壤里生根开花，被学界称为"成就了中国文学翻译事业的一个奇迹"。

第 9 章　翻译中的意义再现

> The power of words, then, lies in their associations—the things they bring up before our minds. Words become filled with meaning for us by experience; and the longer we live, the more certain words recall to us the glad and sad events of our past; and the more we read and learn, the more the number of words that mean something to us increases.
>
> —The Anonymous

问题导入

1. 阅读并试译下面的句子。

   A business can reduce the costs of handling sales inquiries, providing price quotes, and determining product availability by using electronic commerce in its sales support and order-taking processes.

   译文　_____

   _____

   _____

2. 说明你在翻译时如何确定词汇在上下文中的意义。在翻译上述例句时你认为有需要查阅的词汇吗？如果有的话，请画线标出。

3. 说明翻译中遇到的问题，并和同学们讨论解决问题的方法。

   难点：_____

   解决方法：_____

翻译知识讲座

翻译中的意义再现

提到翻译，人们总避不开直译（literal translation；word-for-word translation）和意译（free translation；sense-for-sense translation）之类的说辞。无论是直译还是意译，翻译从根本上讲是意义的转换，而意义的转换既无法仅仅停留在字面上，也不能彻底摆脱原文而做到绝对自由。因为语言是由形式和内容构成的：形式具体可见，而内容则是附着于形式之上的。从形式上讲，词汇可以组合成语句，语句可以组合成篇章，所谓"因字而生句，积句而成章，积章而成篇"。然而，句子意义并不等于句中单个词汇意义之和，语篇意义也不是篇中单个句子意义之和。就单词而言，我们也无法仅靠查阅词典便将其中的意义原封不动地移植到译文中去。请看一例：

例 1 For example, the advent of sailing ships in ancient times opened new avenues of trade to buyers and sellers.

参考译文： 例如，历史上大型帆船的出现就曾为买卖双方开辟了新的贸易渠道。

例句中的 avenues 一词用法比较新颖。avenue 有两种常见意义：a) a street in a city or town（如美国著名的 the Fifth Avenue 第五大街）；b) a wide straight road with trees on both sides, especially one leading to a big house。而在例句中，avenues 所表达的并非这两种常见意义，而是由此引申出的另一种意义或喻义：a choice or way of making progress toward sth。例如：

例 2 Several avenues are open to us.

参考译文： 多条道路（选择、途径）摆在我们面前。

例 3 We will explore every avenue until we find an answer.

参考译文： 找到答案之前，我们会探索各种途径（方法、手段）。

由此可以看出，词汇意义的确定一方面需要根据上下文进行选择，同时也取决于译者个人的用词特点。

例 4 More recent innovations, such as the printing press, the steam engine, and the telephone, have each changed the way in which people conducted commerce activities.

参考译文： 再后来的一些发明创新，如印刷机、蒸汽机和电话等的出现也都改变了人们从事贸易活动的方式。

例句中的 press 一词很容易被忽略，在日常表达中 press 使用频率很高，使用者大都以为自己业已熟谙其义，因此在翻译过程中容易想当然地译成"新闻界"。显而易见，例句中的 press 所指并非"报纸""新闻界""新闻记者"等，而是指"印刷机"（a machine for printing books, newspapers, etc.）。

不同类型的意义有些可以从词典中觅得踪迹，有些需要译者对源语语言和文化深入了解方可感受到，需要译者的主观参与。当在词典中查不到可以使用的恰当表达时，如果译者能够吃透原文，对原文的内涵信息融会贯通，还是可以根据汉语的特点进行适度引申并找到恰当的语言表达方式。

例 5 Many other retailer websites include a link to separate sections for overstocks or clearance sales of end-of-season merchandise.

参考译文： 许多其他零售商的网站上都设有一个链接，可以链接到季末积压商品或清仓甩卖产品专区。

看到 clearance 一词，一般都会想到这是动词 clear 的名词形式，意思是"清除；排除；清理"，如 forest clearance（林间空地）。但是当这个词用于商务语境时，可以指"清仓"，如 clearance sales（清仓甩卖），也可以指"审查许可"或"审核批准"，如 security clearance（安全许可）。具体词义需要根据上下文来判断，而不能先入为主，仅凭对这个词的熟悉而忽略上下文，从而误解其意。

词义的选择过程是译者根据语境对词典释义的选择过程或对词典已有释义的动态引申过程，因为翻译不仅仅是翻译词汇的表层意义，更是翻译词汇在特定语境中动态的引申意义。著名词典编纂家葛传槼介绍词汇学习方法时曾经说过："我曾经被人'谣传'，说我少年时代曾经通读过 The Concise Oxford Dictionary of Current English。事实上我从未这样做过。我只是在这本词典中仔细读过 a、about、above、account、across、act、after、again、against、age、agree、air、all、and、any、as、at、away、back、bad、be、bear、beat、because、become、before、begin、behind、between、bit、book、both、break、bring、build、burn、burst、business、but、by 等等。不但弄懂每个词的确义和它的种种习语的确义，而且弄懂每个举例，还把它记住。我直到现在还认为我当时用的这番工夫是给我终身受用不尽的。"这段话说明了两个问题：一是词语往往具有多义性，越是常用词，意义越是丰富。二是要想提高语言运用能力，掌握词汇的多种意义非常重要。从翻译角度讲，在具有一定词汇量的基础上，掌握一个单词的多种意义的重要性不亚于掌握多个不同的单词。

一般说来，英语词义比较灵活、宽泛而多变，词义对上下文的依赖性较大，独立性较小。汉语词义较为严谨，词的含义范围比较狭窄、精确、固定，词义的伸缩性和对上下文的依赖性较小，独立性较大。但总体来说，无论是英文还是中文，词汇的意义只有在语境中才会明晰，缺乏特定的语境，词语意义就会具有多变性。因此，我们可以通过下面的过程来选择词义：

1. 查阅词典，理解原文；
2. 分析语法，吃透原文；
3. 理顺逻辑，跳出原文。

翻译时查阅词典并用搜索引擎检索相关词汇的意义是非常必要的。试译下面四个句子：

例 6 Many other businesses have emulated the company's global networked business model in recent years.

例 7 A business can reduce the costs of handling sales inquiries, providing price quotes, and determining product availability by using electronic commerce in its sales support and order-taking processes.

例 8 A man may usually be known by the books he reads as well as the company he keeps; for there is a companionship of books as well as of men; and one should always live in the best company, whether it be of books or of men.

例 9 Books introduce us into the best society; they bring us into the presence of the greatest minds that have ever lived.

例 6 中的 emulated 一词比较生僻，翻译时通常会去查阅词典，但是例 7 中的 inquiries, quotes, availability，例 8 中的 company 和例 9 中的 society 则是常见词汇，很容易被忽略。第一次试译之后，请查阅词典后再次翻译一遍，然后比较自己前后两次的译文看有哪些区别。参考译文如下：

参考译文 6： 近年来，众多公司纷纷效仿该公司的全球网络商业模式。

参考译文 7： 公司采用电子商务支持销售并接受订单，可降低处理销售询价、提供报价和判断产品供货情况的成本。

参考译文 8： 见其交友，知其为人；观其所读之书，也可知其为人。与书为友如同与人为友，都应与最佳最善者常相伴依。

参考译文 9： 书籍引导我们与最优秀的人物为伴，使我们置身历代伟人巨匠之间。

查阅工具书是选择词义的重要手段，但是，词典中的释义往往是词汇的静态意义，而词汇在使用中却因为具体情景而具有动态意义，仅靠词典显然不足以应付翻译中出现的词汇理解问题。词典是不可或缺的，但更为重要的是译者应深入了解词汇使用的语境。同时，作为翻译学习者，我们不能在汉译英时尊重译语（英语），在英译汉时又转为尊重源语（还是英语），应始终尊重译入语的语言个性。翻译时如果不能尊重译入语的语言个性，那就违反了翻译的根本规律。因此，我们要深入了解英汉两种语言各自的语言个性，并根据译入语的语言个性，对源语中词汇的静态意义进行语境化引申和动态延伸，形成符合译入语表达习惯的译文；既要再现原文的意义，又要避免翻译腔，保证译文流畅地道。因此，要准确把握词义，必须把词汇静态的基本意义与动态的延伸意义相结合，寻找静态词义在特定语境中的动态表达。

商务语篇翻译与解析

Electronic Commerce

Over the thousands of years that people have engaged in commerce with one another, they have adopted the tools and technologies that became available. For example, the advent of sailing ships in ancient times opened new avenues of trade to buyers and sellers. (1) More recent innovations, such as the printing press, the steam engine, and the telephone, have each changed the way in which people conducted commerce activities.

For decades, firms have used various electronic communications tools to conduct different kinds of transactions. Banks have used (2) EFTs (electronic funds transfers) to move customers' money around the world, all kinds of businesses have used EDI (electronic data interchange) to place orders and send invoices, and retailers have used television advertising to generate telephone orders from the general public for all kinds of merchandise.

To many people, the term "electronic commerce" (sometimes shortened to e-commerce) means shopping (3) on the part of the Internet called the World Wide Web. In fact, electronic commerce is much broader and encompasses many more business activities than just web shopping. A broader definition of electronic commerce is business activities conducted using electronic data transmission via the Internet and the World Wide Web. The three main elements of electronic commerce include:

- Consumer shopping on the web, called business-to-consumer (or B2C);
- Transactions conducted between businesses on the web, called business-to-business (or B2B);
- The transactions and business processes that support selling and purchasing activities on the web.

Firms are interested in electronic commerce because, quite simply, it can (4) help increase profits. All the advantages of electronic commerce for business entities can be summarized in one statement: Electronic commerce can increase sales and decrease costs. Advertising done well on the web can get even a small firm's promotional message out to potential customers in every country in the world. (5) A firm can use electronic commerce to reach narrow market segments that are geographically scattered. The web is particularly useful in creating virtual communities that become ideal target markets for specific types of products or services. A virtual community is a gathering of people who share a common interest, but instead of this gathering occurring in the physical world, it takes place on the Internet. Moreover, (6) a business can reduce the costs of handling sales inquiries, providing price quotes, and determining product availability by using electronic commerce in its sales support and order-taking processes.

(7) Just as electronic commerce increases sales opportunities for the seller, it increases purchasing opportunities for the buyer. Businesses can use electronic commerce in their purchasing processes to identify new suppliers and business partners. (8) Negotiating price and delivery terms is easier in electronic commerce, because the web can provide competitive bid information very efficiently. Electronic commerce increases the speed and accuracy with which businesses can exchange information, which reduces costs on both sides of transactions.

Electronic commerce provides buyers with a wider range of (9) choices than traditional commerce, since they can consider many different products and services from a wider variety of sellers. (10) This wide variety is available for consumers to evaluate 24 hours a day, every day. Instead of waiting days for the mail to bring a catalog or product specification sheet, or (11) even minutes for a fax transmission, buyers can have instant access to detailed information on the web. Some products, such as software, audio clips, or images, can (11) <u>even</u> be delivered through the Internet, which reduces the time buyers must wait to begin enjoying their purchases.

The benefits of electronic commerce also extend to the general welfare of society. Electronic payments of tax refunds, public retirement, and welfare support cost less to issue and arrive securely and quickly when transmitted over the Internet. Furthermore, electronic payments can be easier to audit and monitor than payments made by check, which can help protect against fraud and theft losses. To the extent that electronic commerce enables people to work from home, we all benefit from the reduction in commuter-caused traffic and pollution. Electronic commerce can make products and services available in remote areas. For example, distance education is making it possible for people to learn skills and earn degrees no matter where they live or when they are available for study.

However, (12) <u>some business processes may never lend themselves to electronic commerce</u>. For example, perishable foods and high-cost items such as jewelry or antiques may be impossible to inspect adequately from a remote location, regardless of any technologies that might be devised in the future. Some of the (13) <u>disadvantages</u> of electronic commerce today stem from the rapidly developing pace of the underlying technologies. However, these disadvantages will disappear as electronic commerce matures and becomes more available to and accepted by the general population.

难点解析

（1）press 一词经常指"新闻界"，此处与 printing 搭配，和 the steam engine、the telephone 并列使用，指"印刷机"。要特别注意 each 一词有突出和强调的作用，在翻译中需要用适当的表达予以再现。

（2）本句有两个首字母缩略词，这也是现代语言的一个特点，主要是为了语言表达的简洁和便利。这类词汇很多，一般在上文会有全称。有些首字母缩略词可以不翻译（如 WTO），有些需要按照汉语的习惯进行重新缩略（如下文的"电商"）。此外，本句中的 move 一词不能简单译为"移动"或"运动"，而应根据上下文适度引申，将其译为"转账"。在商务英语中，order 常用的词义为"订单"，常和 place 连用，意为"下订单"，take order 意为"接受订单"。

（3）on the part of 是一个固定词组，意为"在……方面、就……而言"。如：The agreement has been kept on the part of the factory. 工厂方面遵守了协议。There is no objection on the part of the owner of the house. 房主没有任何异议。此处可译为"在互联网上"。

（4）help 指 make it easier for sth to happen（促进、促成），如：This latest development doesn't exactly help. 这一最新进展对事情并没有真正的好处。本句 help 可以虚化不译，直接译出其后的动宾结构即可。

（5）本句中的 geographically scattered 不能译为"地理位置上分散在各地"，不符合汉语表达习惯，可译为"分散在各地"。本句中的 reach 需要进行词义引申，不妨试译一下，再与附录中的参考译文进行比较。market segment 亦作 market segmentation，是商务用语，可译为"市场细分""细分市场"等。市场细分是企业根据消费者需求不同，把整个市场划分成不同消费者群的过程，其客观基础是消费者需求的异质性。市场细分的目标是为了聚合，即在各种需求的市场中把需求相同的消费者聚合到一起。

（6）inquiry 和 quote 在商务英语中具有不同含义。前者是"询盘"，后者意为"报盘"，都是特定的商务行为。business 一般作抽象名词使用，意为"商业、买卖（尤指作为职业）、贸易"，如 international business；也可作可数名词使用，指"商业机构、公司、商店"，如 She runs a thriving grocery business. 她经营着一家生意兴隆的食品杂货店。availability 是常用词汇，此处若生硬套用其词典释义"可利用性、可获得性"，会影响译文的可读性。翻译时要联系上下文，尤其是与 product 的关系，合起来不妨译为"产品供货情况"。

（7）seller 和 buyer 在文中多次出现。在本文中 seller 的同义词有 supplier，另外 firm 和 business 也可视为 seller 的同义词，可根据上下文译为"卖方、销售方、供货方"；另外 retailer 在某些上下文中也属于同义表达，译为"零售商。"buyer 指"买方、购货方"，有些上下文中的 customer 也可理解为 buyer。英语表达忌重复，因此经常变换表达方式，而汉语中重复用词现象较普遍，英汉翻译时要注意英语这种不同词汇表达同样意义的现象。

（8）delivery terms 此处译为"交货条款"，terms 在商务文本中经常用作"条款、条件"之意，如 the terms of the contract（合同条款）。要注意区分作为 term 复数的 terms 和独立词汇 terms 意义上的区别，不可简单地将其一概视为 term 的复数形式。bid information 意为"价格信息"。competitive 本意为"有竞争力的"，此处可引申为"更好的、更优惠的"。

（9）choices 在这里指"可供选择的东西"，根据上下文可进一步引申为"可供选择的产品和服务"。

（10）this 此处用来衔接上下文，强调消费者可获得产品和服务的便利。句中 every day 与前面的成分用逗号隔开，进一步突出其便利性。翻译时要注意表达出这种强调的语气。

（11）even 出现了两次，强调意味很明显，以凸显电子商务的优势。这样的小词语气强烈，意味丰富，翻译时不可忽视。

（12）lend oneself to sth 有两种常见含义：a) lend one's name to sth; allow oneself to be associated with sth（参与某事），如 She lent her name to many worthy causes. 她参与了许多有意义的事情。b) lend itself to sth; be suitable for sth（适合某事物），如 a novel which lends itself well to dramatization for television. 适合拍成电视剧的小说。此处是第二种意义，全句可译为"有些商业流程也许永远都无法采用电子商务"。

（13）disadvantage 的词典释义包括"不利条件、阻碍成功或进步等的事物、不便之处"等，此处可根据上下文及汉语表达习惯适当调整措辞，译为"不尽如人意之处"。

商务知识讲座

电子商务

电子商务源于英文 Electronic Commerce，是指通过使用互联网等电子工具，使公司内部、供应商、客户和合作伙伴之间，利用电子业务共享信息，实现企业间业务流程的电子化，并配合企业内部的电子化生产管理系统，提高企业的生产、库存、流通和资金等各个环节的效率。电子商务可通过多种电子通信方式来完成。但现在人们所探讨的电子商务主要是以 EDI（Electronic Data Interchange，电子数据交换）和互联网为基础来完成的。作为一种新型的商务模式，电子商务具有普遍性、便捷性、整体性、安全性、协调性等特征。

EDI 于 20 世纪 60 年代末期产生于美国，是指将业务文件按一个公认的标准从一台计算机传输到另一台计算机上去的电子传输方法。由于 EDI 大大减少了纸张票据的使用，因此，人们也形象地称之为"无纸贸易"或"无纸交易"。

20 世纪 90 年代以来，因为计算机的广泛应用、网络的普及和成熟、信用卡的普及应用以及电子安全交易协议的制定和政府的支持与推动，电子商务的发展进入了国际互联网时代。与基于 EDI 的电子商务相比，基于互联网的电子商务具有费用更低廉、覆盖面更广、功能更全面、使用更灵活等明显的优势。

从贸易活动的角度分析，电子商务可以在多个环节实现，由此也可以将电子商务分为两个层次：较低层次的电子商务如电子商情、电子贸易、电子合同等；最完整的也是最高级的电子商务是利用互联网网络进行全部的贸易活动，即在网上将信息流、商流、资金流和部分的物流完整地实现。企业可以从寻找客户开始，一直到洽谈、订货、在线付（收）款、开具电子发票以至电子报关、电子纳税等都通过互联网一气呵成。

电子商务可以通过构建企业内部网、实现局域网与互联网的连接以及运行电子商务应用系统软件来实现。

电子商务可提供以下服务：

1. 售前服务，企业可利用网上主页和电子邮件在全球范围内做广告宣传；客户可借助网上检索工具迅速地找到所需要的商品信息。

2. 售中服务，即咨询洽谈、网上订购、网上支付等商务过程，甚至包括直接试用产品的机会等。

3. 售后服务，主要包括帮助客户解决产品使用中的问题，排除技术故障，提供技术支持，传递产品改进或升级的信息以及搜集客户对产品与服务的反馈信息。网上售后服务不仅响应快、质量高、费用低，而且可以大大降低服务人员的工作强度。

电子商务的应用有以下三种类型：

1. 企业内部电子商务，即企业内部之间通过内部网的方式处理与交换商贸信息。

2. 企业间的电子商务（简称为 B2B 模式），即企业与企业之间通过互联网或专用网方式进行电子商务活动。

3. 企业与消费者之间的电子商务（简称为 B2C 模式），即企业通过互联网为消费者提供一个新型的购物环境——网上商店，消费者在网上购物并支付。

按照不同标准，可对电子商务进行不同的分类。按商业活动运作方式可分成完全电子商务和不完全电子商务两类。

1. 完全电子商务：可以完全通过电子商务方式实现和完成整个交易过程。

2. 不完全电子商务：无法完全依靠电子商务方式实现和完成完整交易过程，需要依靠一些外部要素，如运输系统等来完成交易。

电子商务要健康发展，一个关键因素就是安全问题，这也是全球普遍关注的一个问题。随着全球网络信息安全体系的形成和电子商务的日趋成熟，电子商务将为更多的大众所熟悉和接受。

作为一种商务活动过程，电子商务对社会经济的作用远远超过商务本身，并对就业、法律制度以及文化教育等带来巨大的影响。

翻译练习

I. 思考题

1. 什么是意义？翻译和意义有何关系？
2. 结合实例说明翻译中词义选择的重要性及其原因。

II. 从"Electronic Commerce"中摘录给你深刻印象的句子或词组。

1. _____
2. _____
3. _____
4. _____
5. _____

III. 商务术语翻译

access control list	
acquiring bank	
banner exchange site	
click-through rate	
commerce service provider	
digital signature	
distance education	
e-card	
electronic cash	
electronic clearance	

electronic funds transfer	
electronic product code	
electronic wallet	
e-logistics	
enterprise resource planning	
file transfer protocol	
logical security	
personal identification number	
physical security	
private-key encryption	
public-key encryption	
rational branding	
smart card	
stored-value card	
target market	
virtual community	
web hosting	
web mall	
web portal	

IV. 句子翻译

1. Due to the global reach of the Internet, business organizations are able to send messages worldwide, exploring new markets and opportunities. This breaks down geographic limitations and reaches narrow markets that traditional businesses have difficulty accessing.
2. Through the Internet, different levels of product information can be accessed online globally, which makes it easy for customers to compare and evaluate.
3. E-commerce brings the universal access of the Internet to the core business processes of buying and selling goods and services. It helps generate demand for products and services and improve order management, payment, and other support functions. The

4. The emergence of electronic commerce started in the 1970s with the earliest example of electronic funds transfer, which allowed organizations to transfer funds between one another electronically.
5. Then another technology, electronic data interchange, was introduced. It helps extend inter-business transactions from financial institutions to other types of businesses and also provides transactions and information exchanges from suppliers to the end customers.
6. The open structure of the Internet and the low cost of using it permit the interconnection of new and existing information and communication technologies, offering businesses and consumers an innovative and powerful information system and another form of communication.
7. Moreover, e-commerce can involve electronic funds transfer, supply chain management, e-marketing, online marketing, online transaction processing, electronic data interchange, automated inventory management systems, and automated data collection systems.
8. Originally, the enterprise system was known as enterprise resource planning, which supports a broad set of activities by multi-module application software that helps a manufacturer manage the important parts of its business. These include product planning, parts purchasing, maintaining inventories, interacting with suppliers, providing customer service, and tracking orders.
9. Using the Internet for conducting e-commerce will not assure a business of being able to compete favorably with large established competitors.
10. Setting up a professional web presence can be a big project and setting up an e-commerce system on top of that can be yet another big project.

(Note: Item starting with "overall goal is to cut expenses by reducing transaction costs and streamlining all kinds of processes." appears at the top of the page as continuation.)

V. 篇章翻译

E-commerce is becoming more social and more connected to the offline world.

Those who cherish privacy will recoil in horror, but for digital exhibitionists it is a dream. At a web start-up, users can now publish their purchases. Whenever they swipe their credit or debit card, the transaction is listed on the site—to be discussed by other users. "Turn purchases into conversations" is the firm's mantra.

The above-mentioned firm is among the latest entrants in the growing field of social commerce. Firms in this market combine e-commerce with social networks and other online group activities. They aim to transform shopping both online and offline. The firm's boss points out that the Internet has already disrupted the content industry and commerce will be next.

The first generation of e-commerce sites, which hit the web in the late 1990s, was essentially digitized mail-order catalogs. Many websites collected user reviews and recommendations, but they did not sell anything—and many collapsed during the dot-com crash. Only a small number of firms brought together selling and social feedback, to great effect. By means of collaborative filtering, they made suggestions based on other buyers' purchases.

The second generation of e-commerce firms is quite different. Few emerged from Silicon Valley. Indeed, they tend to drive customers to actual shops. Many make their money from flash sales—brief offers of steep discounts on products—that are advertised to registered members.

翻译名家

高健（1929—2013），著名散文翻译家，数十载投身于翻译教学与实践，在英语诗歌、散文汉译方面成就卓著。他既有大量精品译著，又有翻译理论著述，曾荣获中国翻译协会授予的"资深翻译家"称号，被称为"阵地翻译家"。高健的译作"精致周到、隽美考究、纯净圆熟"。他的《英美散文六十家》由于广受译界赞誉而被收录于"世界文学名著丛书"，他本人也被列入《中国翻译家辞典》《中国社会科学家辞典》等。

高健以大量翻译实践为基础，批判地继承和发扬了中国传统翻译理论的精华，形成了以"语言个性理论"为核心，以"语性论""相对论""协调论""复式语言论"和"停顿论"为基本理论框架的翻译思想理论体系。从他对语言个性的总结和概括，可以看出他驾驭语言的深厚功力。高健的译论虽缘于诗歌和散文翻译，但是对学习者认识源语和目的语的语言个性、认识翻译、提高翻译的灵活性和创造性都很有益处。

高健认为，每种语言都有它自己所独具的性格、习性、脾气、癖好、气质，都有它自己所独具的倾向、性能、潜力、可能性和局限性，等等，该语言的使用者需对此有一个通盘了解，对它的运作方式、搭配范围、表述习惯、灵活幅度、扩展的条件与限度等要做到烂熟于胸，了无窒碍。

第 10 章　翻译与语境

> Language comes to life only when functioning in some environment.
>
> — M. A. K. Halliday

问题导入

1. 选择符合自己翻译习惯的选项，并分析其优势和不足。

    （1）先通读全文，了解文章的主题和要点，之后再下笔翻译；

    （2）先查好所有生词的词义，之后再逐句翻译；

    （3）边阅读边动手翻译；

    （4）阅读一句翻译一句；

    （5）阅读一段翻译一段；

    （6）其他 _____。

2. 用你习惯的方式翻译下面的句子。

    European agricultural interests wanted protection from US farm products, and US manufacturing firms wanted insulation from European competitors. Barriers to immigration arose as well.

    译文 _____

    _____

    _____

3. 与同学一起讨论你采用的翻译方法的优缺点，以及如何改进你的翻译方法。

    优点：_____

    缺点：_____

    改进方法：_____

翻译知识讲座

翻译与语境

随着翻译理论的发展，翻译中的语境因素正日益受到人们的关注，研究者从不同的角度探讨了语境在翻译中的作用。在翻译实践中，语境因素对于理解和表达都会产生重要影响，正如纽马克（Newmark, 1981）所言："对于所有翻译，语境（包括文内语境和文化语境）都是最重要的因素，其重要性大于任何法规，任何理论，任何基本词义。"

语境即语言表达的环境，其中包括语言本身的环境以及交际所涉及的社会文化因素。交际中的语境因素可以分为三个层面：一是狭义的语义语境，包括微观与宏观层面的搭配与构成方式；二是情景语境，即交际活动的话题和交际双方的背景知识；三是语用语境，涉及交际的目的和交际双方的社会文化背景知识（Hatim, 2001）。从翻译角度，可将语境大致归纳为两类：一是文内语境，通常指上下文，即词语在文中的搭配、语法功能和在句中的词序。这一层面的语境贯穿于整个语篇，对原文的理解与把握至关重要，忽略文内语境会直接导致原文理解与译文表达的失误。二是文化语境，即语言所处的社会环境，包括文化背景和读者的共享知识。文化语境提供了关于原文的深层社会信息，对翻译过程中语篇的正确理解极为重要。

1. 语境与理解

翻译是以意义传递为中心的语言转换行为，因此意义转换是翻译中最为重要的问题，意义表达和传递的准确性与得体性常常是考量翻译结果的首要标准。在翻译过程中，语境对正确理解原文的意义具有不可或缺的作用，其具体表现如下：(1) 有助于消除信息的歧义和多义性；(2) 能够明确某些指称词的所指对象与内容；(3) 能提供说话人或作者省略的信息。除此之外，语境还有助于译者理解原作者的写作意图和创作风格，从而为我们提供文本所指涉的社会活动背景知识。需要指出的是，翻译活动中的语境是动态的，语境中的意义也随着语境变化呈现出动态特征。因此，要准确把握原文的意义，就必须对语境因素进行详细分析。

在翻译过程中，语境分析对正确理解与传递原文信息都会产生重要影响，忽视语境对意义的制约作用，必然会导致语义理解上的失误。在英语中一词多类、一词多义及一词多用现象可谓比比皆是。不少情况下，只有借助语境分析，才能对特定搭配或结构中的词语意义加以确定。我国杰出的史地学家和翻译家冯承钧提出史学翻译必须充分利用中西史料，通过史料对比还原文本产生的语境，确定词汇的精确意义。同样，商务文本内容涉及商务活动的方方面面，其语言表述方式有别于其他文本类型，尤其在用词方面具有鲜明的商务特色。因此，在翻译过程中，译者需要根据具体的商务语境明确特定搭配中词语的意义，区分词语的一般意义和专业意义。

例 1 We have drawn on you at sight a draft for the invoice value to be collected through the Bank of China.

参考译文： 我们已按发票金额向你方开具即期汇票，由中国银行托收。

collect 的一般意义为"收集、搜集"等，而在本句中，collect 则具有特定的专业意义，应将其译为"托收"。

某些情况下，词义的确定不仅依赖于狭义的文内语境或微观与宏观的语言搭配及结构，而且还需要考虑词语所涉及的具体文化背景。在商务文体中，广义语境中的文化背景知识包括商务知识以及商务活动参与者所共享的知识与原则。鉴于此，在商务文本翻译过程中，我们既要重视文内语境，也不能忽略与商务知识相关的文化语境对词义理解的影响。请看以下例句：

例 2 Shipment is effected during June.（装船）

例 3 We have done our best to hasten shipment.（装运）

例 4 Quality must be the same as your last shipment.（船货，到货）

例 5 Please extend shipment for 30 days.（装船期限）

在上述四个句子中，shipment 一词看上去没有区别，而实际上却存在着某些差异，所表达的是海运的不同流程，不能简单地将其理解为同一种意义。因此，不同语义的理解与意义的确定一方面要依据句子的语法结构，同时还要考虑专业方面的背景知识。只有这样，才能正确理解词义并找到得体的转换形式。

2. 语境与表达

语境对语义的准确表达也同样具有重要意义，在翻译过程中，离开语境的参照作用，对词语、句子乃至语篇的理解很可能会出现错误，进而导致表达方面的失误。

例 6 In this case, sensing techniques are necessary to understand the time signature of the channel and some second order statistics.

原译1 在这种情况下，需要感知技术来理解通道的时间信号和一些二阶统计量。

原译2 这种情况下往往需要利用传感技术来获取信道的时间节拍和一些二阶统计量。

如果没有特定的语境作为参照，这两种译文似乎都说得通，原译 1 中 sensing techniques 译为"感知技术"，但是如果置于现代物流的语境中，这种译法明显有误。物联网技术中的 sensing techniques 来自 sensor（传感器），特指"传感技术"，它是支撑现代物联网的支柱技术，因此在现代物流情境下，sensing 有其特定意义。同样，signature 也不可翻译为"签字""签名"，在现代物联网技术中 time signature 是一个整体，译为"时间节拍"。

不同的语言对语境的依赖程度往往有所不同，这种现象被霍尔（Hall，1990）区分为"高语境"和"低语境"两种情况。英语属于"低语境"模式，语言表述注重外在的形式，比如运用不同的语法策略来表现各成分之间的逻辑关系，同时也十分注重表达的准确性。汉语则属于典型的"高语境"模式，其特点是偏重意合，语法手段不甚明显，注重内在关系、隐含关系和模糊关系（潘文国，1997）。在表述过程中，汉语使用者所用语言本身往往并不能完全表达真实的交际意图，具体的意图常需要依靠交际环境和交际双方的关系来推断。汉语文本多强调言外之意，要求读者具备从字里行间寻找逻辑关系的能力以及运用文化背景知识解读文本的能力。

尽管英汉两种语言对语境的依赖程度不同，但在翻译过程中，译者的理解与表达都需要对语境进行分析与把握。语境分析的对象包括原文中的搭配关系、语法手段，以及与此密切相关的词语、句子和篇章的意义或信息。而在表达过程中，则需要充分考虑英汉两种语言的行文特点，不能简单复制原文的表层句法结构，以避免因过分异化而使译文晦涩难懂。

例 7 In other words, rolling up these activities, from original raw material supply to the final delivery of a finished product to a customer, under a single logistics management ensures a continuous flow of materials and goods.

参考译文： 换句话说，就是在统一的物流管理范畴内，把从原材料供应到成品送达客户的所有行为整合起来，保证原料和商品的不间断流动。

原句的主语很长，动名词短语的宾语又有后置定语，但是因为英语有明显的语法手段，清楚地表明了它们之间的关系，所以没有产生任何歧义。翻译时要考虑文化语境，根据汉语的表达习惯，按照主次层层断开，并且要把后置定语提前。

鉴于语境在翻译过程中的重要性，译者在翻译时不仅要关注原文的语言本身，而且要分析原文语篇所涉及的语境知识。通过分析文内语境，了解词语的选择和搭配、句式的特点和衔接，确定原文词汇和句子的意义；通过分析语篇的社会语境，确定语篇所指涉的商务活动的背景知识和相关社会文化知识，消除理解方面的歧义，从而使译文更加精准地道。

商务语篇翻译与解析

The Logistics Management

(1) Historically, the movement of goods inwards and shoving goods outwards were always considered to be quite separate entities. They invariably fall within quite separate spheres of management responsibility. There was little or no cross-referencing, or indeed much cooperation, about such vital issues as operational plans or indeed the costs involved; management tended to (2) be very territorial.

Now, of course, things are very different. (3) With the concept of logistics taking hold in most firms, it is seen to be both economically and operationally preferable that these functions should be fully integrated to ensure an efficient flow of goods, of relevant documentation, and of essential information through the complete supply chain. In other words, rolling up these activities, from original raw material supply to the final delivery of a finished product to a customer, under a single logistics management ensures a continuous flow line of materials and goods. This has many readily identifiable benefits: permitting a global view of total logistics costs within firms, and presenting greater opportunities to achieve cost savings.

The logistics industry looks at integration in a variety of ways and spanning a number of functions, for example, where the customer demands just-in-time (JIT) deliveries, the supplier needs to ensure that an integrated materials management system is in place to provide a flow stock into and through the production and packaging phases. (4) <u>This has to be done in such a way that</u> sufficient finished products are available in time for delivery to meet the customer's schedule. Or put another way, the customer will not receive his/her JIT deliveries if the supplier does not have the stock of goods to meet the demand. Integrated systems will ensure that these vital flows of materials, components, and finished products are ready on time, to specification and at an acceptable cost.

These days, information technology provides the facility to examine the efficiencies and costs of the various elements that make up an integrated logistics system and the system as a whole. A task that was hitherto laborious and long-winded is not completely impossible. The modern communication allows people to connect with the other side of the world via the Internet and telephone (5) <u>in mere seconds</u>. Such a scenario demands also that the supply of material and delivery of finished goods should also be on a global scale with finished goods capable of being delivered across the globe to customers within short time scales. And acceptable cost bounds just as efficiently as deliveries to customers on the home market.

Many of the barriers to global trade have been swept away, and firms now look to market their products beyond their traditional home markets. But it is no good marketing products to overseas potential customers unless they can be sure that the orders can be delivered within an acceptable time scale and at an acceptable cost. (6) <u>There is a call for international logistics: in determining</u> what mode of transport should be used, what packaging is necessary, what legal requirements or restraints have to be complied with, and so on.

An effective overall logistics strategy will consider each of (7) <u>these questions</u> and develop suitable policies and systems to deal with each and every aspect of the material flow in an integrated manner. Such a strategy will seek to arrange the sourcing, grouping, kitting, and shipment of the various components to achieve the logistics objectives of the organization.

难点解析
（1）historically 在句中作时间状语，但所强调的并非历史事实，而是通过对比历史与现在来反映物流行业的发展，因此译作"过去"反而要比"在历史上"更为简洁明确。the movement of goods inwards and shoving goods outwards 意思较为笼统，不宜照字面直译为"货物的向内运转和向外推出"，应将模糊概念具体化，译为"货物的入库和出库"，意思显然清楚得多。
（2）be very territorial 系表结构在翻译中可改为动宾结构，这样的译文更易被读者理解和接受。
（3）本句中 with 部分是伴随状语，翻译成汉语时可处理为独立的分句，并将原文的主语 the concept of logistics 处理成宾语，firms 处理为分句主语。本句中还出现了形式主语 it，真正的主语是后面的 that 从句，翻译时注意顺应汉语表达习惯，比如考虑增添主语"人们"等。
（4）This has to be done in such a way that... 表示上述情况所导致的结果，可考虑只翻译 that 后面引导的结果，而酌情省略其他部分，如果一味追求逐词对应，译文势必会显得累赘。
（5）in mere seconds 作时间状语，用于强调现代通信的快捷，翻译时应注意适当调整，以突出原文的信息重点：人们之间相互联系的方便与快速。
（6）介词短语 in determining... 表达了国际物流的必要性。本句译为汉语时不易处理，因为汉语缺乏与 there be 结构对应的表述方式和相应的语法手段，如将其直译为"有一种对国际物流的需要……"，显然是不通顺的。变通方法是将 there be 句式移至句末，处理成独立的分句。
（7）在本句中，these questions 指上文 what mode of transport should be used, what..., what..., and so on 所罗列的内容，通过指称手段的运用，两段之间自然地衔接起来，而不会产生任何歧义。翻译时要注意传达出这种前后的逻辑联系，these questions 不宜译为"这些问题"，而应译为"上述问题"。

商务知识讲座

国际物流

物流即货物的流通，现代物流行业涉及信息、运输、仓储、材料搬运与包装等种种业务，需要协调各项专业技术才能成功运作。与此同时，现代物流还应以物料供应商和服务供应商等客户为导向，不断开拓有效的供给链，把内外流通环节整合为统一管理的供应链。物流对企业的生存和发展至关重要，有效的物流能够使企业以最低的成本实现既定的客户服务目标，通过控制材料、产品、库存成品的流通实现企业降低成本、增加利润的目标。

国内物流环境相对比较稳定，而国际物流因为必须要适应不同国家和地区的环境，往往充满不确定因素。不确定因素的产生一是因为国际物流涉及的距离远、时间长，二是由于国际物流过程涉及政治、文化、规章制度以及语言等多方面因素。有学者把国际物流成本及其复杂性概括为 4 个 D，即 Distance（距离）、Documentation（单证）、Diversity in culture（文化差异）和 Demands of customers（顾客需求）。国际物流涉及不同国家和地区，物流活动的距离更长、单证更复杂。在产品和服务方面，顾客需求变化莫测，需要解决文化差异问题。因此，国际物流能力的扩展，不仅包括国际运输能力和供应链作业，还包括了解多元文化和掌握多种语言的能力。

物流企业在开发国际物流市场时，必须充分考虑国际物流的复杂性及其所面临的障碍，制定统一的国际物流战略。在统一的物流战略指导下，充分考虑国际与国内作业的区别，采取灵活的应对措施应对各国、各地区的贸易或金融壁垒，以实现全球层面作业。

第一，国际物流的完成周期长，缺乏一致性和灵活性。完成周期长，导致更高的存货需求，一致性的降低增加了物流计划的难度。这样一来，在等待国际装运交付产品的到达和清关期间，就要不断对存货和存货空间进行评估。

第二，全球作业要求产品和有关部门单证使用多国语言，有些特殊产品必须具有地方特征，这些语言差异和地区差异增加了物流作业的复杂性，同时也增加了物流作业的时间和劳动强度。鉴于此，物流企业必须熟悉各地港口的作业规则和单证规范要求，在装运交付前必须翻译好物流单证和相关的海关文件，合理安排运输模式并准确估计运输时间。

第三，尽管国际物流需要统一的信息系统与各个企业之间的作业协调，但是由于国家和地区之间的信息处理差异会影响信息通畅，信息成本费用也会随之增加。此外，供应链上不同的企业目的不同，也为协调带来困难，从而最终导致国际物流企业缺乏一体化的物流信息系统，竞争力由此而受到抑制。因此，企业需要加强和完善内部信息系统，确保信息畅通，通过提高整体素质来增强自身的竞争力。

第四，由于涉及领域广泛，国际物流企业必须与全世界零售商、批发商、制造商、供应商和服务供应商保持合作关系，因此建立承运人和专业化服务供应商的联盟对国际物流尤其重要。建立联盟可节省维持合同关系所花费的大量时间，而且国际联盟能够提供日常通道和专业人员，以减少潜在的风险。

随着经济、技术和社会的发展，现代物流产业正在融入新的物联网当中，成为其中的一部分。物联网，简而言之是通过信息技术将各种物品与网络相连，帮助人们获取所需物品相关信息的网络。物联网不仅可以实现物与物、人与物之间的实时信息交换，还能够在此过程中实现对物品的智能化识别、定位、跟踪、监控和管理。物联网技术的出现不仅推动现代物流走向智能时代，也关系到社会经济发展和科技创新。未来，物联网技术将促使现代物流从实体网络升级为数字网络。随着全球化经济和物联网技术的双轮驱动，物流企业将拥有持续发展的动力，能够实现规模经济并提升盈利能力。

翻译练习

I. 思考题

1. 什么是语境？语境和意义的关系是怎样的？
2. 结合实例说明语境对翻译准确性的作用。

II. 从"The Logistics Management"中摘录给你深刻印象的句子或词组。

1. _____
2. _____
3. _____
4. _____
5. _____

III. 商务术语翻译

added-value service	
automatic replenishment	
cargo damage rate	
consolidation center	
contract logistics	
cross-dock/docking	
customized logistics	
distribution center	
distribution logistics	
distribution processing	
drop shipment	
fill rate	
freight forwarder	
freight management	
global trade item number	
goods-tracked system	
integrated logistics	
inventory cost	
inventory cycle time	
just-in-time (JIT)	
lean logistics	
logistics cost control	
logistics management information system	
logistics outsourcing	
logistics performance management	
logistics planning	

logistics strategy	
multi-modal transportation	
physical distribution	
production line system	
regional distribution center	
reverse logistics	
seamless transportation service	
sorting and picking system	
sporadic freight transportation	
stock-out rate	
supply chain management	
through transportation	
time-definite delivery	
transportation of truck-load	
warehouse management system	
zero-inventory technology	

IV. 句子翻译

1. The presence of a distribution center (DC) allows a supply chain to achieve economies of scale for inbound transportation to a point close to the final destination, because each supplier sends a large shipment to the DC containing products for all locations the DC serves.
2. Inventory aggregation is a good idea when inventory and facility costs form a large fraction of a supply chain's total costs. It is useful for products with a large value-to-weight ratio and for products with high demand uncertainty.
3. To manage supply with the goal of maximizing profit, companies must manage their capacity through the use of workforce flexibility, subcontracting, dual-facilities, and product flexibility. They must also manage supply through the use of inventory by emphasizing common parts and building and holding products with predictable demand ahead of time.

4. The importance of logistics management has increased in today's environment, marked by the use of speed as a competitive edge (to deliver customers' orders, for example), development of exciting new computer technologies, and increased realization that overall operating costs are extremely sensitive to the various costs of handling and holding inventory.

5. Although one mode of transportation may get the job done for a given shipper, intermodal shipping is often the choice, which involves the use of two or more modes of transportation. Some modes, such as railcars, can move products economically; others, such as trucks, can complete the delivery in a timely fashion.

6. Logistics in the global marketplace is a lot different from logistics in the domestic market and since the economy is becoming a global economy, many companies will have to change the way they do things if they don't want to become obsolete.

7. Containerized systems have revolutionized sea freighting by overcoming the problems associated with handling wide varieties of vastly different materials. The further development of roll-on/roll-off ferries has enabled road-based distribution systems to extend across the sea with no additional re-handling or transshipping.

8. The cost of transport in relation to the market price of the goods carried has an important effect on the demand for shipping services; total distribution costs generally account for between 8% and 15% of the market price of the commodities.

9. Quality of service is a paramount consideration in the competitive world of shipping and international trade today. The service provided must be customer-oriented, with emphasis being placed on providing a reliable service and handling the goods and documentation in an effective way.

10. When companies enter growing global markets such as Eastern Europe, China, and South America, expanding their supply chains becomes a strategic challenge. Such strategic challenge can be solved by the wide range of application areas for Internet of Things.

V. 篇章翻译

At a women's brand store in Manhattan the other day, Fabienne Michel made a routine purchase of khaki shorts. But she left the store without something equally routine: her receipt. The sales clerk had sent it to Ms. Michel by email. "It's easier," said Ms. Michel. "You can reprint it, save it, or make folders in your email."

Major retailers have begun offering electronic versions of receipts, either emailed or uploaded to password-protected websites. And more and more customers, the retailers report, are opting for paperless receipts. "As consumers, we're changing the way we shop," said Jennifer Miles. "Customers are starting to want electronic receipts."

Many people like keeping searchable records on a computer—e-receipts come in handy during tax season. Others see the paper versions as an anachronism, wasteful of resources (an estimated 9.6 million trees are cut each year for receipts in the United States, according to a digital receipt company) and as irrelevant as printed bank statements and mutual fund reports. And face it, paper receipts can be annoyances, burrowing into the bottoms of purses, getting lost in glove compartments, or fattening up wallets—only to be pulled out and puzzled over long after their usefulness has expired.

In the early 21st century, a few companies introduced electronic receipts at their retail stores. More mainstream retailers found the checkout system difficult to replicate. Now, paperless receipts have become a rite of passage for retailers trying to integrate the digital experience into their brick-and-mortar stores.

翻译名家

冯承钧（1887—1946），著名史地学家和翻译家，他潜心译述工作，在史地和交通领域撰写、翻译、校注了大量作品。他通晓法文、英文、比利时文、梵文等语言，充分利用自己的语言能力吸收和整合了前人成果，使我国的史地学翻译达到了前所未有的水平。

冯承钧一生译著不断，其代表作包括《马可波罗行纪》《佛学研究》《西突厥史料》《成吉思汗传》等。冯承钧在史地学翻译中主要采用翻译与校审、订证相结合的方法，对不少人名地名考证辨误，充分发挥了其高超的翻译水平。首先，冯承钧考订了地名和人名，并基于大量的翻译经验总结了地名和人名翻译方法，即优先采用元代史料中的译名；元史中没有的则用唐、宋史料中的译名；史料中也没有的必须用元人古时的读音来翻译。其次，冯承钧编纂了地名词典，他在翻译考证的基础上，撰著《西域地名》，为后人研究西域交通史、元代史等带来极大的便利。第三，冯承钧提出了翻译古代地名人名的三个条件：1）名从主人；2）掌握汉字古读，尤其是元代读法；3）了解北部和西部地区的若干方言。

第 11 章　翻译中的文化因素

> For truly successful translating, biculturalism is even more important than bilingualism, since words only have meanings in terms of the cultures in which they function.
>
> ——Eugene A. Nida

问题导入

1. 下面是一则商务发票中描述商品特征的部分内容，请试译。
   Commodity: cow wet blue, unsplitted, TR1 selection, medium size 42 sq. ft., average area, minimum 38 sf., free of hump.

   译文：_____
   _____

2. 和同学们一起讨论，找出翻译中的难点，并分析原因。

   难点：_____

   原因：_____

翻译知识讲座

翻译中的文化因素

　　文化指的是一个群体共同遵守的一系列相互关联的价值观、风俗习惯、法律制度等方面的总和。语言和文化密不可分，语言由文化决定并且反映文化的内涵。文化背景不同，语言的外延意义及其被赋予的联想意义也会大不相同。同一个词或同一种表达方式在不同的文化背景下会具有不同的意义，由此可能引起误解。比如 politician 一词，在英国英语中，该词为中性词，也不乏一定成分的褒义，同汉语中的"政治家"大致相当，而在美国英语中，politician 则与另一词 baby-kisser 大致相当，意为专门吃政治饭的"政客"。这说明，要学好一门语言，不仅应掌握语音、词汇、语法等语言知识，而且还要学习该语言所承载的文化信息。就翻译而言，语际转换看似是语言层面的对等转换，实际上更是文化之间的转换。

1. 文化因素与商务翻译

文化需要通过语言来表达，故而文化差异无疑会体现于语言表述中。首先，物质文化对语言的影响是多方面的，其中涉及地理位置、生活方式、服饰和艺术等。比如受地理位置影响，英国的 west wind 是温暖而湿润的，所以才有雪莱的《西风颂》，而在我国，西风常见于秋冬季节，故此汉语中的"西风"往往有萧索与寒冷之意。其次，制度文化方面的差异也会体现在语言上，不同的语言体现了不同的制度和法律。以法律中的"不可抗力"为例，源于法语中的"force majeure"在原文化语境中特指自然灾害，但是我们知道在我国"不可抗力"作为免责条款，不仅指自然灾害，也可以指战争、罢工等人为造成的阻止合同履行的社会因素。至于理念文化层面的差异，不仅可见于语言的词汇等微观方面，有时候还反映在宏观的语篇层面。从语篇层面来看，受思维方式影响，英语行文结构严谨，逻辑缜密，句式层层环套，汉语则形式疏放，铺排流散，行文似珠玉满盘，错落自然。换言之，英语多受形式约束，枝蔓之处必用形合，汉语则多表现为意合，情非得已，才屈从于形式接续，有悖于此，动辄加以承接，必然会累及节奏，阻断语气（刘全福，2011）。

鲁迅先生强调翻译具有强大的文化功能，了解文化方面的差异性及其在语言中的表现，无疑对翻译具有重要的指导意义。同其他文体的翻译一样，商务文本翻译也需要注意文化差异以及由此而引起的语言差异问题。不少人以为，商务语篇不过是格式化文本，在全球化背景下，商务文化差异及其在语言中的表现正趋于消弭。然而事实却并非如此。在全球商务沟通中，各个国家和地区通过对比反而增强了跨文化交际意识，也加强了自身的文化认同感。商务语篇翻译也同样需要对所涉及的两种文化之间的差异有所了解，或至少需要了解并掌握两种文化背景下所产生的商贸知识、商务流程、法律制度等，只有这样，才能避免因文化差异而引起的语言及语义失误。以本章"问题导入"中商务发票的翻译为例，假如对相关的商务及商贸文化不甚了解，即有可能出现有悖于商务规范的常识性错误，比如在 cow wet blue, unsplitted, TR1 selection 一语中，皮革按皮性分为头层皮、剖面皮或二层皮和再生皮，其表述形式分别为 top-grain、split leather 和 recycled leather、unsplitted 所指为无剖面皮革，TR1 selection 指的是牛皮等级，这里的 TR1 应译作"一级品皮"。free of hump 是指皮面平整光滑。

除了专业的商务术语的翻译，商务翻译中句子、句群乃至篇章的翻译无一不受文化因素的制约。请看一则宾馆的公告：

例 1 Dear Guest: In the interest of making a contribution to lessening environmental pollution and reducing waste, you are invited to place your used towels on the handrail for further use. If you wish your towels to be washed daily, please place them in the bathtub.

参考译文： 尊敬的宾客：为了支持环保事业，减少浪费，我们恳请您的帮助，如果无须更换毛巾,请将毛巾放回架上;如需要更换,请把毛巾放在浴盆内。谢谢您的合作!

此例中英文要求客人支持环保,对客人的要求直截了当,而相对应的中文告示则不然。中国文化重视人际关系,作为服务行业,宾馆首先要和客人建立良好的关系。因此在翻译中没有严格按照英文原文,用"你"作主语,而改用"我们",并加上"恳请"和"您"这类措辞,让客人感受到尊重,有享受服务的感觉。因此中文告示显得委婉,语气更柔和。由此可见,在商务文体翻译中,文化因素也同样是一个不可忽视的重要问题。

商务文本翻译所涉及的文化因素可以分为两大类:一是源语和目的语本身所反映的文化差异及其所引起的语言表述差异;二是商务文本所涉及的专业知识和商务文化知识,比如国际贸易、国际金融及国际商法等方面的相关专业知识,又比如商务信函简洁清晰而不失礼貌等隐性规则。这两类文化因素都会对商务文本的翻译产生影响,其中第二类的影响更加具体而直接。以国际贸易合同翻译为例,译者必须掌握中英两种文化环境中合同的专业术语、用词和句式特点,而且还要掌握关于合同的专业知识,以及合同文本的规范。

例2 Applicant, within 30 days upon receipt of notice of approval from competent authority, shall go through industrial and commercial registration.

参考译文: 申请人应在接到主管机关批准之后30日内办理工商登记手续。

英文合同的表达往往句子冗长,结构复杂,还往往使用从句,将状语、同位语或定语插入主句中间,这是合同英语的一大特点。上例中的 within 30 days upon receipt of notice of approval from competent authority 为插入的状语,但是为了避免造成歧义,译成汉语时,这个状语通常放于它所修饰的动词之前或之后,由副词或介词短语来充当,结构上也比较简洁。

2. 商务文本中文化因素的翻译策略

文化因素的翻译涉及两种常见的翻译策略:归化和异化。所谓归化,指的是遵守译入语语言文化当前的主流价值观,对原文采用保守的同化手段,以迎合本土的典律、出版潮流和政治需求;所谓异化,则是指一定程度地保留原文的异域性而故意打破译入语语言常规的翻译策略。这两种翻译策略反映了译者对待源语和译入语之间文化差异的不同态度。归化其实就是要淡化文化差异,使译文更好地被译入语读者理解和接纳,异化则要在译文中反映出原有的差异,给译入语读者带来不同的文化体验与感受。归化和异化各有利弊,前者可保证译文通顺易懂,后者则能够保留外国的原质文化(鲁迅,2005),还可以引进某些独特的表达方法。我们不应将两种策略对立起来,而要根据翻译文本的类型和翻译的目的加以取舍。在商务翻译中,译者根据自身的认知,在实现语用等效的动态过程中平衡不同文化因素,灵活使用归化和异化两种翻译策略。这强调了语境因素对翻译决策的限制,避免了功能目的翻译理论对译者主体性的过度夸大。由于商务翻译传递的意义是在译者与语境互动中构建的,翻译中的选择也必须顺应动态语境,既考虑语言语境、情景语境和文化语境的客观存在,又考虑译者基于认知能力和认知倾向对语境的动态构建与顺应。商务翻译中的语境制约正是通过译者的选择顺应来实现,是译者根据不同文化语境及语境中的文化要素进行译入语重构,实现商务交际目标的过程（徐珺、肖海燕，2015）。比如广告翻译旨在打动读者，激发其购买欲望，因此主要采用归化策略，商务合同所强调的是严谨性与权威性，因而翻译时应该主要以原文为指向，为忠实于原文意义，有时甚至不惜牺牲译文的通顺与畅达。翻译过程中，译者应合理取舍，灵活掌握。

首先，翻译之前应通读全文，明确所译文本的类型及其所涉及的语言文化因素以及相关的专业知识。以商务信函为例，商务信函翻译要遵从礼貌原则，行文应简洁清晰，还要符合其特定的文体特征，体现商务信函的特点和专业水准。为了体现商务信函的专业性和礼貌原则，译文应尽量使用简洁的书面语，也可以套用汉语商务信函中约定俗成的惯用语。

例 3 There are quantities of this item here, in different weights and sizes, with varied colors and shapes. The price is very reasonable and the quotation will be given upon request.

参考译文： 我方现有各种不同重量、不同体积、颜色丰富、形状各异的该货品，数量甚巨。价格合理，受函报价。

其次要考虑中西语言文化差异的影响，仔细分析原文用词特点与篇章结构特征，认真思考翻译过程中可能遇到的因语言文化差异而产生的转换问题。

例 4 The Buyer shall have the right to claim against the Seller for compensation of losses within 60 days after arrival of the goods at the port of destination, should the quality of the goods be found not in conformity with the specifications stipulated in the Contract after re-inspection by the China Commodity Inspection Bureau and the Buyer shall have the right to claim against the Seller for compensation of short weight within 60 days after arrival of the goods at the port of destination, should the weight be found not in conformity with that stipulated in the Bill of Lading after reinspection by the CCIB.

参考译文： 若货物经中国商品检验局复检后发现质量与本合同之规定不符，买方有权于货物抵达目的港后的 60 天内向卖方提出索赔。若经中国商品检验局复检发现货物重量与提单所示不符，买方有权于货物抵达目的港后的 60 天内向卖方提出短重索赔。

译文按照原文所含的两层意义断句，每个分句中列出索赔的条件和时间，这样合同就不会产生歧义，同时也符合汉语句式较短的特点。

最后还应严格遵守商务翻译的一般标准，文化差异的化解应以原文信息的准确传递为前提。商务翻译的标准可大致概括为"准确"二字，这也是由商务文本的文体特征所决定的。

例 5 The date of the receipt issued by transportation department concerned shall be regarded as the date of delivery of the goods.

参考译文： 由承运机构所开具的收据日期即被视为交货日期。

在本句中，后置定语 concerned 一词体现了英语独特的思维方式，若采用异化策略将其笼统地表述为"有关的"，即会因语义模糊而无法准确地再现原文所包含的信息，可以依照商业流程稍作变通，使原文信息得以完整而准确地再现。

文化因素的翻译有归化和异化两种策略，两者各有利弊，翻译过程中不能简单地运用其中一种原则，宜互相补充，灵活取舍。具体到商务文本的翻译过程，译者既要考虑源语和译入语之间的文化差异，尊重译入语读者的阅读习惯，同时又要体现商务文本的礼貌原则和专业性，遵从商务文本简洁清晰而不失礼貌的隐性规则。

商务语篇翻译与解析

Intercultural Communication

Today's world can (1) <u>be characterized as</u> a global village. (2) <u>The international and domestic changes in the past few decades have brought us into direct and indirect contact with people who, because of their cultural diversity, often behave in ways that we do not understand</u>. Thanks to the rapid expansion of worldwide transportation and communication networks, it is no longer difficult to find social and professional situations in which members of once isolated groups of people communicate with members of other cultural groups. Communication satellites, sophisticated television transmission equipment, and the World Wide Web now allow people throughout the world to share information and ideas at the same time. It is now possible for a person in one country to communicate with a person in another country within seconds.

As the population of the world has increased, it has become more difficult to remain detached and isolated from global tensions and conflicts. When people of different nationalities and ethnic origins, (3) <u>who frequently speak different languages and hold different convictions attempt to work and live together</u>, conflicts can easily arise. We should not forget that the reality of a global economy makes today's contacts far more commonplace than in any other period of the world's history. Multinational corporations now participate in various international business arrangements such as (4) <u>joint ventures, licensing agreements, turnkey projects, subcontracts, and management contracts</u>. Each country's economy is now tied to the economic fortunes of others. These and countless other economic ties mean that it would not be unusual for you to work for an organization that does business in many countries or for you to conduct business in remote parts of the world.

In a world of international interdependence, the ability to understand and communicate effectively with people from other cultures takes on extreme urgency. However, we may find intercultural communication different from communication within our own cultural group. Even if we overcome the natural barriers of language difference, we may (5) <u>fail</u> to understand and to be understood. Misunderstanding may even become the rule rather than the exception. And, if we are unaware of the significant role culture plays in communication, we may place the blame for communication failure on those other people. This is unfortunate because our real problem is culture and the difficulty of communicating across cultural boundaries.

(6) It is widely recognized that one of the characteristics separating human from other animals is our development of culture. The development of human culture is made possible through communication. It is through communication that culture is transmitted from one generation to another. Culture and communication are intertwined so closely that Hall maintains that "culture is communication" and "communication is culture." (7) In other words, we communicate the way we do because we are raised in a particular culture and learn its language, rules, and norms. Because we learn the language, rules, and norms of our culture by a very early age (between five and ten years old), we generally are unaware of how culture influences our behavior in general and our communication in particular.

When we communicate with people from other cultures, we are often confronted with languages, rules, and norms different from our own. (8) Confronting these differences can be a source of insight into the rules and norms of our own culture, as well as being a source of frustration or gratification. Therefore, what we have to learn is to understand culture, communication, how culture influences communication, and process of communication between people from different cultures. Such knowledge is extremely important. In fact, it is necessary if we are to fully comprehend the daily events of today's multicultural world. It will help us not only analyze our intercultural encounters in order to determine where misunderstandings occur, but also determine how these misunderstandings can be minimized in future interactions.

难点解析

（1）be characterized as 意为"以……为特点"，本句如直译为"当今世界以地球村为特点"，显然不符合汉语表达习惯。汉语修饰成分多为形容词或形容词词组，如"四川菜的特点是麻辣"等，故此将其转译为形容词"典型的"可谓得当。

（2）本句较为冗长，其中 who 引导的定语从句修饰 people，而定语从句中又出现了原因状语。由于定语从句较为复杂，译为前置定语会有些拖沓。鉴于此，本句可拆分成两个部分，定语从句另行译出，如此一来，主、从结构之间内在的转折关系也就明朗了。

（3）非限定性定语从句与主句联系不甚紧密，翻译时通常可处理为独立成分。画线部分为非限定性定语从句，被处理为独立状语，原文中 people 与 speak 及 hold 之间的逻辑关系也就无法保留，而只能将两个动词省略，并将原来的宾语提前用作主语，如此变通后，译文就更加自然了。

（4）商务英语术语的翻译需要予以重视。这些术语意义相对稳定，翻译时不能随意处之，而应该遵从约定俗成的原则，例如 joint ventures（合资企业）、licensing agreements（许可协议）、turnkey projects（工程总承包）、subcontracts（分包工程）、management contracts（管理合同）等。

（5）fail 一词常具有否定意义，类似的例子还有 lack、miss、deny、exclude、run out of、keep (from)、overlook、absence、ignorant、free from、short of、exclusive of、beyond、without、above、except、save、but 等。除此之外，某些英语固定结构也可用于表达否定意义，例如 more...than、rather than、know better than 等。需要指出的是，它们并非否定词语，其所谓的否定意义，主要是从英汉翻译角度而言的，也就是说，将上述词语或结构译成汉语时，常常需要运用"不……"或"没有……"等否定形式进行转换，这种正说反译法的目的在于顺从汉语表达习惯，使译文更自然。

（6）原文中多次使用被动语态，目的在于强调论述的客观性。汉语尽管不排除被动表达，但使用频率远不及英语。此外，某些英语被动语态也无法完全移植到汉语中，故而常常需要进行语态转换，将 it is widely recognized 译为"众所周知"即是典型的例子。separate...from 的字面意义是"把……从……独立出来"，此处可译为"人类与动物的显著区别就在于……"。

（7）本句虽然不长，但是却包含两个从句：一个是 the way 引导的方式状语从句，另一个是 because 引导的原因状语从句。而且 the way we do 这种英文表述结构还很容易束缚我们的思维，造成翻译腔。此时，应该吃透原文，顺应译文表达，可舍形取义，译为"我们以自己的方式"。

（8）本句中的 a source of 意为"来源、出处"，此处需要根据词典释义和语境引申其意义。insight 虽然是名词，通过 into 这个介词引出了洞察或深入了解的对象，翻译时可以译为汉语的动词。

商务知识讲座

跨文化交际

跨文化交际是指不同文化背景的人们之间传递信息、知识和情感，以及彼此理解和沟通的过程，涉及社会学、心理学、人类学、管理学等许多领域。随着经济全球化的发展趋势和国际商务活动的日益频繁，跨文化商务交际的地位日渐突出，成为跨文化交际学中的焦点。跨文化商务交际指不同文化背景的人在从事商务活动中产生的交际行为。企业将产品推向国际市场，跨国公司管理设在不同国家和地区的子公司，都涉及跨文化商务交际。

跨文化交际的前提条件是对文化的了解。文化犹如洋葱，层层剥开才能探求文化的内核。文化包括物质层、制度层以及理念层。第一层是物质层，这是直观可见的，包括语言、服饰、仪式、艺术等；第二层是制度层，既包含成文的法律法规，也包括约定俗成的风俗习惯；第三层是理念层，主要包括抽象的思维模式和核心价值体系，通常起决定和主导作用，是文化的核心层，也是一种文化区别于其他文化的重要因素。跨文化交际比较复杂，超越了简单的语言层面的交流，涉及信仰、价值观等核心元素。根据不同文化的价值取向，学者们将文化划分为不同类型，其中最有影响的是霍夫斯塔德（Hofstede, 1991）的衡量价值观的维度。他将文化划分为个人主义—集体主义、高权力距离—低权力距离、不确定因素的高回避—低回避、男性主义—女性主义四组类型。从交际模式的角度区分，根据语境在交际中的作用，霍尔（Hall，1990）将文化划分为高语境与低语境两种类型。这些文化类型的划分明确了最基本的文化组群特征，给从事国际商务的人们提供了简化的文化信息，使他们能够推断来自不同类型文化背景的人们的交际方式，从而在商务活动中理解文化差异，避免文化冲突。

　　文化差异不仅体现在价值观和交际方面，而且表现在不同的商务活动中。文化差异加大了商务交际的难度，因此跨文化交际能力在商务活动中是不可或缺的，往往决定着商业活动的成败。商务人士的跨文化交际能力体现在他们是否能够理解文化差异，能否根据不同的文化环境采取适合的交际方式。比如，在商务写作中，不同文化对商务写作的规范不同，从事商务活动的人员必须分析交际对象的文化背景、态度和情感，选择恰当的措辞和最适当的交际渠道。了解和尊重当地的文化，特别是遵守特定的商务礼仪不仅有助于提高跨文化商务交际的成功率，而且有助于树立良好的公司形象。

　　跨文化交际能力体现在国际营销、跨国公司管理等各个方面。如今，文化环境已成为国际营销的关键因素。在国际营销中，必须对价值观差异进行研究，尊重各个文化群体的价值观。营销方式涵盖了语言和非语言交际两方面的内容，而且与产品所要传达的文化意义和理念息息相关。如果国际营销中忽视了消费者的文化背景，违背了消费者的宗教礼仪，可能会带来严重的负面影响。美国迪士尼公司初到欧洲，因为对消费者的饮食习惯和度假习惯缺乏了解，禁止在乐园内售卖酒精饮品而受到游客抵制，乐园酒店也不能及时有效应对退房高峰的客流，从而引发了一系列问题，导致迪士尼乐园的品牌形象受损，成为国际营销的反面教材。跨文化交际能力对跨国公司的管理也至关重要，精明的企业领导能够意识到多样化的团队带来的竞争优势，多样化团队可以提供多元化的视角和观点，帮助企业理解不同市场，也能够让企业具备更强的人力资源优势。

　　跨文化交际能力有助于跨国公司协调企业文化与当地文化，有利于员工产生认同感，从而使管理更有效。可以说，一个企业的成功，不仅取决于它的生产能力，而且取决于它的文化能力，在国际商务活动中，更取决于它的跨文化交际能力。

翻译练习

I. 思考题

1. 阐述文化因素对文本的意义及其对语篇结构产生的影响。
2. 结合实例说明文化因素对商务英语文本翻译的准确性有什么作用。

II. 从"Intercultural Communication"中摘录给你深刻印象的句子或词组。

1. _____
2. _____
3. _____

4. _____
5. _____

III. 商务术语翻译

barrier to communication	
communication style	
communicative distance	
cultural adaptation	
cultural attribution	
cultural dimension	
cultural empathy	
cultural faux pas	
cultural iceberg	
cultural imperialism	
cultural sensitivity	
culture shock	
decoding	
encoding	
face maintenance theory	
high-context culture	
interaction skill	
intercultural awareness	
intercultural communication competence	
intercultural knowledge	
intercultural management	
intercultural marketing	
interpersonal identity	
loss of identity	

monochronic	
non-verbal communication	
polychronic	
power distance	
pragmatic failure	
tolerance of difference	

IV. 句子翻译

1. Concern with the difficulties cultural diversity poses for effective communication has given rise to the marriage of culture and communication and to the recognition of intercultural communication as a field of study.

2. In most cases, the Chinese discourse patterns seem to be the inverse of English discourse conventions in that definitive summary statement of main arguments is delayed till the end.

3. Each person has, around him or her, an invisible bubble of space which expands and contracts depending on a number of things: the relationship to the people nearby, the person's emotional state, cultural background, and the activity being performed. Few people are allowed to penetrate this bit of mobile territory even for a short period of time.

4. How far you experience culture shock will depend on a number of factors, including your personality, how different the culture is from your own, the social support you receive, and the purpose of your stay.

5. Today, international businesspeople increasingly find themselves working in multi-cultural environments, dealing with differences in everything from communication styles and social etiquette to core values.

6. Every large grouping of human beings has its own collection of ideas and habits, passed on from one generation to the next. These ways of thinking and behaving are usually the ones which have best helped members of the group to deal with their surroundings.

7. Through increased cultural awareness and understanding, the ability to peacefully coexist with people who do not necessarily share our life styles or beliefs could benefit us not only in our own neighborhood but could be the decisive factor in maintaining world peace.

8. The art of negotiating is hard enough in your own country, dealing with colleagues who think like you, process information as you do, share a common set of values, and speak the same language. Now consider a situation where there is little shared knowledge and

few common values and a different language is spoken, and you can readily see just how complicated negotiating international transactions can become.

9. Culture is like an iceberg. It's very beautiful but very dangerous. Only a small part of culture is visible. For instance, food, dress, paintings, architecture, and dance are apparent to eyes. But a greater part of culture is hidden under the water, such as beliefs, attitudes, perceptions, and values. They are out of our awareness. This makes our study of culture difficult.

10. As strangers in the new land, they are subject to a greater or lesser necessity to conform to the communication patterns of the host society. Permanent immigrants or long-term settlers generally have a greater need to conform than temporary sojourners, yet no one is completely free from having to understand and manage the various communication patterns sanctioned and operating in the host culture.

V. 篇章翻译

Organizational culture is typically understood as a system of shared values and norms that define and guide appropriate attitudes and behaviors. Culture is represented by artifacts (e.g., images, symbols), values, and assumptions held in common by the members of an organization. These elements then create norms that act as a "social glue" and guide behavior. From a cultural perspective, formulating a precise definition of organizational culture will require an integration of top-down signifiers provided by leaders and founders, as well as agreed-upon norms influencing individual behaviors.

It is well-recognized that an organization's culture to some extent has become the ubiquitous clarion call for both organizational successes and organizational failures. In fact, some scholars believe that it has embraced the opaque nature of the construct, leading to a lack of understanding of how organizational culture truly affects organizational outcomes.

Case studies in the US, Japan, and China have revealed that organizational culture can function in the following three aspects of the company operations: First, it can enhance employees' interpersonal motives (cooperation, competition, and autonomy); second, it can increase the company's productivity and creativity; and third, it can promote organizational viability and overall performance. The importance of organizational culture becomes salient as the organization becomes institutionalized and rigid over the course of its existence. Its importance lies in its ever-changing cultural forms and innovation throughout the life cycle of a firm.

翻译名家

鲁迅（1881—1936），我国著名文学家、思想家、革命家、教育家，五四新文化运动的重要参与者，中国现代文学的奠基人之一，在翻译领域具有重大贡献。

鲁迅坚持通过译作的传播逐步改良社会，改变国人的生活方式和精神世界。鲁迅在翻译中主要采用异化策略，开创了"硬译"这种特殊时期的翻译方法，被称为"硬译之祖"。鲁迅强调为了引进外国的原质文化，"硬译"无疑是首选策略，即他所描述的"除了几处不得已的地方，几乎是逐字译"的方法。硬译是对当时以归化为主流翻译方式的反叛，鲁迅发现主流译作的弊病在于把外国的新思想置于中国原有的儒家礼仪之中，完全丧失了翻译改造社会的初衷。他选择翻译被压迫民族和国家的文学作品，让中国读者理解和感受压迫下的抗争。在翻译过程中，为了保留原作的精神和力量，他力求忠实，再现原文中的意义，如果实在找不出更好的语言表述，他宁可创造生硬晦涩的方式进行翻译。通过"硬译"，鲁迅抛弃了迎合大众口味和追求流畅的本土化翻译，将翻译变成了文艺革命的利器，达到了教育青年人和有识之士的文化及政治目的。

鲁迅以"开民智"为己任，翻译了大量西方思想佳作，充分发挥了翻译的文化和政治功能，成为挽救民族危亡的译者楷模。

第 12 章　翻译症与对策

> One must be wary of "translatorese"—a queer language that counts words but misses their living force.
>
> ——John Ciardi

问题导入

1. 比较下面的原文和译文，并对各译文的优缺点进行点评，尤其注意几个译文中 surplus 和 enter 的翻译。

   原文　It is widely reported that there is a huge surplus of diamonds ready to enter world markets.

   译文1　一个被媒体广为报道的事实是，有大量多出来的钻石随时准备进入世界市场。
   译文2　许多报道指出，可随时进入全球市场的钻石储量惊人。
   译文3　有关钻石严重富余、可随时投放全球市场的报道比比皆是。
   译文4　据媒体广泛报道，钻石的库存量十分惊人，并可随时投放全球市场。

   点评：_____
   _____
   _____
   _____

2. 译文1中"一个被媒体广为报道的事实是"在意义表述上是否正确？在形式特征上是否符合汉语习惯？可读性如何？造成这种译文的原因何在？
   _____
   _____
   _____
   _____

翻译知识讲座

翻译症与对策

所谓翻译症是指在翻译过程中因过分拘泥于原文表达形式而出现的种种不合乎目的语规范从而损害译文可读性的问题，如语义不通、表达不畅等。翻译症不能简单地等同于误译。许多情况下，表现为翻译症的译文往往并不存在对原文内容理解上的错误，而只是不符合或不完全符合目的语的表达规范。因为理解和表达是翻译过程中两个相对独立的阶段，能正确理解原文并不一定意味着能准确恰当地表达原文的意义。

1. 翻译症的表现

孙致礼（2003）指出，翻译症主要体现在两个方面：一是语言不通，往往让读者不知所云，甚至把读者引向歧路；二是语言不顺，既违背了汉语表达规范，又影响读者的阅读兴趣。下文将从语义、文辞两方面入手，结合一些真实译例加以探析。

（1）语义不通，晦涩难懂

译文语义不通由多种原因造成，如词不达意、语序混乱、转承不当等。

例 1 The railroads did not stop growing because the need for passenger and freight transport declined, but because it was not filled by the railroads themselves.

初看这个句子，似乎并无难点，于是很快翻译为："铁路并没有因为客货运输的需求下降而停止增长，而是因为铁路自身的需求尚未满足。"但是细读译文，会觉得意义含混不清，且逻辑不通。

其实，原文是英语中的一种特殊句式——否定转移。否定转移是指表示原因的状语从句如果和否定的主句一起使用，此时的否定词不是修饰主句中的动词，而是会转移到原因状语从句，即否定原因状语从句。就本句而言，主句中的 not 并不是否定 stop，而是否定 because 引导的原因状语从句。

参考译文： 铁路运输量停止增长，不是因为客货运输的需求下降，而是因为铁路运输量不饱满。

例 2 We believe that they are wrong, and that oil is close to a peak. This is not the "peak oil" widely discussed several years ago, when several theorists, who have since gone strangely quiet, reckoned that supply would flatten and then fall. We believe that demand, not supply, could decline.

原译 我们认为他们错了，石油需求量已几近峰值。这里所说的峰值不是几年前广泛讨论的"石油供应峰值"，当时一些如今保持出奇安静的理论家估计，石油供应量将达到峰值，随后将开始下降。我们认为，是石油需求量而非石油供给量下降。

参考译文： 我们认为，他们错了，石油的确已接近峰值。但这里所说的"峰值"并不是供给量的峰值。几年前曾有几位理论家认为石油供给量已经达到峰值，此后会持平，继而会走低。他们当时的讨论可谓热烈，而现在却全都沉默得出奇。我们认为，现在接近峰值的是需求量，有可能从此走低的也是需求量，而非供给量。

原译将插入语 when several theorists, who have since gone strangely quiet 译为 theorists 的前置定语，从而产生形如"当时一些如今保持出奇安静的理论家"的句子，影响了语义的流畅表达。参考译文则将此定语部分与上下文的相关信息结合，拆分为两个独立完整的句子，避免了语义的混淆。另外，对于原文没有直接表述但十分关键、不交代清楚便可能引起误解的内容，参考译文进行了强调："我们认为，现在接近峰值的是需求量，有可能从此走低的也是需求量，而非供给量。"虽然此处译文字数可能略多，但对消除误解、明确原文语义内容而言还是有意义的。

（2）文辞欠佳，冗杂拖沓

翻译中的某些表达并不直接影响原文意义的传递，但由于语言表述存在种种瑕疵，同样令人难以卒读。

例 3 We are now discovering that regional and national differences are not dissolving and that Europeans think and act very differently from one another.

原译 我们现在正在发现，地区的和国家的差异并没有在溶解，以及欧洲人想的和做的都彼此很不一样。

参考译文： 我们渐渐发现，欧洲各国、各地区之间的差异依然存在，其观念与做法更是千差万别。

原译在再现原文主要信息方面基本无误，但言辞表达欠妥。首先，we are now discovering 中的现在进行时仅表示一个不间断、逐渐发展的过程，而非强调目前正在进行，译文中"现在正在"四个字多而无当。其次，这里的 regional and national 并非泛指，而是专指欧洲，最好在译文中给予明示。第三，把 dissolve 一词译为"溶解"，明显照搬词典释义，未考虑到词与词之间的搭配要求。第四，"想的和做的"在语义上没有问题，但一是较为啰唆，二是用词过于生活化；建议用四字格替代，如"所想所做、所思所为"等，或者像参考译文一样，用"观念与做法"等较为正式的词汇。细心的读者还会发现，在原译中短短的一句话中有四个"的"字，赘词过多影响了译文的简洁与流畅。

请研读以下译例，分析比较参考译文相比原译的改进之处。

例 4 This lack of unity is Europe's third and most profound crisis, one that underlies the continent's economic and political woes.

原译 团结的缺乏，是位于欧洲这个大洲经济和政治弊病之下的，最为深刻的第三个危机。

参考译文： 除了政治、经济两方面的顽疾，欧洲还潜藏着第三种危机，也是最深刻的危机——不团结。

例 5 The sort of environmental policies that are reducing the thirst for fuel in Europe and America by imposing ever-tougher fuel-efficiency standards on vehicles are also being adopted in the emerging economies.

原译 一些环境政策通过强制车辆符合更严格的燃油效率标准而使得美国和欧洲减少了对石油的需求，而这些环境政策也已经为新兴国家采用。

参考译文： 新兴经济体也开始仿效欧美，通过实施更严格的车辆燃效标准来减少对燃油的迫切需求。

2. 克服翻译症的对策

余光中（2002）曾对翻译症做过分析，他认为有以下三方面的原因："第一，见字而不见句；第二，以为英文的任何字都可以在中文里找到同义词；第三，以为把英文句子的每一部分都译过来后，就等于把那句子译过来了。"事实上，英语有很多词汇在汉语中都没有现成的对应词汇，英语句子在译成汉语时，往往需要根据汉语语言个性增加或删除一些词汇，有些甚至需要大动手术，调整句子中词汇的顺序，方能成为文通字顺的译文。

在具体的翻译转换过程中，准确理解原文意义，理清原文的逻辑关系是第一步。接着，在选择适当的目的语词汇来表达时，应注意所选词汇的引申意义和深层内涵。此外还应注意调整译文语序，避免对原文结构和语序亦步亦趋，应依据汉语表达习惯灵活调整。

例 6 Intense competition, a growing number of channels changing customer behavior, and commoditized products make brand management and the process of creating a differentiated brand experience particularly important and complex. This complexity grows as firms expand operations into new markets and in new languages. Cultural differences, a lack of local marketing expertise, fragmented channels, and an absence of marketing process coordination all lead to a disjointed brand experience.

原译 激烈的竞争、越来越多的渠道改变了客户行为，以及商品化的产品使得品牌管理和创造差异化品牌体验的过程变得尤为重要和复杂。随着公司向新市场和新语言拓展业务，这种复杂性也在增加。文化差异、缺乏本地营销专业知识、渠道分散以及缺乏营销流程协调，都会导致品牌体验脱节。

原译读起来非常拗口，有些地方晦涩难懂：一是"商品化的产品""向新市场和新语言拓展业务""品牌体验脱节"等词组的意义不清晰，令人费解；二是整个句子读起来不顺畅，中文表达的是英文的思维方式，"激烈的竞争""越来越多的渠道改变了客户行为"和"商品化的产品"这三个并列的成分有的是短语，有的是句子，结构不平衡；"使得……变得……"是典型的欧化汉语。针对原译存在的问题，翻译时应该深入理解原文，将原文意义融会于心，然后再根据汉语特点重新组织句子。

参考译文： 商业竞争日益加剧，影响消费行为的渠道越来越多，产品日渐出现低价化趋势，这些都凸显了品牌经营管理和品牌差异化体验的复杂性和重要性。企业在不断开拓新市场发展新业务，需要使用新的语言，此时情况就更为复杂。文化差异、管理本地市场的专业知识匮乏、渠道管理混乱、营销环节失调都直接导致了对品牌体验的不一致。

从词汇层面来看，参考译文将 commoditized 一词的意义进行了引申，避免了语义模糊；将 make 一词的词义根据汉语特点进行融会贯通，译为"凸显"，避免了欧化汉语表达；将抽象名词 lack 和 absence 转换为谓语动词。从句子结构来看，参考译文使用了三个并列的主谓结构"商业竞争日益加剧""影响消费行为的渠道越来越多"和"产品日渐出现低价化趋势",实现了句子结构的平衡,符合汉语结构特点。随后用"这些"来实现前后内容的关联,达到了有效衔接,避免了较长的主语与谓语距离过远可能带来的语义模糊问题。最后一句中使用四个并列的主谓结构,意义清晰明确,读起来结构平稳。

试分析比较译例 7 的各种原译的优劣之处,并说明参考译文的改进体现在哪些方面。

例 7 Luckily for the clean-tech industry, a much larger investor stepped in to replace the retreating venture capitalists—the federal government.

原译1 对清洁技术产业来说幸运的是,一个实力更强的投资者介入,步了撤退中的风险投资家之后尘——美国联邦政府。

原译2 让清洁技术产业倍感庆幸的是,风投尚未撤尽,实力更为雄厚的投资者就来了——美国联邦政府。

原译3 清洁技术产业运气真是不错,风投前脚刚走,后脚就来了个更大的投资者——美国联邦政府。

原译4 清洁技术产业可谓时运亨通,风投尚未撤尽,更大的投资者翩然而至——美国联邦政府。

参考译文 1: 清洁技术产业的一大幸事便是:在风险投资公司接二连三地撤资之时,一家实力更为雄厚的投资者——美国联邦政府——接踵而至。

参考译文 2: 在风险投资公司接二连三地从清洁技术产业撤资之时,一家实力更为雄厚的投资者——美国联邦政府——接踵而至,这是清洁技术产业的一大幸事。

总之,要克服翻译症,译者应注意以下三个方面:一是要深刻认识英语和汉语在语言、思维、文化上的差异,树立正确的翻译观,形成开放、包容、灵活的翻译理念,避免把忠实、对等等概念狭隘化、绝对化;二是要掌握丰富的转换技巧,并佐以大量的练习,积累丰富的实战经验;三是要加强语言表达方面的基本功,培养正确、敏锐的语感。

商务语篇翻译与解析

Currency Risk

Currency risk results from changes in exchange rates between a bank's domestic currency and other currencies. (1) <u>It originates from a mismatch when assets and liabilities are valued in different currencies</u>. That mismatch may cause a bank to experience losses as a result of adverse exchange rate movements when the bank has an open, on- or off-balance-sheet position, either spot or forward, in an individual foreign currency. In recent years, a market environment with freely floating exchange rates has practically become the global norm. This has opened the doors for speculative trading opportunities and increased currency risks. (2) <u>The relaxation of exchange controls and</u>

the liberalization of cross-border capital movements have fueled a tremendous growth in international financial markets. The volume and growth of global foreign exchange trading has far exceeded the growth of international capital flows and has contributed to greater exchange rate volatility and therefore currency risk.

Currency risk arises from a mismatch between the value of assets and that of capital and liabilities denominated in foreign currency (or vice versa), or because of a mismatch between foreign receivables and foreign payables that are (3) expressed in domestic currency. Such mismatches may exist between both principal and interest due. Currency risk is speculative and can therefore result in a gain or loss, depending on the direction of exchange rate shifts and whether a bank is net long or net short in the foreign currency. For example, in the case of a net long position in foreign currency, domestic currency depreciation will result in a net gain for a bank and appreciation will produce a loss. Under a net short position, exchange rate movements will have the opposite effect.

(4) In principle, the fluctuations in the value of domestic currency that creates currency risk result from changes in foreign and domestic interest rates that are, in turn, brought about by differences in inflation. Fluctuations such as these are normally motivated by macroeconomic factors and are manifested over relatively long periods of time, although currency market sentiment can often accelerate recognition of the trend. Other macroeconomic aspects that affect the domestic currency value are the volume and direction of a country's trade and capital flows. Short-term factors, such as expected or unexpected political events, changed expectations on the part of market participants, or speculation-based currency trading, may also give rise to currency changes. All these factors can affect the supply and demand for a currency and therefore the day-to-day movements of the exchange rate in currency markets. In practical terms, currency risk comprises the following:

• (5) Transaction risk, or the price-based impact of exchange rate changes on foreign receivables and foreign payables—that is, the difference in price at which they are collected or paid and the price at which they are recognized in local currency in the financial statements of a bank or corporate entity.

• Economic or business risk related to the impact of exchange rate changes on a country's long-term or a company's competitive position. For example, a depreciation of the local currency may cause a decline in imports and greater exports.

• Revaluation risk or translation risk, which arises when a bank's foreign currency positions are revalued in domestic currency or when a parent institution conducts financial reporting or periodic consolidation of financial statements.

(6) Other risks related to international aspects of foreign currency business are incurred by banks conducting foreign exchange operations. One such risk is a form of credit risk that relates to the default of the counterparty to a foreign exchange contract. (7) In such instances, even a bank with balanced books may find itself inadvertently left

with an uncovered exchange position. Another form of credit risk peculiar to exchange operations is the time-zone-related settlement risk. This arises when an exchange contract involves two settlements that take place at different times due to a time-zone difference, and the counterparty or the payment agent defaults in the interim. The maturity mismatching of foreign currency positions can also result in interest rate risk between the currencies concerned: A bank can suffer losses as a result of changes in interest rate differentials and of concomitant changes in the forward exchange premiums, or discounts, if it has any mismatches with forward contracts or derivatives of a similar nature.

There are many activities of banks that involve risk taking, but there are few in which a bank may so quickly incur large losses as in uncovered foreign exchange transactions. This is why currency risk management deserves the close attention of the bank's board and senior management. (8) The board of directors should establish the objectives and principles of currency risk management. These should specifically include setting appropriate limits to the risks taken by the bank in its foreign exchange business and establishing measures to ensure that there are proper internal control procedures covering this area of the bank's business. Within this framework, specific policies and limits should be determined by a risk management committee such as the asset-liability management committee. The policy guidelines should be periodically reviewed and updated to properly match the bank's risk profile with the quality of its risk management systems and staff skills.

The policy guidelines should also reflect changing circumstances in domestic and international currency markets, (9) accommodating possible changes in the currency system—for example, in the form of capital controls introduced as the result of political decisions or underlying macroeconomic conditions of particular countries that would affect the currency exchange rate. In addition, the policies should specify the frequency of revaluation of foreign currency positions for accounting and risk management purposes. In principle, the frequency of revaluation and reporting should be commensurate with the size and specific nature of the bank's currency risk exposures.

难点解析

(1) 产生翻译症的一大原因在于过分拘泥于原文的形式，导致译语表达不地道、不自然。如果不能合理调整句序，It originates... 一句可能被译成："它来自当资产与负债被用不同的货币来评估时的某种不匹配"，令读者费解。通过调整句序，可以把"A 来自 B"这一结构变成"B 产生 A"，且使 B 成为相对独立的命题，这样译文逻辑更加清晰。此外，应摒弃见到 when 就不假思索地译为"当……的时候"的习惯，此处可依据上下文的需要弱化其意义，使译文更加符合汉语的表达习惯。

(2) 本句中 relaxation 和 liberalization 这两个并列的抽象名词反映了英语静态、抽象的思维特征。照搬此结构，译成"外汇管制的放松与跨境资本流动的自由化推动了国际金融市场的巨大发展"

也未尝不可，但这样的译文忽略了汉语以动词为主线和倾向动态的思维习惯，失去了汉语的特质，因此不宜提倡。

（3）翻译时比较容易出现的一个问题就是照搬词典释义，例如本句中的 expressed 译成"表达"，就会造成歧义。

（4）本句中的 in principle 不宜译成"原则上"。事实上，不少词典均把该短语解释为 in theory，即"理论上"；根据上下文的不同，还可能将其译为"一般情况下"等。另外在翻译本句时还要注意调整语序，按汉语的逻辑顺序来重新组织译文。

（5）在翻译过程中常常需要将原文的句子结构打散、重构，包括改动其标点等。Transaction risk... 一句作为上文 the following 的三个同位语之一，整体上作为一个名词短语而存在，只不过通过 or 与 that is 进行了扩充。鉴于英汉语表达习惯上的差异，翻译时要注意调整语序，变换结构，才能使译文准确达意，且顺畅自然。下文中的 Economic or business risk... 和 Revaluation risk or translation risk... 情况类似。

（6）本句是被动语态，结构并不复杂，如照搬原句的结构将其译为"其他与货币生意的国际方面相关的风险可以被做外汇业务的银行招致"，则其行文拖沓、结构凌乱，且与汉语的逻辑格格不入，是典型的翻译腔。因此，有必要将原文拆分，按汉语的语言和思维习惯进行重组。

（7）本句有两处容易造成译文语义不清或表达不畅。首先，a bank with balanced books 中的 books 并非"书"，而是"账本"及其所代指的各种报表。其次，find itself... 结构很容易被初学者译为"发现它自己……"，从而出现类似"发现它自己被无意间和无抵扣外汇仓留在了一起"这样的句子。翻译时要多加留意。

（8）本句与下一句 These should... 一句在内容上衔接较为紧密，可考虑将两句合并为一句，译成"董事会应该建立起货币风险管理的目标与原则，为银行在外汇业务中所承受的风险设定具体的、适当的限制，并采取措施以确保将外汇业务纳入内部安全控制的流程"。

（9）accommodate 一词含义相当于 to adapt or fit，而不是其常见的"招待、提供食宿"等释义。另外，该动宾结构层次较复杂，其后还套有定语从句，翻译时要注意理清这些层次，并灵活调整译文语序。

商务知识讲座

国际金融

国际金融是国家和地区之间由于经济、政治、文化等联系而产生的货币资金的周转和流动。国际金融由国际收支、国际汇兑、国际结算、国际信用、国际投资和国际货币体系构成，它们之间相互影响，相互制约。譬如，国际收支产生国际汇兑和国际结算；国际汇兑中的货币汇率反过来对国际收支有重大影响；国际收支的许多重要项目又同国际信用和国际投资直接相关。

国际金融是一种全球性的经济活动，错综复杂，千变万化，它与国际贸易等其他国际经济往来密切交织在一起,往往牵一发而动全局。随着国际间贸易、非贸易的经济联系不断发展,国际间金融活动的范围和规模也随之日益扩大,各国经济相互依赖性加强。同时,随着垄断财团高度集中于发达国家,发展中国家的干预日益加强,国际金融所涉及的范围也更加广泛,其中主要包括:国际收支、外汇与汇率、国际货币、国际金融市场、国际金融机构、国际金融业务活动与操作等。

第二次世界大战以来,跨国银行的发展突飞猛进,成为战后国际金融领域一个令人瞩目的现象,其在国际经济中的重要性也日益为人所重视。联合国跨国公司中心对跨国银行定义如下:跨国银行是指在海外相当数量的国家和地区至少拥有五个或五个以上分支机构的商业银行。如果跨国银行的经营管理完全是全球化的,而非以母国为中心,那么它又可以被称作多国银行。

在现代国际经济运行中,各国跨国银行所处的社会经济环境与对应的经济发展阶段不同,相应的发展战略也会有所区别。但一般说来,现代跨国银行的基本特征主要有以下四个:第一,跨国银行一般具有全球战略目标,这是现代跨国银行区别于其他银行机构与非银行金融机构的重要特征。第二,跨国银行往往实施集权化管理以确保全球战略目标的顺利实现及自身系统的有效运行。第三,跨国银行资金实力雄厚,业务范围广阔。跨国银行拥有的资产少则数十亿美元,多则上千亿美元。雄厚的资产实力使其在现代国际金融市场中处于主导地位。第四,跨国银行一般极为重视联合贷款。在提供巨额贷款时,跨国银行往往与其他大银行或非银行金融机构组成贷款银团进行联合贷款,并由跨国银行作为银团贷款的牵头行。

跨国银行的海外分支机构形式多种多样,一般说来,主要包括代理行、代表处、分行、子银行、联属行、联营银行等形式。代理行是指与其他国家银行建立往来账户,代理对方的部分业务,为对方提供服务的银行。代表处是跨国银行设立在海外最简单的机构。分行是跨国银行一个很重要的形式,它并非独立的经济实体,而是总行的一个组成部分。子银行是独立的经济实体,是在所在国注册的银行。如跨国银行在另一银行中拥有股份,但持有的比例尚不足以绝对控制其经营管理,则该银行称为跨国银行的联属行,此时,跨国银行只是该银行的一个普通参与者。联营银行也是合资银行,它是由多个不同国家的银行合资建立的国际银行,其中任何一家银行都不能绝对控股(即持股50%以上)。

跨国银行的影响具有两面性。一方面,跨国银行可以促进国际贸易和投资的发展,促进银行业的发展和竞争,有利于国际资本流动和国际收支平衡。近年来,由于国际金融市场的迅速发展,以及银行业务电子化、网络化以及现代通信手段在银行业务中的应用,集中统一的跨国银行经营业务变得越发方便。另一方面,跨国银行的发展在给国际银行业带来空前繁荣的同时,也带来了巨大的潜在风险。跨国银行可以很容易地在主要国际金融市场上转移资金和开展业务,利用各国在管理上的差异和漏洞规避管制。跨国银行可能强化金融资本对国际经济运行的控制,导致国际金融市场动荡,弱化各国货币政策的效力。

对跨国银行的监管主要来自母国、东道国和国际机构。母国对本国银行海外业务的监管主要包含以下几个方面:对设立海外分支机构的监管,对海外分支机构业务经营范围的监管，对海外分支机构日常运营的监管，以及对海外分支机构经营外汇的监管。东道国对跨国银行的监管主要由以下几点构成：对跨国银行市场准入的监管，对跨国银行市场运作的监管，对跨国银行业务限制的监管，对跨国银行资本市场并购的监管，以及对跨国银行日常报告的监管。鉴于跨国银行可能带来的负面作用，就跨国银行业务经营的监督和管理进行国际协调和国际合作就显得尤为重要。当前对跨国银行监管最突出的成果是 1983 年的《巴塞尔协议》及其后续文件，主要相关机构为 1975 年成立的巴塞尔银行监管委员会。跨国银行的国际监管主要包括以下几个方面：强调对跨国银行的合作监管，强调监管国际银行业的资本充足水平，强调银行业务的风险管理，以及强调对银行业的有效监管和信息披露。

翻译练习

I. 思考题

1. 什么是翻译症？造成翻译症的原因何在？
2. 结合实例说明如何避免翻译症。

II. 从"Currency Risk"中摘录给你深刻印象的句子或词组。

1. _____
2. _____
3. _____
4. _____
5. _____

III. 商务术语翻译

agreement deposit	
auto-pledge financing	
bank's acceptance bill	
banker's draft	
banker's promissory note	
bill discount	
call deposit	

call option	
collateralized debt obligation	
commercial acceptance bill	
demand deposit	
dividend payable	
equity of stakeholder	
excess reserve	
financial bond	
financial instrument	
general reserve	
gold lending	
gold swap	
guaranty deposit	
hybrid capital bond	
inter-bank borrowing	
intra-bank lending fund	
legal deposit reserve	
loan commitment	
long-term deferred expense	
monetary gold	
mortgage-backed securities	
option contract	
overdraft account	
packing loan	
paid-in capital	
paper gold	
pledge loan	

put option	
rediscount	
secured loan	
securities issue guaranty	
securities lending	
short-term financing bond	
special drawing right	
standard gold	
syndicate loan	
time-demand deposit	
treasury deposit	
value-preserved bond	
vault cash	
working capital loan	

IV. 句子翻译

1. An improved world economic environment could ease the erosion of bank capital resulting from domestic loan losses.
2. Hedge-fund managers are the smartest investors around. With keen eyes and sharp brains, they spot and exploit inefficiencies in the markets. Or at least that is what the industry tells its clients.
3. In a separate statement on Sunday, the central bank reiterated that it intended to maintain a stable monetary policy.
4. The stronger-than-expected lending and money supply figures suggest that Beijing is firmly on track to unveil more pro-growth steps as inflation eases, which reduces the risk of a hard landing in the world's second-largest economy.
5. One wonders how well these books are selling today, now that the European dream has become a nightmare for many, with the euro teetering on the brink of collapse and the union that produced it mired in a triple crisis that will take years, if not decades, to resolve.
6. These elite groups commonly have close connections with foreign countries and

promote the latter's interests, as well as their own, more effectively than the interests of the "masses" in these countries.

7. In its schedule of benefits, New York offers the most generous measure of compensation in the entire country, and it can be safely said that it has the best balanced schedule.
8. Non-involvement works best when the industry is highly competitive and competition is likely to achieve socially desired behavior. This is especially so regarding the pricing of products, since competition can bring prices down.
9. Other things being equal, the easing of demand for bank credit would tend to imply a more ready availability of such credit to those borrowers who still sought it.
10. Concerns about risk in lending to particular countries, however, may well lead banks to focus their lending more strongly on countries whose perceived creditworthiness has improved, or at least not deteriorated.

V. 篇章翻译

The deep international economic linkages among countries that provide the channels for negative spillovers across borders also enhance the scope for beneficial policy coordination. Indeed, efforts to stimulate aggregate demand through expansionary monetary and fiscal policies, to recapitalize insolvent financial institutions, and to restore the functioning of credit markets through the provision of liquidity are more likely to be taken—and are more likely to be effective—if there is broad agreement among the major governments on policy direction.

Governments' willingness to coordinate their policies can help reestablish confidence by ruling out beggar-thy-neighbor responses to the crisis. The danger of special interests using trade policy to protect particular industries is especially severe in a downturn. As for financial policies, measures taken to recapitalize commercial banks with public funds have introduced pressures for banks to concentrate lending activity on the domestic market (the so-called home bias in lending practices), at the expense of cross-border lending.

In the years leading up to the crisis, a defining feature of global finance in developed countries was the escalating integration of the household sector into capital markets. Excessive credit creation, made possible through the technology of asset securitization, yoked consumer spending to the expansion and profitability of the banking industry, with both serving as engines of economic growth. As household ownership of equities and bonds increased, households' wealth and income became more closely linked to capital markets, forging closer linkages between the real economy and financial markets—and increasing the likelihood of political intervention when trouble appears.

翻译名家

余光中（1928—2017），著名作家、诗人、学者、翻译家，一生从事诗歌、散文、评论、翻译，被誉为文坛的"璀璨五彩笔"。余光中驰骋文坛逾半个世纪，涉猎广泛，被誉为"艺术上的多栖主义者"。其代表作有《白玉苦瓜》（诗集）、《记忆像铁轨一样长》（散文集）及《分水岭上：余光中评论文集》（评论集）等，其诗作如《乡愁》《乡愁四韵》，散文如《听听那冷雨》《我的四个假想敌》等，广泛收录于语文课本。

余光中认为翻译也是一种创作，一种"有限的创作"。他认为，以英文译中文为例，两种文字在形、音、文法、修辞、思考习惯、美感经验、文化背景上如此相异，字、词、句之间就很少有现成的对译法则可循。因此，一切好的翻译，犹如衣服，都应是定做的，而不是现成的。要买现成的翻译，字典里有的是；可是字典是死的，而译者是活的。他用轻松幽默的文笔描述了种种翻译流弊，比如公式化的翻译体，一口气长达四五十字、中间不加标点的句子，消化不良的句子，头重脚轻的修饰语，画蛇添足的所有格代名词，生涩含混的文理，毫无节奏感的语气，等等。他指出，译者的外文程度不济固然是一大原因，但中文周转不灵，词汇贫乏，句型单调，首尾不能兼顾的苦衷，恐怕要负另一半责任。因此，他极力提倡译者提高中文水平，防止"恶意西化"的狂潮，防止中文式微的现象危及中华民族的文化生命。

附录1　商务语篇翻译参考译文

第1章　心理契约

在讨论组织与员工的关系时，心理契约是一个非常有用的概念。心理契约是指员工和雇主对他们之间工作关系的性质的一种不成文的心理期待。这种心理期待是个性化的，具有主观性，且主要是对"公平"的期待，因而员工很难清晰地界定。

员工和雇主之间不成文的心理契约既包括一些有形指标（如工资、福利、员工生产效率、出勤率等），也包括一些无形指标（如忠诚、公平待遇、工作保障等）。很多雇主可能会尽量把他们对员工的期望详细写入员工手册或规章制度汇编中，但是这只是整个"契约"关系中的一部分。

曾几何时，员工可以凭勤奋和能力换取一份薪水见涨、福利不错、升职有望的稳定工作。但是随着组织开始减员，辞退一些忠心耿耿的老员工，越来越多的员工就会开始动摇对雇主的忠诚。与心理契约密切关联的是心理归属感。如果员工感觉自己在组织中拥有一定的支配权和其他可感受到的权利，他们对组织的忠诚度可能会更高。这里要讨论的是心理契约中员工心理期待的变化情况。

雇主提供	员工贡献
令人满意的薪酬和福利	不断提高的技能与生产率
职业发展机会	合理的工作时间
工作与家庭之间的灵活平衡	必要时的额外奉献

影响个人与组织之间关系的因素有两个，即经济变化和不同年代的人的心理期望的变化。这些因素在很多方面影响着心理契约。

经济的繁荣与萧条是影响员工心理期望的主要因素。回想一下网络公司和科技迅猛发展、大行其道时的"就业市场"就可以管中窥豹。很多人，尤其是那些拥有技术背景的年轻人心理期望很高：高起薪、入职安置费、股票期权、宽松的工作环境以及不断的职位升迁等。然而，随着网络经济泡沫的破灭，这些人却不得不面对一个截然不同的就业市场，雇主提供的薪酬和工作环境也大为不同。

已有很多论述都谈到不同年代的人的不同心理期望，其中大部分仅对不同年龄段的人作了总体概括。以下是通常的年代标签：

- 成熟世代（1909—1945年出生）
- 婴儿潮世代（1946—1964年出生）
- X世代（1965—1980年出生）

- Y 世代（1981—1996 年出生）

区分上述每个年龄段的特征并不重要，重要的是要强调同一年代标签的人心理期望不同，不同年代的人心理期望也不同。对雇主来说，期望的差异带来了各种挑战。例如，婴儿潮世代和成熟世代的很多人都很关心工作保障与经验，而年轻的 Y 世代的人则期望快速得到回报，更易对管理者和组织作出的决策提出质疑。再设想一下，如果让一个成熟世代的管理者去领导 X 世代和 Y 世代的人，或者让 X 世代的人去管理比他年长、比他经验丰富的婴儿潮世代的人，情况又会怎样？不同的人有不同的期望，因此不同年代出生的人之间的差异可能会在组织中不断诱发挑战与冲突。其中一个最突出的差异体现在对组织的忠诚方面。

员工确实很看重心理契约，希望雇主能信守这种"约定"。很多员工还是想得到工作保障与安定，得到一份有意思的工作、一位受人爱戴的上司以及不错的薪酬和福利等。如果这些条件不能满足的话，员工为组织效力的热情可能就会减退。如果组织合并重组、大量裁员、业务外包、雇用大量临时工或兼职人员，员工更没有理由为一份没有稳定感的工作而效忠雇主。这一点在美国一些公司中已经很明显。这些公司大量裁员，股价下跌，导致许多员工人心散乱，士气低迷。越来越多的雇主意识到在竞争十分激烈的劳动力市场，如果员工忠诚度偏低，组织中关键岗位人才就更容易流失。这也证明了拥有一支具有奉献精神且忠心耿耿的工作团队非常重要。

对心理契约的研究表明了员工最关注什么，以及当他们的期望得到满足或得不到满足时，他们会作出什么反应。研究发现，员工的关注和这些关注得到满足之间的差距与员工的工作满意度和离职的可能性有相关性。因此可以说，这项研究证实了很多人都会有的一个符合逻辑的猜想，即当雇主未能满足员工的心理契约"义务"时，员工就会对工作不满意，也越可能离职。另外，员工期望雇主能通过业绩评价体系，提供个人发展机会，对个人的工作业绩给予反馈。如果雇主能够理解员工期待的"新"心理契约，那么员工就会感到满意，就更有可能较长时间留任。

第2章　国际贸易

　　国际贸易指的是两个或多个国家之间进行的涉及使用两种或多种货币的货物或服务交换过程。国际贸易能使全球生产力得到更加有效的利用。

　　为何会出现国际贸易？答案直接来自国际贸易本身的定义——居住于两个不同国家的交易双方认为各自能从一桩出于自愿的交换中获得利益。这简单的事实背后隐含着许多经济学理论、商业惯例、政府政策与国际冲突。

　　国际贸易的发展带来了诸多利益。国际贸易让消费者选择面更宽，满意度更高；规模经济降低生产成本，从而也降低了消费者所应支付的价格；国际贸易加剧竞争，可防止本地出口商对本国市场的垄断性控制；国际贸易还能刺激经济增长，促进科技发展，提高生活水平。

　　总之，国际贸易可增加经济财富，为思想交流及国家与地区基础设施建设和资源发展提供机遇。贸易有益于国家之间的往来，促进旅游业和教育事业的发展，为国家或地区带来稳定的政治和经济局面。通过促进经济增长和增加就业，国际贸易在消除贫困方面发挥了重要的作用。业已进入出口市场、对进口产品依赖性加大、投资环境改善从而更具国际竞争力的国家，其发展速度较未参与国际贸易的国家更加迅猛。

　　国际贸易对国民经济具有重要的直接和间接影响。一方面，出口能刺激国内经济中的其他经济活动。另一方面，进口也不例外。举例来说，南方酒业集团的酒类出口为澳大利亚和全世界软木塞供应商及葡萄种植者等带来了大量订单，同时还为该公司的澳大利亚员工带来了工资收入，为股票持有者带来了红利收益，而所有这些又为当地汽车经销商、超市和其他行业创造了收入。进口也能向国内供应商施加压力，促使其降低价格并提升竞争力。

　　面对国外竞争，国内供应商如不能及时作出反应，会导致工厂停产、工人失业。进口还能创造就业岗位，促进竞争。尽管在世界贸易相关讨论中出口是一大突出话题，我们切莫忘记每一次出口同时也是进口。或许由于每个国家都重视收支平衡，而在收支平衡中，出口又被认为比进口更具有积极意义，因而进口就逐渐背上了"恶名"。视进口为"坏事"这种看法当然是愚蠢的。作为消费者，我们很少有人愿意生活中缺少日本和德国的科技产品、美国的娱乐产品、法国的美酒，也很少有人不想隔三岔五地到太平洋的珊瑚岛或亚洲某个充满异域风情的度假区游历一番。假如不进口这些商品，不购买这些服务，作为消费者，我们的生活将会苦不堪言，我们的工厂也将会落伍。在探讨国际贸易和投资理论时，这一点也不能忽略。我们需要牢记，每一单出口同时也是进口！

　　国际贸易与专业化生产的迅速增长为贸易存在的经济原因提出了如下问题：日本为何主要出口制成品而进口原材料？美国与荷兰的农业差异为何如此之大？而最为重要的是，敞开国门参与国际贸易，国家究竟是获益还是受损？要回答这些问题，还要从比较优势理论那里寻求答案。该理论认为，通过专门从事提供自身生产效率最高或具有比较优势的商品或服务，一个国家就能提高其生活水准与实际收入。专门化生产的益处也会受到运输成本的影响。货物和原材料要输送到世界各地，运输成本缩小了贸易的盈利空间。

　　将比较优势理论稍作延伸，在两种或多种产品上拥有绝对优势的国家开展对外贸易仍是有利可图的。例如，比之世界其他国家和地区，美国在钢材和计算机方面的人均产出（或单位产出）都要高出许多。然而，假如美国出口计算机（生产力相对较强）而进口钢材（生产力相对较弱）的话，则仍然能够获益。同样，另一国家即使在一些产品的生产上绝对处于较低的水平，同美国进行贸易也能够获利。

第3章　跨国公司

跨国公司指的是至少在两个国家从事生产或提供服务的公司或企业。跨国公司也被称为多国企业或多国公司。根据生产设施的配置，跨国公司通常可分为三类：1）横向一体化跨国公司管理位于不同国家或地区的生产企业，以生产相同或相似的产品；2）纵向一体化跨国公司管理某些国家或地区的生产企业，为其他国家或地区的生产企业提供上游产品；3）多元化跨国公司管理位于不同国家或地区的生产企业，这些企业在结构上为横向或纵向一体化。

跨国公司20世纪以前就已存在，但直到20世纪60年代，才最终成为国际舞台上的主力军。1900年，只有欧洲公司才是跨国经营方面的主角，至1930年，美国跨国公司开始崭露头角，1960年则标志着公司多国化经营这一新时期的开端。1960年至今，每10年当中，国际上外国直接投资存量增长均超过了2倍，而20世纪前半期却只增长了1倍。20世纪后半叶，跨国公司逐渐活跃起来，这主要归因于交通、通信和信息处理领域的技术创新，这些创新使得企业能在全球范围内开展盈利丰厚的业务，同时又能继续保持及时有效的组织控制。凭借高速发展的通信和交通技术，跨国公司业已成为超越国家边界与限制的强劲力量，贸易、商务、货物、服务和观念的流动也因此更为畅通无阻，并因此造福于全人类。

上述所言强调了跨国公司的重要性与潜力，之所以能下这样的结论，有四个方面的原因。首先，跨国公司在某种程度上是维护和平的强大力量。从自身利益出发，跨国公司试图努力促进税收、专利版权法、贸易惯例及全球经济活动所有规则的统一，从而能在共同规则下求得发展，服务大众市场。第二，跨国公司所推行的生产与服务国际化有力地推动了全球进步所必需的电子化发展水平。第三，发展中国家谋求发展所急需的大部分技术业已研发出来，且为私营部门拥有和控制。这些专利性技术的创造无不是耗资巨大，因而一旦为公司拥有便被视为极其珍贵的财产。第四，国际公司在技术传输方面具有特殊能力。这里所说的技术远不只是通常所谓的高科技，还包括了管理能力和营销技能。跨国公司所能发挥的最有效的作用并不在于资源转移本身，而在于按照特定的发展机遇与项目，将资本、技术、管理技巧等资源作为精心搭配的生产要素组合形式进行运作所产生的影响。

在当今世界经济舞台上，跨国公司发挥了至关重要的作用，其所从事的活动大大推动了经济全球化进程。解决世界经济问题所需的许多技术、管理人才和私人资本都掌控在跨国公司手中。

几乎所有主要的跨国公司均来自美国、日本或西欧国家。支持者说，跨国公司为那些需要发展的国家创造了就业机会和财富，而且提升了这些国家的技术水平。另一方面，批评人士则指出，跨国公司会向政府施加不适当的政治影响，对发展中国家进行盘剥，同时也会为自己的国家带来失业问题。1992年，联合国曾试图通过谈判达成一项跨国公司自愿行为准则，但这一想法却因遭到政府和公司反对而最终无果。2000年6月，经济合作与发展组织颁布了跨国企业指导方针，这套方针由非政府组织和行业工会协助起草，旨在促进跨国公司与其所在社群之间的良好关系。

第4章　制定全球市场营销战略

制定全球性市场营销战略，以求在全球市场上进行有效竞争，这是当今企业所面临的最为关键的挑战。无论是针对邻近本土的若干市场，还是全球范围内的多个市场，企业都必须制定一个充满活力的长期战略，从而为企业带来可持续的竞争优势。同时，这一战略还必须能使企业对全球市场日渐复杂的情况和快速变化进行预测、作出反应并进行调整。

然而，根据参与国际市场的程度与经验，企业制定有效的全球市场战略时所面临的具体问题亦有所不同。企业参与市场的过程可划分三个阶段：1) 进入市场初期阶段；2) 地方市场拓展阶段；3) 全球合理化阶段。初次进入国际市场时，企业主要关注的是评估并挑选出对其产品和服务最具诱人机会的国家，并为如何利用好这些机会制定出富有竞争力的市场进入战略。一旦成功立足于国际市场，企业管理层往往会将注意力转向地方市场的拓展。初期阶段，这需要企业拓宽产品系列、增加新的产品种类、开发新产品并调整市场策略，从而能在地方市场进行更为有效的竞争。之后，随着地方市场的拓展，企业必须在全国市场范围内建立起协调及控制经营的机制。随着企业全球业务的逐渐发展，为提高企业在全球范围内的经营效率，促进企业内部知识和技能的传播，企业在不同国家之间进行合理化及统一业务的压力也会随之而来。企业必须制定战略，以充分利用其在全球市场的竞争优势及全球市场业务所带来的潜在合作机会。

由于背景、资源、能力及竞争实力方面的差异，不同的企业在全球市场所追求的发展方向也大为不同。然而，以往大多数关于全球市场战略的讨论和研究都将关注的焦点聚集在大型跨国企业，尤其是那些来自工业化国家的企业。人们普遍认为，面对国内市场增长疲软及外来竞争加剧的现实，来自此类市场的企业都会尽力在欠发达国家市场上销售其产品和服务，并在国际范围内最大限度发挥其在国内市场上的竞争优势。随后，他们会尽力巩固自己在这些市场中的地位，并最终建立全球范围内的主导地位。

不过，全球商业市场不再由来自工业化国家的大型跨国企业独领风骚。现在，全球市场内还存在众多其他类型的公司，其中就包括数量不断增多的中小型公司。随着一度受到保护的本土市场面向国外竞争者开放，来自新兴经济体的本土市场领头羊正将其商业触角伸向国际市场。国家垄断企业也正在进行私有化并参与到竞争中来。

这类企业无法享用与大型跨国企业同等的资源与实力，也没有全球市场战略所依托的市场地位和权力。跨国大型企业得益于自身的规模及广泛的资源网络，小企业需要灵活应变并专注于制定市场战略，来自新兴市场的大型企业以及由国有企业转型而来的企业则需要考虑如何在国际市场最大限度发挥其国内优势。再者，这些企业往往尚处于进入国际市场的早期阶段。工业化国家的跨国企业进入国际市场通常已有很长一段历史，已处于进入市场后的第二或第三阶段，而多数刚进入国际市场的企业仍处于第一阶段，正在寻求如何在国际市场上站稳脚跟，仍在确立目标市场或区域及竞争对手。因此，这些企业所面对的挑战、竞争威胁的性质、关键决策与战略重点均不相同，需注重的功能性目标也不一样。

无论处于国际市场的哪个发展阶段，管理者都面临着同样的任务，即制定出能使企业在全球市场获得成功的战略。但是，根据企业参与国际市场程度的不同，成功的内涵会体现出极大差异，获取成功的手段也同样有所区别。早期阶段，成功的战略只要求能够适用于若干市场并能实现适度的销售目标。随后，成功可能意味着与世界范围内的主要竞争对手抗衡，这需要对资源进行大范围部署，并持续不断地密切关注全球不同地区的多个市场前沿。

  无论是哪一种战略，其内在的必要条件都是要为特定发展阶段的成功创造广泛条件，并为企业过渡到下一阶段搭桥引路，这也是任何一种战略赖以存在的基础。在第一阶段（进入市场初期阶段），除制定市场进入战略外，企业还必须建立机制，学习（一种持续的学习义务）国际市场的相关信息及如何在某一国家的市场内进行成功的经营。处于第二阶段（地方市场拓展阶段）的企业业已成功登上国际市场大舞台并开始涉足于多个市场。在进一步拓展过程中，行业不同、基本战略条件不同、企业拓宽经营的意愿不同，适合企业的战略也各不相同。随着企业的不断学习，本阶段的重点是立足于各个市场。该目标达成后，重点将逐渐转向如何改善各国范围内市场的协调和控制。处于第三阶段（全球合理化阶段）的企业已然在国际市场上站稳了脚跟，正努力对全球范围内的业务加以合理化，以获取由全球化经营所带给企业的合作机会。在本阶段，企业仍处于学习和建设过程，优先考虑的是如何巩固企业的市场地位，建立全球范围内的领先优势。

第5章　保险的性质

保险是一种复杂而精细的机制，因此很难对其进行界定。但简单而言，保险有如下两个基本特点：

- 将风险从个体转移至群体；
- 群体中所有成员在平等的基础上分担损失。

从个体角度我们可将保险定义如下：对个体而言，保险是一种经济手段，个体借此将如果没有保险可能面临的不确定性大额损失（被投保的突发事件）转变为确定性的小额成本（保费）。

保险最主要的作用是创造出安全保障以应对风险。对个体而言，保险并不能降低某一事件发生的不确定性，也不会改变该事件发生的概率，但的确能够减少与该事件相关的经济损失的概率。从个人角度而言，房屋所有人为房屋购买适当金额的保险，万一房屋发生火灾，可减少因此产生的经济损失。

有人似乎认为，假如没有遇险，他们便无从获得赔偿，这样一来，购买保险的钱就等于是浪费了。有人甚至认为，假如保险期限内没有发生损失，那么就应该退还保费。这两种观点本身都很无知。说到第一种观点，我们已知道保险合同可使投保人免于承担不确定的风险，这也正是保险的价值所在。即使保险期限内投保险情没有发生，投保人也已经获得了回报，即出险后获得赔偿的承诺。

至于第二种观点，我们必须认识到，保险规则之所以能够运行，原因是很多人共同分担了个别投保人不幸出险的损失。如果将保费返还给多数没有遭受损失的投保人，就意味着没有资金支付个别人所蒙受的损失。因此，保险本质上是一种风险分担手段，即对个人而言是毁灭性的损失由所有投保人共同分担，这正是保险赖以存在的基础。

除借助风险转移为个体降低风险外，保险还通过支付一定费用的方式降低损失，从而减少总体经济风险。这些费用是通过大数法则评估而得出的。由此我们可以为保险下第二个定义：从社会角度而言，保险是一种经济手段，通过将足够数量且险种相同的投保人集结为一个整体，使损失对整体具有可预测性，从而达到减少乃至消除风险的目的。

保险无法避免损失，也不能减少对整个经济所造成的损失。相反，保险可能会带来风险，增加为避免风险所付出的成本。保险可能会诱发对承保人的诈骗行为，此外也会有投保人因投保而松懈或疏于防范风险。再者，由于既要承受损失本身，又要承在平等基础上分担风险而产生的额外费用，整个经济也可能会承受保险机制运行所带来的额外费用。

也许我们应该就保险的性质进行最终的界定。常有人说，保险是一种赌博形式。"你赌的是自己的命，保险公司则赌的是你不会送命"，或者"我下300美元的赌注与保险公司打赌，万一房屋被烧，我就能拿到10万美元"。这些说法显然是错误的。赌博过程中，赌局未成立前是不会产生损失的，因此也就不存在风险。而对于保险，无论保险合同是否存在，损失风险都是存在的。换言之，保险和赌博的根本区别在于赌博本身会带来风险，而保险则提供了转化现存风险的手段。

第6章　转让定价

和国内企业一样，跨国公司同样追求税后收益的最大化。然而，不同的东道国对跨国公司有着不同的税务要求，且往往彼此冲突，从而成为跨国公司必须面对的挑战。跨国公司一般都会谨慎从事，在合理利用税收优惠政策与规避惩罚性税收之间另辟蹊径。

跨国公司经常借助转让定价和避税港这两种手段来降低总体税负。转让定价指母公司的某个分公司或子公司为其向其他分公司或子公司提供的商品或服务制定的价格。转让定价对跨国公司而言非常重要，其原因是多方面的。跨国公司在多个国家设有子公司，经常在它们之间进行货物、技术和其他资源的转移。据估计，跨国公司内部交易占美国国际货物贸易的40%。转让定价也会影响跨国公司监管各子公司的经营情况，并据此对子公司管理人员予以奖惩。此外，转让定价还会影响跨国公司向母国及各东道国支付的税额。

在实际操作中，转让定价的计算方法有两种，一是基于市场，一是脱离市场，二者常取其一。

基于市场的定价方法以公开市场所确定的价格作为同一母公司各单位之间商品转移的价格。假如一家科技公司打算由韩国向其位于美国的某子公司出口用于组装个人电脑的内存条，它就可以直接以该内存条的公开市场价作为美国和韩国子公司之间的转让定价。

基于市场的定价方法有两大优点。首先，这种方法减少了交易单位之间的价格纷争。在公司内部流转中，定价越高，卖方业绩就会越好，而买方的业绩也就会越差。鉴于母公司视子公司收益率高低向其派发管理奖励或投入资金，子公司管理人员非常重视本单位在母公司账面上的表现，因此在转让定价上锱铢必较，各不相让。然而，在母公司看来，这种纷争无异于浪费公司资源。公司财会记录一经汇总，其税前总利润即已确定，无论子公司收益率因转让定价而得以提高或降低，均不能对其产生影响。因此，基于市场的转让定价在深层次上是公平的；假如争执双方都能认识到这一点，诸如此类的内部纷争便会大为减少。

其次，基于市场的定价方法可以激励卖方提高效率，从而提高跨国公司的总体收益率。如果卖方只能以市场价为公司内部交易价，其管理者就会认识到，单位收益率的提高有赖于其对成本的控制能力。此外，他们也会认识到，如果他们能够使所售产品的成本低于国外竞争者，母公司基于市场的转让定价就会对他们的努力给予充分认可。在奖金与升职预期的刺激下，单位管理者将全力以赴提高效率和利润率。

转让定价也可以用脱离市场的方法进行确定。买卖双方可通过协商来议定价格，也可基于成本作出大致的估算，比如用成本加固定加价的方法来确定价格。母公司提供的某些服务所产生的费用，诸如综合经营管理费和母公司所拥有的技术与知识产权的使用费，也可算作子公司销售业绩的一部分。

跨国公司普遍采用脱离市场的方法来确定转让定价，部分原因在于某些商品和服务只可能在公司内部进行交易，而无外部市场可言。以一家知名汽车公司位于西班牙的制造厂所生产的某种发动机为例，其唯一市场就是该公司位于比利时、德国和英国的汽车装配厂。鉴于该发动机并不存在外部市场，这家汽车公司可以运用生产成本外加管理费和利润的方法来确定其转让定价。

用脱离市场的方法进行定价有利有弊。其弊端之一在于，虽然转让定价对母公司总的税前收入没有影响，但却会影响买卖双方上报的利润，从而使双方管理人员为转让定价争论不休，造成时间和精力的浪费。脱离市场的转让定价还可能降低卖方效率。既然转让定价是在卖方成本基础上加价而成，卖方就可以通过脱离市场的方法进行定价将一切新增成本统统转嫁到公司的其他成员身上，从而不再想方设法降低成本。

然而，如运用得当，脱离市场的转让定价也能给跨国公司带来好处。母公司可以巧妙确定内部交易价格，以降低纳税总额。例如，面对以从价原则征收的进口关税，跨国公司可以采用压低卖方价格的方法来降低税基、减轻税负。此外，这样的定价方法还可使跨国公司大大减少其应纳所得税的总额。假设某跨国公司有两个东道国，其中一个征收的企业所得税较高，而另一个则较低，该公司就可以提高位于高税率国家的子公司买进时的转让定价，并降低位于低税率国家的子公司的转让定价。这样一来，前者的账面收益率降低了，而后者的却提高了。其最终效果是：跨国公司的利润由征税较多的高税率国家转移到了征税较少的低税率国家，从而降低了公司的总税负。

第7章　世贸组织争端解决机制

1995年乌拉圭回合谈判将建立争端解决机制问题列入议题，并就此达成了《争端解决谅解》协议。协议规定，世贸组织成员之间出现争端时，既可由世贸组织总干事出面斡旋，也可由争端各方在一致同意的前提下申请仲裁，还可按规定流程启动争端解决机制。启动争端解决机制之前，争端各方须先行磋商。如磋商未果，诉方可于60日内要求成立三人专家组进行听证，形成中期报告，然后形成最终报告。如某成员对最终报告既不执行，也不上诉，专家组可就如何促使其执行提出建议。因客观原因导致裁定暂无法执行时，可允许该成员"在一段合理期限内执行"。争议方可持最终报告向世贸组织常设上诉机构中的三名专家提起上诉，该机构由七名专家组成，相当于世贸组织的"最高法庭"。

按照规定，如某成员败诉，且于此后一定合理期限内未采取任何举措，争端各方可先就补偿展开磋商，"以待日后充分履行"。所谓"补偿"，一般是指被诉方向诉方提供其他方面的减让，典型表现为削减有损诉方利益的其他贸易壁垒。然而，补偿须基于"自愿"，因此实际操作中非常罕见。如争端各方在合理期限20天后依然未就补偿问题达成一致，诉方可向争端解决机构申请暂停向被诉方提供的等值减让。值得一提的是，"暂停减让的程度……应等同于权益遭剥夺或受侵害的程度"。例如，在世贸组织认定欧盟非法禁止美国向其出口含激素牛肉并造成美国1.168亿美元经济损失的情况下，世贸组织可授权美国对来自欧盟的产品施行价值1.168亿美元的惩罚性关税。

总的来讲，在帮助成员解决因违反协议而引发的争端并使相应裁定得以执行方面，争端解决机制还是相当成功的。不少争端刚进入磋商阶段就得到了解决。虽然拖延时有出现，尤其在需要订立新法的时候，虽然拒不执行的情况也偶有发生，但事实表明，大多数国家总体上还是最终执行了裁定。成员之所以执行这些裁定，主要不是因为对鲜有实施的报复措施有所顾虑，而是因为只有这样做才最符合他们的利益。之所以如此，是因为总体看来，在世贸组织这种处处需要谈判的体系中，守规则、重信誉会给他们带来更多好处。此外，他们也必须考虑与重要贸易伙伴之间的关系。

有证据表明，虽然某些最不发达国家在运用该机制时尚有困难，但就发达国家与发展中国家而言，其运用已相当广泛，并与其在世界贸易中所占的份额大致成正比。例如，1995年至2000年，由高收入国家提起的诉讼占诉讼总量的70.2%，而发展中国家占29.8%。然而，在接下来的五年，即2001年至2006年，发展中国家提起的诉讼却占了多数，高达52.1%。虽然这些数字主要反映的是以印度、巴西为代表的出口份额较大的发展中国家的情况，但也同样涉及较小的发展中国家巧妙而有效地利用该体系与贸易大国角力的情况。另外，南南争端的增加也颇为引人注目。总而言之，近来的发展趋势表明，发展中国家对世贸组织争端解决机制越来越熟悉，对争端的处理也越来越有信心。

世贸组织争端解决机制有如下几个特点尤为值得关注。首先，世贸组织本身既不负责调查，也不鼓励诉讼。虽然世贸组织会审查成员的贸易政策，但并没有核心监管机制——审查意见完全靠成员主动履行。被诉方无法中止诉讼，而诉方却有权随时撤诉，在被诉方尚未执行裁定时也是如此。

第二，争端解决机制的运作方式体现了世贸组织作为政府间组织的特点。虽然世贸组织允许聘请私人律师进行辩护，或在某些场合允许非政府实体以"法庭之友"的身份出庭陈述，但有权提起诉讼的却只有政府，私人无权诉讼。因违反协议而造成私人利益受损时，私人无独立追索权，必须通过政府提起诉讼。同理，报复的对象也仅限于被诉国。然而，报复同样可能殃及某些出口企业，致使其收入受损，即便这些企业与此纠纷毫无干系，只是身处该国而已——这便是有人认为补偿以外的形式都应被禁止的原因。

第三，《争端解决谅解》并未明确规定采用赋予判例约束性的普通法体系。由此而言，所谓必须遵从的先例并不存在。理论上来讲，专家组的每次裁定都是独一无二的——只有当事成员能够采用协议中有关"增加或减少权利义务"的条款。然而在实际操作中，先例的作用却举足轻重：在专家组和上诉机构报告脚注中，援引和尊崇其他报告中的推论过程的情况比比皆是。世贸组织上诉机构通过规范裁定并确保其前后一致来行使监管这一重要职能。因此，《争端解决谅解》已实际构建了一套接近普通法的体系。

第四，世贸组织的裁定并非令出必行。在实际操作中，是否执行裁定由成员自主决定，虽然这么做不尽符合法律规定。成员甚至有可能冒着违背协议而遭到贸易报复的风险拒不执行裁定。从法律上来讲，报复只是权宜之计，并不能替代执行。但实际上，报复有可能成为争端的最终后果。这也就意味着，报复机制可以像安全阀一样，起到释放压力的作用。

第五，世贸组织争端解决机制无意对胜诉方因等待执行而遭受的损失进行赔偿，这一点与普通法体系中的合同案件截然相反。其优点在于可避免因此类赔偿数额和支付而引起新的纠纷，而弊端则在于有可能会促使预期败诉的一方尽可能拖延下去。在明白了只有拖下去、推迟执行才最为有利的时候，各方均可能出现违反规则的行为。

简言之，世贸组织争端解决机制是一种融合了多种司法评议在内的非常独特的仲裁体系。只要有一方申诉，各方就需启动相应程序。仲裁小组以各成员此前议定的规则为基础展开调查，形成结论。裁定对各方均有约束力，拒不执行或拒不赔偿可能导致减免中止，不服裁定者亦可提起上诉。然而，与国内法律体系中的仲裁程序相比，世贸组织的争端解决体系相对较弱，其主要原因有以下四点：一是裁定无法确保执行；二是先例无严格约束力；三是诉讼资格不全面——能提起诉讼的只有政府，而非所有的受害者；四是救济手段有限。

第8章　贸易壁垒

在国际贸易中，商品进入不同的政治领域，就可能会产生贸易壁垒。贸易壁垒是对贸易的一种限制，没有限制的贸易则是自由贸易。贸易壁垒最常见的形式是关税，关税的征收对象通常为进口商品。非关税壁垒也是一种贸易壁垒，又被称为非关税措施，其作用也是限制全球贸易。

关税有不同的种类。出口关税是对输出一个国家的商品征收的税种，而进口关税则是对进入一个国家的商品征收的税种。关税可根据计算方式的不同进行分类。从价关税是一种按照进口或出口商品价值的百分比进行计算的税种。例如，20% 的从价关税是指要征收相当于相关商品价值 20% 的关税。按其他方式计算的关税包括从量关税，以商品的数量、重量或体积为基础进行计算，也包括复合关税（又称混合关税），计算该税时要综合考虑从价关税和从量关税。

关税也可按照其功能或目的进行分类。反倾销关税是对定价低于市场公平价格，并有可能给本国生产商带来损害的进口商品所征收的关税，也被称为惩罚性关税。反补贴关税是另外一种形式的惩罚性关税，在本国生产商遭受巨大或实质性影响后进行征收，尤其是对已获得出口国家政府补贴的进口商品进行征收。反补贴关税的目的是抵消进口商品所获得的补贴，并提高进口商品在本国的销售价格。

禁止性关税又称为排他性关税，其目的在于大幅度减少甚至全面禁止某一产品或商品的进口，一般在进口商品数量超过一定允许范围时使用，也可用于保护本国生产商。另一种关税是最终关税，根据进口产品的用途进行征收。例如，同一种产品用于教育而非商业用途时，所缴纳的关税亦不相同。

除关税外，国际贸易中还存在非关税壁垒。非关税壁垒包括数量限制或配额，由一个国家实施，也可通过两个或两个以上的国家协定实施。数量限制包括国际商品协定、自愿出口限制以及有秩序的市场安排。

行政法规是另外一种非关税壁垒，包括进行贸易必须满足的一系列要求（如费用、执照、许可、当地成分要求、金融债券和存款）和政府采购行为。第三种非关税壁垒为一系列必须满足的技术法规，如包装、标签、安全标准和多种语言产品说明要求等。

1980 年，《技术性贸易壁垒协议》（又称《标准准则》）正式实施，旨在确保行政和技术行为不会构成技术壁垒。关税与贸易总协定标准委员会开展了其他旨在促进统一标准以消除非关税壁垒的工作。1994 年，关税与贸易总协定标准委员会由新成立的世贸组织所取代。目前已有超过 131 个政府接受了世贸组织所实施的技术性贸易壁垒中的条款。

如果根据某个国家或地区的利益制定某些标准及检验流程，然后在国际贸易中强制实施，这些标准及检验流程就构成了技术性贸易壁垒。美国商务部 1998 年的报告《美国国家出口策略》将"由各国政府和地区经济集团在全球内操纵的国际产品标准和检验流程"视为美国海外竞争的主要威胁。《技术性贸易壁垒协议》规定，世贸组织应保证国际标准制定过程的正确性与透明度。然而，美国商务部所列举的事实证明，出于狭隘的地域或市场利益方面的原因，某些标准被强加于国际贸易过程，此外，一些国家的政府和地区经济集团（如欧盟）还公开采用某些标准和相关做法来获取市场的垄断地位。因此，美国已成为呼吁制定技术和贸易中立标准的国家之一，尤其是制定针对拉美和亚洲市场的标准。

其他技术性贸易壁垒包括环境、健康和安全认证等方面的要求。在欧洲，这些要求涉及禁止进口使用荷尔蒙饲料的牛肉及以噪声污染为由不允许老旧型号的飞机着陆等方面。

《1988年综合贸易与竞争法》通过后，美国国务院定期向国会提交《经济政策和贸易国家报告》。这些报告详细列举美国出口的主要障碍，不仅包括关税、制裁、禁运和技术准则，也包括燃料短缺、现代通信系统匮乏、银行系统落后及购买力低下等当地情况。

关税和其他贸易壁垒对消费和生产的影响是确定无疑的。它们提高了进口产品的国内售价，因此会降低进口产品的销量，而且关税和贸易壁垒还使得该产品的国内售价提高，从而可能刺激该产品在当地的生产。关税支持者认为，这种国内生产的增加是可取的，而反对者则认为，从经济角度而言，国内生产的增加不会带来效益。总的来说，国际贸易中的关税和贸易壁垒会降低贸易量，抬高进口产品价格。自由贸易倡导者认为，这两种结果都不是人们希望看到的，而贸易保护主义的支持者则认为，由于种种原因，关税的存在是必要的。

第9章　电子商务

人们在进行贸易的几千年间，一直在利用已有的各种工具和技术。例如，历史上大型帆船的出现就曾为买卖双方开辟了新的贸易渠道。再后来的一些发明创新，如印刷机、蒸汽机和电话等的出现也都改变了人们从事贸易活动的方式。

几十年来，公司间通过各种电子通信方式进行各种类型的交易活动。银行使用电子资金转账实现了客户资金全球转账，各类公司通过电子数据交换下订单、寄发票，零售商们通过电视广告提高大众的电话订购量。

很多人认为，"电子商务"（有时简称电商）这一术语就是指在互联网上的购物活动。其实，电子商务的范围更广，还包括许多其他的商务活动。电子商务的一个更广泛的概念是指在互联网上通过电子数据传输进行的商务活动。电子商务的三个主要组成部分是：

- 消费者在网上购物，也被称为企业与消费者之间的电子商务（简称为B2C）；
- 企业之间通过网络达成的交易，这类商务活动被称为企业间的电子商务（简称为B2B）；
- 辅助网上销售及购买活动的交易和商务流程。

公司对电子商务感兴趣的原因很简单，它有助于增加盈利。电子商务给公司带来的好处能用一句话表述：增加销量，降低成本。网上广告做得好，即使是一家小公司，其促销信息也可传递给世界各个国家的潜在顾客。公司可利用电子商务将业务拓展到分散在各地的小细分市场。在创建虚拟社区，为某类产品或服务开拓目标市场时，互联网的作用尤其明显。网上虚拟社区是由拥有共同兴趣爱好而聚集的人群所构成，只不过这种聚集不是在真实世界，而是在网络上。此外，公司采用电子商务支持销售和接受订单，可降低处理销售询价、提供报价和判断产品供货情况的成本。

电子商务不仅为卖方提供更多的销售机会，它同时也让买方拥有更多的购买机会。各商家在采购流程中采用电子商务来确认新的供货商和商业伙伴。由于网络能快速高效地提供更优惠的价格信息，电子商务中的价格协商和交货条款谈判变得更为简便。电子商务提高了公司间信息交流的速度和准确度，降低了交易双方的成本。

与传统商务相比，电子商务为买方提供了更多可供选择的产品和服务，因为他们有更多机会考察多个供货商提供的产品和服务。对买方来说，他们可以全天候评估分析多种多样的产品和服务，而且可以天天如此。他们再也用不着花上几天时间等待邮寄的产品目录和产品说明，甚至都不用花上几分钟来等候传真，即刻就能找到网上提供的详细信息。有些产品（如软件、音频文件或图像）甚至可以直接通过互联网传送，这同样减少了买方等待的时间，他们即刻就能享受自己购买的东西。

电子商务也有益于社会的整体福祉。通过网络采用电子方式进行退税、支付退休金和福利不仅安全快捷，而且能降低成本。此外，电子支付比支票支付更易审查监督，从而有效避免欺诈或盗窃带来的损失。电子商务还使人们在家工作成为可能，由此可减少上下班通勤带来的交通流量和污染，给整个社会带来益处。从这个角度来说，我们每个人都是受益者。电子商务还可为偏远地区的人们送去产品和服务。例如，远程教育使人们能够随时随地学习技能、获取学位。

然而，有些商业流程也许永远都无法采用电子商务。比如，容易变质的食品和珠宝、古董等昂贵的商品，不管将来发明什么样的技术，都难以从现场之外的地方进行充分检验。现今，电子商务还有些不尽如人意之处，因为它的支持技术发展太快。但随着电子商务的逐步成熟，以及电子商务的广泛使用、广为接受，这些不足也将会消失。

第10章　物流管理

　　过去，货物的入库和出库通常被当作独立的概念，也总是分属独立的管理职责范围。两者之间几乎没有或完全没有参照性，甚至也没有太多的配合，在诸如运营计划或实际成本之类的重要问题上，都倾向于严格按照不同领域加以管理。

　　现在情况则完全不同。大多数公司采用了物流概念，从经济效益和操作便利方面考虑，人们更倾向于把供应和销售功能集成起来，确保货物、相关单证和必要信息在整个供应链中的有效流动。换句话说，在统一的物流管理范畴下，把从原材料供应到成品送达客户的所有行为整合起来，确保从原料到商品的不间断流动。这样做的好处显而易见：便于全面掌握公司的物流总成本；提供更多节约成本的机会。

　　物流产业重视多种方式的集成并拓展其多种功能。例如，当客户要求准时配送时，供应方就需要确保有一个完整的材料管理体系，能在整个生产和包装阶段提供不间断库存，确保有充足的成品，并按照客户要求交货。换言之，当供应方货物库存无法满足需求时，客户就无法及时收到货物。集成的物流系统能确保原材料、配件和成品的动态流动，以合理成本按时、按规格备齐，随时供应。

　　如今，信息技术为检验集成物流系统的不同组成部分及其本身的效率和成本提供了便利条件，以往费时费力的任务现在也可能完成。现代通信技术使人们短短数秒便能通过网络和电话与世界另一端的人取得联系。这就要求原料供应和成品交货也应在全球范围内进行操作，成品能在短时间内交付到全球各地的客户手中，而且交付成本和效率应与对国内客户的交货相同。

　　全球贸易的许多障碍都已被清除，企业现在期望将其产品推向传统本土市场以外的市场。但假如企业不能确定是否能在可接受的时间范围和成本范围之内完成订单配送，那么向国外潜在消费者推销产品就不可取。决定采用何种运输模式，采用何种包装，需要遵守哪些法律规定或限制，凡此种种，都需要国际物流的参与。

　　全面而有效的物流战略应考虑到上述每一个问题，并制定适当的政策与体系，以应对集成物流中出现的各个方面的问题。该物流战略旨在合理安排不同部件的采购、配套、拼装和装运，以实现公司的物流目标。

第11章　跨文化交际

当今世界可谓是一个典型的"地球村"。在过去几十年间，国际和国内发生的变化使我们得以直接或间接地与不同的人交往。由于文化多样性，我们往往无法理解这些人的行为方式。不难发现，由于世界运输系统和通信网络的迅速发展，在某些社交场合或专业场合，曾经闭塞的人们也能够与来自其他文化背景的人们进行交流。通信卫星、先进的电视传输设备和互联网使世界各地的人们能够同时分享信息和思想。现在，身处不同国家的人们可以进行即时交流。

随着人口的增长，人们越来越难以远离和摆脱全球的紧张局势与冲突。当不同国家与民族的人们尝试在一起工作和生活的时候，因为语言差异、信仰不同，很容易发生冲突。我们应牢记，由于经济的全球化，交流比以往任何时期都更为普遍。现在跨国公司参与了各种国际商务活动，如合资企业、许可协议、工程总承包和分包工程以及管理合同等。每个国家的经济都与其他国家的经济息息相关。所有这些以及其他数不胜数的经济纽带表明，你可能会为一家在许多国家都有业务的公司工作，你也可能会在世界上某个遥远的地区经营业务。

在国与国之间互相依存的世界里，了解不同文化背景的人并与之有效交流已成为当务之急。但我们也发现，跨文化交际不同于同一文化内部的交际，即使克服了语言障碍，我们也可能不理解别人或不被别人理解。误解不是例外，而是普遍现象。此外，如果我们忽视了文化之于交际的重要作用，就可能把交际的失败归咎于他人。遗憾的是，我们真正的难题是文化，真正的障碍是跨文化交际。

众所周知，人类与动物的显著区别就在于人类发展了文化，人类文化的发展得益于交际，通过交际，文化得以代代相传。文化和交际相互依存，这就是霍尔所谓的"文化即交际""交际即文化"。换言之，我们以自己的方式进行交际，原因是我们在特定的文化中成长，学会了这种文化的语言、规则和规范。因为我们从幼年（5到10岁之间）便开始学习语言、规则和规范，故而无法意识到文化如何影响我们的日常行为，特别是交际行为。

与来自不同文化背景的人进行交际，我们常会接触到不同的语言及不同的规则与规范，这种接触可能会引起挫折感或满足感，却有助于我们了解自身文化。因此，我们必须学会理解文化与交际，学习文化对交际的影响以及文化背景不同的人进行交际的过程。这方面的知识极为重要，实际上，要真正理解多元文化世界中每天都在发生的事情，这些知识不可或缺。这些知识不仅能帮助我们分析跨文化交际行为，了解产生误解的真正原因，还能帮助我们在未来的交际中尽量减少误解。

第12章　货币风险

国内货币与其他货币之间的汇率变化会给银行带来货币风险。用不同货币来评估资产与负债会导致二者不匹配，从而产生货币风险。在银行持有以单一外币为单位的即期或远期、表内或表外的未平仓资产或负债的情况下，如果二者不匹配，一旦汇率朝反方向变化，银行就会遭受损失。近年来，自由浮动汇率已实际成为世界各地市场环境的标准配置。这不仅向货币投机敞开了大门，也增加了货币风险。而放松外汇管制，允许跨境资本自由流通更是引发了国际金融市场交易的迅猛增长。全球外汇成交量与增幅已远远超出了国际资本流量，从而带来更大的汇率波动与货币风险。

如果以本币为单位评估的资产价值与以外币为单位评估的资本、负债价值之间不匹配（或反之），或以本币为单位的国外应收款项与国外应付款项失衡，均可构成货币风险。在本金与到期利息之间也可能存在这种不匹配的现象。货币风险具有投机性，它可能带来收益，也可能造成亏损，一切取决于汇率变化的走向，以及银行所持的是该外币的净长仓还是净短仓。例如，如果银行持有该外币的净长仓而本币贬值，银行将取得净收益；若本币升值，则银行亏损。在银行所持为净短仓的情况下，汇率波动将带来相反的效果。

理论上讲，各国不同的通货膨胀状况造成了外币与本币利率的变化，继而造成本币价值的波动，最终形成了货币风险。虽然许多情况下，市场情绪可以帮助人们更早地认清波动趋势，但一般而言，诸如此类的波动都是由宏观经济因素造成的，需要较长的时间才能显露。影响本币价值的其他宏观经济因素还有一国的交易量与交易方向、资本量和资本流向。短期因素也可能导致货币变化，例如可预见、不可预见的政治事件，市场参与者预期的改变，货币投机行为的出现等。所有这些因素都能影响到货币的供求，进而影响货币市场每日汇率的变化。在实际操作中，货币风险包括以下几种：

- 交易风险。它是汇率变化通过价格对国外应收款项与国外应付款项造成的影响，由将来收取或支付这些款项时的价格与此前以本币为单位登记在银行或公司的财务报表上的价格之间的差异造成。
- 经济上或商业上的风险。它源于汇率变化给特定国家长期或特定公司的竞争地位带来的影响。例如，本币贬值可能会增加出口、减少进口。
- 重估风险或外币折算风险。在以本币对银行持有的外币仓重新进行估价，或是母公司编制财务报告、定期合并财务报表时，这些风险就会出现。

银行在从事外币业务时，也会带来一些与外币相关的其他风险。下面这种信用风险即是其中一种。在外汇合同另一方不履行债务的情况下，即便银行资产与负债相抵，也会在不知不觉中形成无抵补外汇仓。另一种与外汇业务尤为相关的信用风险是基于时区的清偿风险。当汇兑合同涉及两次因时区差异而发生在不同时间的清偿时，如果合同方或支付机构在两个时间之间的这段时间拒不履行债务，就会产生这样的风险。多个外币仓的到期日不同也会在相关货币之间引起利率风险：如果银行的多个远期合同或与之同质的多个衍生物有任何不匹配，且利率差异发生变化，以及由此引发的远期汇兑溢价或折扣发生变化，银行将遭受亏损。

银行的许多行为都会给银行带来风险，但能像无抵补外汇交易一样在极短的时间内给银行带来巨大损失的委实不多。这也正是银行董事会和高层必须密切关注货币风险管理的原因。董事会应该建立起货币风险管理的目标与原则，为银行在外汇业务中所承受的风险设定具体的、适当的限制，并采取措施以确保将外汇业务纳入内部安全控制的流程。应仿照资产负债管理委员会建立起风险管理委员会，并由其以上述原则为指导决定具体的政策与限制手段。政策纲要应定期审核与更新，使银行的风险概况与其风险管理体系的质量、管理人员的技能正确匹配。

政策纲要还须反映国内外货币市场不断变化的环境，考虑到货币系统可能产生的变化——例如，随着政治决策或潜在的宏观经济条件的变化，某些国家可能采取资本管制，从而给汇率带来变化。此外，出于财会和风险管理需要，风险政策应具体规定重估外币仓的频率。一般而言，重估和编制财会报告的频率应与银行货币风险的规模与性质相匹配。

附录2 参考文献

Arnold, B. J., & McIntyre, M. J. *International Tax Primer* (2nd ed.). Hague and New York: Kluwer Law International, 2002.

Bowker, L. Using Specialized Monolingual Native-Language Corpora as a Translation Resource: A Pilot Study. *Meta*, 43(4), 1998.

Chomsky, N. *Syntactic Structures* (2nd ed.). Berlin and New York: Mouton de Gruyter, 2002.

DeSimone, R. L., & Werner, J. M., & Harris, D. M. *Human resource development* (3rd ed.). Beijing: Tsinghua University Press, 2003.

Fishman, J. A. Language and Culture. In Kuper, A., & Kuper, J. (Eds.), *The Social Science Encyclopedia* (2nd ed.). London and New York: Routledge, 1996.

Griffin, R. W., & Pustay M. W. *International Business: A Managerial Perspective*. Bergen: Prentice Hall, 1995.

Hall, E. T., & Hall, M. R. *Understanding Cultural Differences: Germans, French and Americans*. Yarmouth, ME: Intercultural Press, 1990.

Halliday, M. A. K. Relevant Models of Language. *Educational Review*, 22(1), 1969.

Halliday, M. A. K., & Hasan, R. *Cohesion in English*. London: Longman, 1976.

Hatim, B. *Communication Across Cultures—Translation Theory and Contrastive Text Linguistics*. Shanghai: Shanghai Foreign Language Education Press, 2001.

Hoekman, B., & Mattoo, A., & English, P. *Development, Trade, and the WTO: A Handbook*. Washington, DC: World Bank Publications, 2002.

Hofstede, G. *Cultures and Organizations: Software of the Mind*. London: McGraw-Hill, 1991.

Kramsch, C. J. *Context and Culture in Language Teaching*. Oxford: Oxford University Press, 1993.

Kukulska-Hulme, A. *Language and Communication: Essential Concepts for User Interface and Documentation Design*. New York: Oxford University Press, 1999.

Lawrence, R. Z. *The United States and the WTO Dispute Settlement System*. New York: Council on Foreign Relations Press, 2007.

Leech, G. N. *Semantics: The Study of Meaning*. Harmondsworth: Penguin, 1974.

Mathis, R. L., & Jackson J. H. *Human Resource Management*. Beijing: Peking University Press, 2004.

Mitchell, C. *A Short Course in International Business Culture*. Shanghai: Shanghai Foreign Language Education Press, 2009.

Newmark, P. P. *About Translation*. Clevedon: Multilingual Matters Ltd., 1991.

Newmark, P. P. *Approaches to Translation*. Oxford: Pergamon Press, 1981.

Newmark, P. P. *A Textbook of Translation*. New York and London: Prentice Hall, 1988.

Nida, E. A. *Language, Culture, and Translating*. Shanghai: Shanghai Foreign Language Education Press, 1993.

Nida, E. A., & Taber C. R. *The Theory and Practice of Translation*. Leiden: E. J. Brill, 1969.

Noe, R. A., et al. *Fundamentals of Human Resource Management*. Beijing: Tsinghua University Press, 2004.

Reiss, K. Text Types, Translation Types and Translation Assessment. In Chesterman, A (Ed.), *Readings in Translation Theory*. Helsinki: Oy Finn Lectura Ab, 1989.

Shadikhodjaev, S. *Retaliation in the WTO Dispute Settlement System*. Alphen aan den Rijn: Kluwer Law International, 2009.

Trompenaars, F. *Riding the Waves of Culture: Understanding Cultural Diversity in Business*. London: The Economist Books, 1993.

van Greuning, H., & Brajovic Bratanovic, S. *Analyzing Banking Risk: A Framework for Assessing Corporate Governance and Risk Management* (3rd ed.). Washington, DC: World Bank Publications, 2009.

Wherry, T. L. *Intellectual Property: Everything the Digital-Age Librarian Needs to Know*. Chicago: American Library Association, 2008.

陈光伟．英语词汇习得研究及其对教学的启示．西安外国语学院学报，2003(1).

陈晓峰．知识产权读本．北京：中国传媒大学出版社，2007.

范维杰．谈语法教学中的对比教学．外语与外语教学，1994(1).

范仲英．实用翻译教程．北京：外语教学与研究出版社，1994.

方梦之．翻译学辞典．北京：商务印书馆，2019.

冯庆华．实用翻译教程．上海：上海外语教育出版社，2002.

冯兴石．文化翻译中的"翻译体"现象．山东省农业管理干部学院学报，2003(6).

高一虹．生产性双语现象考察．外语教学与研究，1994(1).

葛传椝．漫谈学习词汇．英语世界，1983(3).

胡明亮．语篇衔接与翻译．成都：巴蜀书社，2007.

胡曙中．语篇语言学导论．上海：上海外语教育出版社，2012.

胡壮麟．语篇的衔接与连贯．上海：上海外语教育出版社，1994.

姜雪．一词多义现象的认知研究．河北科技大学学报(社会科学版)，2005(2).

杰弗里·利奇．语义学．李瑞华等译．上海：上海外语教育出版社，1987.

金隄，奈达．论翻译．北京：中国对外翻译出版公司，1984.

柯平．英汉与汉英翻译教程．北京：北京大学出版社，1993.

李春红，汤雪琪．报关英语中英文单据翻译的实践与应用．中国科技翻译，2009(3).

李福印．语义学概论(修订版)．北京：北京大学出版社，2007.

李国南．辞格与词汇．上海：上海外语教育出版社，2001.

黎难秋．近代杰出史地学、宗教学翻译家冯承钧．上海翻译，2017(1).

李瑞. 知识产权法. 广州：华南理工大学出版社, 2006.
李运兴. 英汉语篇翻译（第二版）. 北京：清华大学出版社, 2003.
连淑能. 英译汉教程. 北京：高等教育出版社, 2006.
廖瑛, 莫再树. 国际商务英语语言与翻译研究. 北京：机械工业出版社, 2005.
刘宓庆. 当代翻译理论. 北京：中国对外翻译出版公司, 1999.
刘宓庆. 文体与翻译. 北京：中国对外翻译出版公司, 1998.
刘宓庆. 新编当代翻译理论. 北京：中国对外翻译出版公司, 2005.
刘宓庆. 新编汉英对比与翻译. 北京：中国对外翻译出版公司, 2006.
刘全福. 英汉语言比较与翻译. 北京：高等教育出版社, 2011.
刘彦奎, 李建华. 高健翻译思想与传统美学的关系探讨. 湖北民族学院学报（哲学社会科学版）, 2012(2).
鲁迅. 鲁迅全集（第十卷）. 北京：人民文学出版社, 2005.
鲁迅. "题未定"草. 中国翻译工作者协会,《翻译通讯》编辑部编. 翻译研究论文集（1894—1948）. 北京：外语教学与研究出版社, 1984.
吕俊, 侯向群. 英汉翻译教程. 上海：上海外语教育出版社, 2001.
吕彦. 知识产权法. 成都：四川大学出版社, 2008.
马红军. 翻译批评散论. 北京：中国对外翻译出版公司, 2000.
马会娟. 论商务文本翻译标准的多元化. 中国翻译, 2005(3).
欧秋耘. 经济语篇翻译忠实性原则探究. 中国科技翻译, 2011(2).
潘文国. 汉英语对比纲要. 北京：北京语言大学出版社, 1997.
潘文国. 汉英语言对比概论. 北京：商务印书馆, 2010.
潘文国, 杨自俭. 共性·个性·视角：英汉对比的理论与方法研究. 上海：上海外语教育出版社, 2008.
秦洪武, 王克非. 英汉比较与翻译. 北京：外语教学与研究出版社, 2010.
沙特尔沃思, 考伊. 翻译研究词典. 谭载喜主译. 北京：外语教学与研究出版社, 2005.
邵志洪. 汉英对比翻译导论. 上海：华东理工大学出版社, 2005.
申小龙. 汉语语法学. 南京：江苏教育出版社, 2001.
申小龙. 中国句型文化. 长春：东北师范大学出版社, 1988.
司显柱. 论语篇为翻译的基本单位. 中国翻译, 1999(2).
孙致礼. 翻译的异化与归化. 山东外语教学, 2001(1).
孙致礼. 新编英汉翻译教程. 上海：上海外语教育出版社, 2003.
谭载喜. 语篇与翻译：论三大关系. 外语与外语教学, 2002(7).
汤宗舜, 文希凯, 蔡小鹏. 英汉汉英知识产权词汇. 北京：专利文献出版社, 1996.
王家平. 鲁迅文学翻译思想及其翻译策略的价值与启示. 首都师范大学学报（社会科学版）, 2017(1).
王菊泉, 郑立信. 英汉语言文化对比研究. 上海：上海外语教育出版社, 2004.
韦利, 吴自选. 从翻译家到对外传播专家：谈沈苏儒先生的翻译观. 海外英语, 2011(10).
翁凤翔. 当代国际商务英语翻译. 上海：上海交通大学出版社, 2006.

伍争荣,缪仁炳.人力资源管理教程.北京：中国发展出版社,2006.
胥瑾.英汉对比与翻译教程.北京：化学工业出版社,2010.
徐珺,肖海燕.商务翻译中的语境顺应研究.外语学刊,2015(5).
许建平.英汉互译实践与技巧(第三版).北京：清华大学出版社,2007.
许钧.翻译论.武汉：湖北教育出版社,2003.
杨丰宁.英汉语言比较与翻译.天津：天津大学出版社,2006.
叶朗,朱良志.中国文化读本(英文版).北京：外语教学与研究出版社,2008.
叶龙,史振磊.人力资源开发与管理.北京：北京交通大学出版社,2006.
余东.论思维模式与英语教学模式.广州大学学报(社会科学版),2003(3).
余光中.余光中谈翻译.北京：中国对外翻译出版公司,2002.
余璐.陈忠诚法律翻译思想探索.上海翻译,2015(4).
张德.人力资源开发与管理(第三版).北京：清华大学出版社,2007.
张德禄,刘汝山.语篇连贯与衔接理论的发展及应用.上海：上海外语教育出版社,2003.
张建国,陈晶瑛.现代人力资源管理.成都：西南财经大学出版社,2005.
张军平.忠实原作内容,发挥译语优势——高健先生的散文翻译风格管窥.运城学院学报,2005(4).
张美平.商务翻译的词义理解与选择.中国科技翻译,2007(2).
张培基.英汉翻译教程.上海：上海外语教育出版社,1980.
郑奕.英汉互译中的逻辑问题.湖北成人教育学院学报,2007(1).
周燕,廖瑛.英文商务合同长句的语用分析及其翻译.中国科技翻译,2004(4).
周志培.汉英对比与翻译中的转换.上海：华东理工大学出版社,2003.
朱永生,严世清.系统功能语言学多维思考.上海：上海外语教育出版社,2001.
朱永生,郑立信,苗兴伟.英汉语篇衔接手段对比研究.上海：上海外语教育出版社,2001.
左飚.环性与线性：中西文化特性比较.社会科学,2001(12).